DADS, TODDLERS AND THE CHICKEN DANCE

DADS, TODDLERS
AND THE
CHICKEN DANCE

PETER DOWNEY

Illustrations by Nik Scott

FISHER
BOOKS™

First published in Australasia in 1997 by Simon & Schuster Australia, 20 Barcoo Street, East Roseville, NSW 2069
A Viacom Company: Sydney New York London Toronto Tokyo Singapore

Library of Congress Cataloging-in-Publication Data
Downey, Peter, 1964-
    Dads, toddlers & the chicken dance / Peter Downey.— North American ed.
        p. cm.
    ISBN 1-55561-242-3
    1. Fatherhood. 2. Father and infant. 3. Toddlers—Care.
    I. Title: Dads, toddlers, and the chicken dance. II. Title.

HQ756.D589 2000
306.874′2—dc2l

                                                            00-034783

Fisher Books
5225 W. Massingale Road
Tucson, Arizona 85743-8416
(520) 744-6110

Fisher Books is a member of the Perseus Books Group.

Find us on the world wide web at http://www.fisherbooks.com.

Fisher Books titles are available at special discounts for bulk purchases in the United States by corporations, institutions, and other organizations.

First printing, December 2000

1 2 3 4 5 6 7 8 9 10—03 02 01 00

This book is dedicated to my parents,
Stan and Hilda,
who taught me that wealth has more to do with family
and less to do with money.

If only the IRS felt the same.

Epigraph

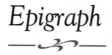

It was the best of times, it was the worst of times . . .
— Charles Dickens, A Tale of Two Cities

It was the best of times, it was the worst of times . . .
— Peter Downey, reflecting on his six years as a dad

Contents

———⌇———

Acknowledgments

Thanks to . . .

- Meredith, my wife and voice of reason, for not once complaining about me shutting myself away to write. I consider myself a lucky man to have found a terrific wife and great mother in the one skin. Thanks for your patience, good advice, levelheadedness, unconditional love and that thing you do when I have a sore back.

- Rachael, Georgia and Matilda, our fantastic girls. You make fatherhood a great joy to me. I love you and am there for you always . . . except between 11 P.M. and 7 A.M., when your mother is there for you.

- Hilda and Stan, my parents, who raised me to believe in family. Thanks for all the baby-sitting, but from now on I really want the kids to go to bed before 10 P.M. and please, no more lollipops.

- Di Jefferson for letting me use her house as a writer's retreat. Sorry about the red wine stain.

- E-Boy Jefferson and Betty B. for letting me use their house for post-vasectomy recovery. Thanks for the coffee and peanut butter on toast.

- George and Tanya for letting us stay in their vacation house for free. This actually has nothing to do with the book, but I figure if I mention their names they might let us stay again sometime.

- Westmead Children's Hospital Safety Unit, the Family Planning Association of NSW and the NSW Child Protection Council for sending envelopes full of stuff.

- Brigitta Doyle, my literary proctologist and the world's most anally retentive editor, for pointing out when I used the word "good" eleven times on the same page.

- And to all the dads and moms (and their kids) who walk the parental road with me, for letting me steal their ideas and anecdotes and dress them up as my own.

Author's Note

—— ⌒⌒ ——

Between the idea and the reality falls the shadow.

— T. S. Eliot

The problem with most books on parenting is that they set up an ideal no parent in the real world can possibly live up to. You can be left feeling angry and frustrated that you're not doing it right.

Many books purport to contain "the secret" to parenting. They have titles like *The Complete Guide to . . .* or *All the Answers to Your Problems about . . .* or *Ten Easy Steps to . . .* or *Everything You Wanted to Know about . . .*

In your local bookstore, you'll find such books shelved under "fiction" or "total baloney."

There is a clear difference between the clinical theory of a textbook and the hard-hitting reality of life with a small child. There are no easy solutions to the daily dilemmas and nocturnal frustrations of parenting. You just have to do your best.

Let me make it clear that I am not a professional parenting expert. I'm a normal guy and an amateur dad. I don't have all the answers. I don't know "the secret." In fact, just the opposite: The more I get into this fathering thing, the more I am aware of my failings as a parent. It is my inadequacies, not my expertise, that makes me the right man to be writing a book like this.

My sole qualification is that I'm the father of three daughters, and they seem to think I'm pretty good at being a dad. I asked them why. Rachael (five) looked puzzled and said, " 'Cause you tell us stories . . . you tuck us in . . . you say 'I love you' . . . you give us kisses and hugs . . ."

Georgia (three) was more straightforward: "You bring us surprises and play fun games with us."

Matilda (one) was less subtle: "Daddy a pooey smell man."

This book is not a "how-to" guide. It's not connect-the-dot parenting for thickheaded men. I raise certain issues, expand on some ideas, plagiarize my friends and leave it up to you to figure out what you think about it all. Ideally, you'll make your own decisions that will help you become a better dad.

This is a personal and subjective book, written from my perspective, background and experience. Obviously, not everybody is like me and parts of the book may not ring true for you, but you should know where I'm coming from.

First of all, I live in a stereotypical, middle-class, atom-splitting family. I have a wife, three children, a minivan, a computer with a huge hard drive and a house in the suburbs. I go to work five days a week. If I grew my sideburns and glued wood paneling to the side of my car, neighbors would mistake me for Mike Brady.

I don't know what it's like to be in a both-parents-working family or a dad-stays-at-home family.

Second, I am the father of girls and only girls. I have never changed a diaper with a penis in it. Our toy room is full of dolls and has never even seen a dump truck. I haven't reared a son and I don't know what it would be like, although my anecdotal observations suggest that boys are louder, harder, stronger, dirtier, smellier and more destructive than girls.

Third, because I'm married to the woman I get into bed with every night, I have used the word "wife" throughout the book when referring to the other half of the parenting team in your family. I did this for four reasons:

- I felt like it.
- Having three less letters, "wife" is quicker and easier to type than "partner."
- Statistically, there are more wives than partners in parenting situations.
- I urinate against the wind of political correctness.

Fourth, I am not the primary caregiver in my family. One of the dangers in writing a book for dads is the misleading implication that I spend twenty-four hours a day thinking about kids' birthday parties and toilet training.

I don't.

Because I go out to work and my wife stays home to work, she bears the brunt of the parenting in our family. I see the kids for half an hour in the morning, a few hours at night, on weekends, holidays and vacations.

This is a book for guys, but in no way does this focus detract from the integral role of the husband-wife team. It's easy for me to be a dad because my wife is such an excellent mother.

But that doesn't let me off the hook. Given my particular domestic situation, I do what I can, when I can, to be the best dad that I can be.

And that is also your task.

About the Title

This book, as you are no doubt already aware, is called *Dads, Toddlers and the Chicken Dance*. I would like to explain what this means.

First of all, this book is about *dads*: regular guys like you and me who find themselves navigating the road of early parenthood.

When I wrote the prequel to this book, *So You're Going to Be a Dad*, I had a particular man in mind. He was your average guy who had just found out that his wife was pregnant. He was getting ready for stage one of fatherhood: the pregnancy, the birth and the months beyond.

This book is written for that same guy, twelve months down the road. He is getting ready for stage two: the post-baby years. He survived the pregnancy, the birth and the first year and is looking ahead to toddlerdom and the early years leading up to school.

Second, this book is about *toddlers*. It's about the years when your baby stops being a baby and becomes a walking, talking, pooping, tantruming monster, hellbent on making your life a misery. I have written about what I have found to be the most significant, interesting and devastating aspects of toddler development.

But wait, there's more! Technically speaking, children are toddlers from one until roughly two years of age, but this book covers ages one through five. I kept the title *Dads, Toddlers and the Chicken Dance*, however, because *Dads, Toddlers, Children between the Ages of Two and Five Years and the Chicken Dance* took up too much room on the front cover.

Which only leaves me to talk about the *Chicken Dance*.

Dads you can understand.

Toddlers you can understand.

"But what the hell is the chicken dance and what has it got to do with me?" I hear you cry.

Let me explain.

One night a few years ago, I was standing half-naked and freezing in the dark, trying to rock a hysterical baby to sleep. I suddenly found my situation so bizarre, so ridiculous and so foreign to anything in my experience that I decided to write a book about the perils of being the father of a baby. That was *So You're Going to Be a Dad.*

A few years later I found myself at a preschool Christmas concert. It was Rachael's theatrical debut. She was supposed to be a sheep, even though she looked like an old car-seat cover with legs. All the moms were chatting together in small groups. All the dads were in the back working their video cameras and checking their watches so they could get back to work in time. And then before I knew it, all the adults had to get up and go to the front. I had no idea what was going on but moments later found myself doing the most ridiculous dance ever created. There we were, hands pecking, butts wiggling, chicken-strutting around the room while making little flapping motions to the annoying tap-tap tune of the musical barnyard.

With a certain sense of déjà vu, I suddenly found my situation so bizarre, so ridiculous, so foreign to anything in my experience that I decided to write a book about the perils of being the father of a preschooler.

To me, the chicken dance is the epitome of fatherhood. Sure, you can go to birth classes, change a diaper, help with feeding, learn lullabies by heart and so forth. But it's when you do the chicken dance that you realize how much dadhood has consumed your life. It is then that you know you have passed the point of no return . . . which is, of course, a good thing.

Doing the chicken dance is a symbolic baptism into the bizarre world of parenting. It symbolizes the total acceptance of your role as dad. The final nail in the diaper pail has been hammered in.

You're not in the back watching like a detached observer. You are right there in the thick of it, giving it all you've got. In my opinion, that is what fatherhood is all about. Even if you do feel like an idiot.

Note: Throughout the book, I had a grammatical meltdown trying to make gender-neutral toddler references, so each chapter alternates between "he" and "she." Just cope with it and convert it to your own situation.

Preface

———⸙———

Being the dad of a toddler is a funny thing. You spend the first year counting down the minutes till your baby begins to walk and talk. Then you spend the next five years telling him to "sit down" and "hush up."

This is a book about being the father of a toddler. I have written it for several reasons:

1. So I could claim my vasectomy as a tax deduction.

2. With my previous book, *So You're Going to Be a Dad*, I had a taste of my Andy Warhol fifteen minutes of fame—and I want more!

   I enjoyed reading my name in reviews (except for that jerk who said I had a *Honey, I Shrunk the Kids* writing style). One guy even called me, "the new Dr. Spock," which I take as quite a compliment—I've always liked science fiction.

   I also did radio and TV interviews and got to "do lunch" with somebody really important from a newspaper. Who knows, next time they might even pay.

3. A sequel just seemed like the logical thing to do. I mean, if it's good enough for *Star Trek*, it's good enough for me.

4. I hold a strong conviction about the importance of the institution of dadhood. It is important (stirring music please, maestro) that today's youth grow up with a family man in the house. I think that fatherhood is something we should deliberately and purposefully pursue.

   Our kids need us. They need our testosterone, our love, our time, our discipline, our patience, our wisdom, our care, our interest. They need us to hold their hands, tuck them in, wipe their bottoms. They need us to teach them about the world and give them a sense of self-esteem. They need us to show them what it means to be in a family and what good relationships are all about. They need us to help them grow into fine people and prepare them for the challenges of life.

   The trite platitudes in the above paragraph are easy to write and even easier to read, particularly in this politically correct climate where "positive parenting" is an assumed role. There is a modern cultural expectation that dads will be involved with their children. But as I'm sure you've already discovered, the reality of fatherhood takes effort, hard work, time, patience, a willingness to learn and shirts that don't stain easily.

> The reality of fatherhood takes effort, hard work, time, patience, a willingness to learn and shirts that don't stain easily.

Given this epic and life-changing task, what training and preparation do we receive to prepare us for the years that lie ahead?

For most, it's a few weeks of prenatal classes, a tour of the maternity ward and a film made in the seventies of a French woman giving birth.

That's it.

This situation would be laughable in any other field.

In business, you have to invest energy constantly into staying on the cutting edge. You have to read industry magazines, go to conferences and seminars, buy new equipment and do lunch with slackers who chat on their cell phones as they eat.

Us guys need to take a page from the rest of our lives and apply the same principles to fathering. We need to train to be good dads. We need to be dedicated and committed. We need to think about what we are doing as dads, read about it, talk about it, evaluate our performance and improve our skills.

If fatherhood is going to be something that is important to you, don't just take it as it comes. Don't just sit there. Work hard at it.

5. To give you the lowdown on what's going to happen to you over the next few years.

When I found out that Meredith was pregnant, I had a sneaking suspicion this fatherhood thing might change my life. This turned out to be one of the biggest understatements of the twentieth century, along with Paul McCartney thinking there might be a living in forming a band.

Now I am the father of three girls under the age of five. And you know what? This fatherhood thing has totally changed my life.

I first realized this when friends commented on my habit of swaying back and forth when I stand talking, a result of years of rocking with a crying baby in my arms.

But that's nothing.

Once I inadvertently cut up the veggies on the plate of a dinner guest. Another time, I absentmindedly excused myself from a business meeting with the words, "Excuse me, Peter has to go tinkle."

Then there was the time I offered my boss a glass of wine but wouldn't let go of it until he said "the magic word." What really annoyed him, however, was when I licked the corner of a napkin and tried to wipe a gravy spot off his wife's chin.

Like I said, fatherhood has totally changed my life. And day by day, as your baby disappears, leaving a toddler in her place, fatherhood will increasingly change your life as well. If it hasn't already. You're a dad and your life is chaos and there's not a thing you can do about it.

6. To help you resolve the dilemma of being a modern father.

We are living in an awkward age, a time of change. The past was supposedly the dark age of fatherhood. Dad was the emotionally detached provider of discipline, authority, finance, major life decisions and Sunday roast carving. He came home from work, grunted at the kids, put on his slippers and read the paper.

We read that men still define themselves through work. Sociologists say men measure their worth by their salary. We read surveys that claim that most men spend less than ten minutes a day with their children. Psychology texts rage about how few men claim to have a close relationship with their father. We hear about the new breed of corporate workaholic who neglects his family as he tries to compete with younger, single colleagues in the workforce.

At the same time, however, we are rushing headlong toward a future where sensitive New Age men wear pastel colors and have tons of time and energy for their children—to play, to talk, to sing and to do the chicken dance without embarrassment. Magazines are full of these alternative dads who are rebelling against the dominant work ethic to spend time with their children: guys who start work at 6 A.M. so they can pick their kids up from school, guys who put their career on hold for years to take care of their children.

So where does that leave the rest of us?

Stuck in the gray area between eras, fumbling about at work by day and with diapers by night; part of both worlds, yet neither; caught in the crossfire between the passing of the old, which isn't quite gone, and the coming of the new, which hasn't quite arrived.

I want to cut down trees, go out to earn a living, lift weights, watch Arnold Schwarzenegger films, drink milk straight from the carton, wash and detail the car and stand around the grill with my friends cooking massively oversized racks of ribs.

But I also want to be a loving father, change diapers, put Band-Aids™ on wounded knees, play peek-a-boo, read nursery rhymes, watch Disney films, do the chicken dance, fly kites, hug and kiss and spend rainy afternoons playing dress-up . . . well, maybe not the "change diapers" part. I can live without that.

Maybe part of this conflict comes from the fact that as I grew up, I never put too much thought into being a dad.

As a child, my goal in life was to be Batman (not the dark Hollywood Batman, but the undies-on-the-outside one) and marry Wonder Woman.

As an teenager, I wanted to be Luke Skywalker, drive a van with chicks spray-painted down the side and marry one of Charlie's Angels (I didn't care which one).

As a young adult, I wanted to marry Meredith and backpack around Europe. Being a dad was never even up for consideration.

Now look at me . . . suburban husband and father of three girls. My undies are still on the inside and there's a minivan in my driveway instead of an X-Wing Fighter. Currently, my only goal in life is to have a mower that doesn't dig dirt circles into my lawn.

I'm gradually accepting this conflict as part of the rich tapestry of a father's life. It's challenging, rewarding and frustrating all at the same time.

I just have to get used to it. And you do too.

7. Finally, I spent close to $3000 on a new computer and I have to write this book to justify the expense to my wife, so she thinks I bought it for writing rather than for the fantastic graphics in "3D Tournament Golf."

CHAPTER 1

Into the
Undiscovered Country

I'M sure you've already discovered that fatherhood is a
wonderful and rewarding experience.

Frustrating, yes.

Tiring, yes.

Life changing, yes.

Sometimes downright awful, yes, yes, yes.

But wonderful and rewarding all the same.

As a dad, your life is probably messy, uncontrolled and
unpredictable. Your house, a picture of chaotic confusion. Your
social life, a portrait of muddled mayhem.

And your sex life . . . just plain crummy.

But you and the wife are starting to come out of that twilight
zone of new parenthood. You've become accustomed to the
terrain. You've adjusted, found your feet. In fact, you've even
started to like it.

But before you get too cocky, look at the road ahead. You will
see a nasty and treacherous bend with a sign on it saying, "Into
the Undiscovered Country." Things are about to change. Your
baby is about to emerge from its cocoon as an entirely new
species: *Toddlerus destructivus*.

Your baby has started to grow. To develop. To metamorphose.
It has started to look human and lose that ridiculously bulbous
head and those disgusting folds of skin around its thighs where
you once lost your car keys.

As you turn that corner, you will discover that being the
father of a toddler is as much a shock to the system as being a
new dad was. The next years are going to be wild. Don't start
thinking that things are going to get better, easier and more
comfortable, because they're not. They're going to get worse.

Instead of your life heading back to what you knew as normal, it will just keep evolving on a bizarre parenting tangent.

If you look carefully, you will see that the parenting road dwindles off into the distance. It's a scary and dark place that will make what you've gone through so far look like a Sunday afternoon tiptoe through the proverbial tulips.

Being the dad of a toddler is more like a Sunday afternoon stomp through a field of landmines.

On the road ahead of you lies really crazy stuff such as first steps, first words, first tantrums, toilet training, nocturnal visitations, absurd conversations, answering difficult questions, bad kids' videos, decorated refrigerators, playgroup barbecues, birthday parties, crayons in the carpet, kids walking in on you during sex, milk and cookies for Santa and, worst of all, kindergarten orientation meetings.

So turn the page and let us enter a new dimension. A dimension of tiredness. A dimension of tantrums. A dimension of fingerprints on every window in the house.

It is the undiscovered country . . . the land of the toddler.

CHAPTER 2
Walking

tod'dler n. *One who takes short, tottering steps.*

AS we head off together into the undiscovered country of toddlerdom, we need a starting point. But where to begin?

It seems to me that regardless of psycho-socio-anthropological theory, in the minds of most parents, children take the step from babyhood to toddlerdom when they begin to toddle.

A baby can't walk. He shuffles along on his stomach like a worm or scoots around on his behind. But as soon as he stands, stumbles forward and inevitably falls flat on his face, he is displaying the behavior of a real human being. He is *toddling* and has, therefore, officially become a *toddler*.

I used to think that babies flopped around on their behinds until one day some synapses connected in their infantile brains and WHAM!, they got up and walked. I had expected that Meredith would call me at work one day and say, "The baby is walking."

It's not like this.

It happens gradually.

Over a long period.

A laborious period.

In stages.

Which is handy, actually, because there is nothing that parenting books love more than to talk about a child's development in terms of a series of sequential steps.

Hey, I don't know about you, but I'm tired of reading about kids' developmental stages.

So let's turn it around and look at the stages that us parents go through as our babies gradually turn into kamikaze walkers.

The Stage of Melancholy

This occurs around the twelve-month mark, give or take several months, and is often referred to as the "Hasn't time flown— where's our baby gone?" stage.

For some, it can even be teary, because Mom and Dad realize that their baby isn't a baby anymore. They can't seem to remember what the baby used to be like when he was really little. It seems like only yesterday they were in the maternity ward. The past months are just a blur.

Some take it a little hard. I know one couple who got depressed because their baby was "growing up." I think they thought that pimples and R-rated films were just around the corner.

As for the baby, he suddenly realizes that the other humans in the house exist on a vertical plane and that he is the only one who uses his stomach as a means of propulsion. And so, in a quest for self-betterment, he decides to reach upward.

He'll be on a reconnaissance mission around the house and will surge up onto the couch like a suicidal whale flopping on a beach.

Suddenly, a hand will reach up and grab the corner of a cushion.

Then another hand.

(From somewhere you will hear the strains of *2001: A Space Odyssey:* "Daah . . . Daah . . . Daah . . .")

A knee will come up.

("Da Daah . . .")

An uncertain foot.

("BOM Bom BOM Bom BOM Bom BOM Bom")

And the baby will cling there desperately, grinning as if he's just conquered Mt. Everest.

Parents seeing this for the first time have been known to burst blood vessels at the exciting thought that their baby is standing.

People rush from all corners of the house.

Dad drives home early from work.

Grandparents are called.

Rivers change course.

The "Where's our baby gone?" stage

Mountains tremble.

Baby falls over.

In the coming weeks, he will do this with increasing frequency.

Once the baby has a little confidence in being upright, he will start with the slo-mo shuffle. This is a low-altitude edging maneuver the baby uses to hoist himself along pieces of furniture. Suddenly, he becomes semi-mobile and can make it around the entire house as long as there's a couch, chair, table or pant leg to hang on to.

The Stage of Great Expectations

One day you will walk into a room and see your baby standing there, not hanging on to the couch or table. You'll pass a Hula-Hoop™ over him to make sure there are no strings or other tricks of the eye.

But it's true.

Your "baby" is standing like a real adult. He has evolved from quadruped to bipedal *Homo sapiens*.

The first step is moments away.

(*There's that music again.*)

("Daah . . .")

Armstrong is about to step off the ladder.

("Daah . . .")

Parental excitement reaches fever pitch.

("Daah . . .")

Video cameras roll.

("Da DAAH . . .")

Hand-held video cameras are held in hands.

(*This is one small step for a man.*)

Only the whine of the charging flash can be heard in the eerie silence.

(*One giant leap for my child.*)

("BOM Bom BOM Bom BOM Bom BOM Bom")

And then, despite the frenzy of parental expectation, *nothing happens*. You wait with the video camera locked to your face, wasting hours of film.

Seconds tick by.

Minutes.

You start making stupid encouraging gestures with one hand while trying to focus with the other.

Our video of Rachael's first steps goes for three hours. For the first two hours and fifty-four minutes, Rachael stands there uneasily looking into the lens, wondering what all the fuss is about. My out-of-focus hand appears repeatedly in the bottom of the picture, snapping fingers and beckoning her to come to me.

She leans toward me, doesn't move her feet and disappears from the screen. Her forehead makes a dull thwack on the tile floor.

> Your child can now stand, but that's about it. The moment he wants to get from A to B, he'll hit the deck and crawl.

That's right. Your child can now stand, but that's about it. He will stay on his wobbly feet if you place him there or he will let go of his support, but the moment he wants to get from A to B, he'll hit the deck and crawl.

The Stage of Success

Eventually, that first step *will* happen . . . usually just before that first fall.

You will invite friends to your house, supposedly to "catch up" or play cards, but really it's so you can show off your new performer.

This rarely works. Many an afternoon has been spent trying to tease, cajole, prod and threaten a toddler into repeating that single step he took almost three weeks earlier.

Don't worry. Your toddler will walk when he's ready and confident. You can't push or hurry him.

Soon he'll repeat that first step, and then the next time maybe one and a half steps. (Well . . . his other foot *did* touch the ground just before his face hit the end table.)

You'll find yourself idiotically running a daily tally of the number of steps taken. You'll find yourself chanting the numbers while your toddler toddles toward you.

"One . . . two . . . that's it, c'mon . . . three . . . four . . . five . . . yes, yes! . . . six . . . seven . . . EIGHT . . . that's your record! . . . nine . . . TEN! We have TEN! I repeat, we have TEN STEPS!"

(Slam.)

The critical thing to remember is not to point out to him that he is actually walking. The moment you do—"Hey, you're walking!"—he'll fall over.

The Stage of Regret

This is also known as the "We never knew how good we had it before" stage. You'll look back fondly to when the baby was just an immobile sloth who stayed put like a turtle on his back. As such, he really didn't affect the set-up or routine of your house.

But then you got what you wished for and now you have an infant tornado. A stumbling, wobbly, out-of-control person who bounces around the house falling over crusts of bread, bumping into tables and chairs, dragging tablecloths down on his head, staggering toward stairs and grabbing at the cords of electrical appliances.

Your every waking moment will be spent in a perpetual stoop as you chase after your toddler. You'll develop a bad back that will stay with you for the rest of your life. And you'll be flat broke because a little pair of kid's plastic beach sandals costs the same as your air-cushioned, computer-designed, leather cross-trainers.

Remember that a few steps don't make a walker. Don't suddenly expect your one-year-old to follow you around the grocery store. He'll still want to be carried or ride in a stroller.

> Don't suddenly expect your one-year-old to follow you around the grocery store.

But week by week his confidence and skill will improve, and soon he'll be independent enough to go on recon missions.

And once your child is on his feet, you're officially the father of a toddler. Ha, ha.

CHAPTER 3
Tantrums

tan'trum n. Toddler outburst of anger or annoyance that causes parents to burst frontal-lobe blood vessels.

ASIDE from taking first steps, the other "toddler" verification is their realization that they can make your life a living hell. To achieve this, they use "the tantrum." Here's how it works:

I am in the supermarket. Matilda says, "I wan' dat," pointing to a forty-pound bag of Doggy Bites.

"No, they're dog biscuits."

Her bottom lip starts to tremble. Her hands form fists and she waves them in the air.

"I . . . I . . . want . . . I . . . wa-wa-want . . ."

There is a bad taste in the back of my mouth.

"I WANT!"

All reason is going.

"I WANT! I WANT!"

Going.

"No."

Gone.

And then it hits.

Screaming.

Not just pretend screaming, but real "my life is in danger" screaming. Legs kicking. Tears flowing. Choking, coughing, sputtering. Total body spasms. Head writhing. Mucus. Saliva. Broken blood vessels. More screaming. Gagging.

Other shoppers start genuflecting and whipping out their crucifixes.

Somebody calls for a priest.

This is what is affectionately known as a "tantrum."

It is an incredible outburst of rage and noise, an uncontrolled explosion of temper. It can happen at any time. Some people refer to the "terrible twos" (which I used to think was a diaper thing) as being *the* age of tantruming. Wrong. Children can have them in varying forms at any time over a number of years.

A tantrum can strike for any reason. It usually occurs because you've stopped them from doing what they want to do (playing with dog poop), going somewhere they want to go (across a busy highway) or having something they want to have (your drill set).

Their frustration is often amplified because they can't really communicate effectively yet and, unlike you and me, they haven't attended any seminars on self-control.

You can be at home, at a friend's place, in the park, the movie theater, the supermarket or the car. The worst times are when they're tired or you're in a hurry . . . oh, and of course, at bedtime. Most toddlers, however, save their performances for public places.

So what do you do when your toddler goes into death throes? How can you possibly deal with a writhing twenty-five–pound nightmare of screaming and tears?

Let's go back to the Matilda–doggy-biscuits episode to illustrate. I had several options at my disposal.

Option One: Act Dumb

I could leave her thrashing around on the floor, turn to the gathered crowd of shoppers, point to her and say in a loud voice, "Whose child is this?"

Option Two: Give In

I could buy the forty-pound sack of Doggy Bites.

The first problem with this is we don't have a dog. Nor do we have a budget that allows for such luxury.

The second problem, as all parenting books will tell you, is that if you give in to a tantrum, you will be rewarding and reinforcing your child's behavior. You will teach her that that's the way to get what she wants. In your toddler's mind, a tantrum will bring tangible results and so the next time you say "no," she'll know that all she has to do is thrash around for a while and you'll give in.

Option Three: The Patience Game

I could say quite sternly that I am not going to buy the Doggy Bites, then leave her thrashing around on the floor of aisle three while I retreat to the potato chips section where, from a safe viewing distance, I could wait for her to finish so we can get on with the shopping.

Of course, this option assumes that you don't exist in the real world, that you have unlimited patience, gobs of time to kill and no other commitments. It also assumes that you can cope with all the "tut-tut" looks from other shoppers who think you are cruel and heartless.

Option Four: Fire with Fire

I could get down on the floor with Matilda and throw a tantrum as well. My wife actually knows someone who knows someone whose neighbor's cousin has done this.
No, really! It was with a young child who suddenly became really embarrassed about the whole situation.

> A tantruming toddler is a little ball of writhing muscle and incredible strength. It's like trying to carry a greased pig receiving 40,000 volts.

One problem with this is that if you're in a supermarket, men in white coats might come and take you away.

I find this method appealing but, to be honest, I just don't have the guts.

Option Five: Fight It

I could grit my teeth, take a deep breath and either drag her around or tuck her under my arm like a football and keep on shopping. Of course, this assumes that I have the strength and stamina of Hercules to be able to do so. A tantruming toddler is a little ball of writhing muscle and incredible strength. It's like trying to carry a greased pig receiving 40,000 volts.

Or I could lose my temper and shout her down.

Both of these methods, however, will do little to end the tantrum. They're more likely to provoke a longer and more vigorous assault.

Option Six: Ignore It

I could just say "bye," leave her where she is and get on with my shopping.

However, this would be irresponsible, dangerous and stupid.

This approach works well in the home, where you can leave them in a safe place to ride out their tantrum. You simply say "No, you may not have a tenth piece of chocolate cake," put them somewhere where they can't hurt themselves, then get on with your life.

But it's not that easy if you're in a supermarket.

There are no easy solutions to a tantrum. You need tremendous mental and physical reserves, oodles of tolerance, patience and preferably a hearing problem.

If the tantrum is in the morning and I'm feeling relaxed but on the ball, I know what to do and I deal with the tantrum in a responsible and mature way. At the end of the day, though, I'm usually tired, impatient, preoccupied and wanting quiet. At these times, I have low reserves of parental wisdom and have found myself yelling at the offender. Afterward, I feel foolish and immature.

But there is good news. Toddler tantrums, as in the screaming-stamping-choking-trembling kind, become less frequent with age. They are replaced with more sophisticated hysterical behavior, such as constant whining, running away from you, an obstinate refusal to cooperate, inexplicable crying over silly little things, a total lack of reason and the repetition of the words "But I want to . . ."

Aaahh, the joys of fatherhood.

The only thing you can do is think in terms of prevention and avoidance rather than confrontation. Some tantrums are avoidable. Don't let them escalate to nightmare proportions. Don't expect too much when your child is tired. Don't put her in tempting or frustrating situations where tantrums are a likely outcome.

Unfortunately, the other 99.99 percent of tantrums are not avoidable.

By the way, in case you're wondering what I did with Matilda in the supermarket, I used my reason, evaluated the situation and made the best decision possible.

I ripped open the bag and gave her a handful of Doggy Bites, which she promptly shoved in her mouth. That kept her quiet.

CHAPTER 4
Toilet Training

EVERYBODY has a few good toilet stories to tell. Along with rehashing episodes of *The Simpsons* and comparisons of ugly driver's license photographs, it is an assured way to launch into hours of riotous conversation at even the most cosmopolitan of dinner parties.

Everyone has at least one friend who's used a bidet incorrectly or was in the cubicle of a 747 when it hit a huge air pocket, with obvious results.

But the best stories come from parents of toddlers.

Parents usually use little discretion when relating long and colorful narratives about their adventures with diapers and their varied contents.

Otherwise-normal guys spew forth phrases such as, "That's nothing—you should've seen the diaper that Justine had the other day! Suffocating? Let me tell you about suffocating, . . ." or "When I went in to his room, the little stinker had taken off his diaper and his hands and mouth were covered in . . . arghh, I can't even bring myself to talk about it without wanting to barf," or "I still don't get it. How'd he get it up around his neck?"

Dads have hours of such tales. It just adds weight to the old saying that trauma etches the memory.

You are no doubt already versed in the mechanics of the infant digestive system and the peril involved in dealing with it up close. It truly is frightening stuff.

When it was time for toddler Rachael to take the great leap forward into bladder control, I read a book on toilet training by a child expert. It was typically dry, devoid of all interest and dripping in clinical formality. But two words stuck in my head. The author referred to a toddler as having a "loaded rectum." The image this evokes always brings a smile to my face. I have visions of a toddler swaggering around, bottom loaded and ready to unleash a brown heap of chaos. With a colon chock-full-jam-packed-bursting with indescribable horrors, they're ready to fire away in your general direction.

This, of course, is why we put them in diapers in the first place. But common sense (and your mother-in-law) keeps telling you that they can't stay in diapers till they're eighteen.

That would cost too much.

Which leads us to a nasty Catch-22: You don't want to take their diaper off because they have no control and the stuff will go everywhere . . . but they can't learn control till they take their diaper off. It's like bike riding. You can have training wheels for a while, but there will have to come a day when you head off at great speed with only two wheels holding you up.

Accidents will occur.

Nevertheless, sooner or later you'll have to start thinking about toilet training. Four things are important for you to come to terms with in your quest to dominate your child's waste products:

1. Easy Solutions

You'll be relieved to know that there is a foolproof way of toilet-training your toddler. It's quick. It's easy. It's 100 percent guaranteed and it will work within just a few days. It's an efficient and clean method that can proceed without much effort or inconvenience at all.

Here's how it works:

Take your toddler and place him near a . . . (*but before the author could finish the sentence, an arrow flew through the window, piercing his chest, killing him instantly. The secret of toilet training would be lost forever. . . .*).

Okay, okay, little joke.

You are no doubt frighteningly familiar with the universal truth that there are no easy answers to the challenges that face us dads. You just have to wade in, do your best and hope the carpet survives.

2. You Can't Rush It

A friend of mine has a book with a title something like *Potty Training in Less Than a Day* or *Ten Easy Steps to the Toilet.* Such books have a useful purpose. You can rip out the pages and use them for toilet paper.

Bowel training, bladder training, toilet training, the removal of diapers and getting through the night without changing the sheets fifty times usually takes a while. Some do it young and get the hang of it quickly. Others take forever and are slow to embrace the change in routine.

> Trying to rush toilet training is like trying to hurry hair growth on your chest. It just doesn't work.

You can't toilet-train a child before he's ready. Trying to rush toilet training is like trying to hurry hair growth on your chest. It just doesn't work. You simply have to do your best and ride out the colonic storm.

3. Don't Stress

Don't worry about it. It's not too bad. All kids get there . . . eventually. How many adults do you see wandering around wearing diapers? It's simply a matter of timing, patience, carpet shampoo and a good washing machine.

4. It's Not Nice

Some books use euphemisms to make toilet training sound clean and sterile. Words like "movements" and "motions" are common. They don't sound too bad, do they? I wouldn't mind cleaning up a movement. Heck, what could be so awful about a motion?

Don't be fooled.

When we're talking about bowels and potties and toilet training, we are talking about sloppy, filthy, stinking sewage. You thought it was bad when the baby did it in a diaper. Wait till your toddler downloads a steaming mound on your couch. Wait till he paints himself with it and it gets everywhere and on everything, including in between the cracks of the polished floorboards and under your fingernails. Yep, there's nothing like a good dry retch to clear your sinuses.

So how do you go about toilet training?

The first thing to consider is the readiness of your child to learn about socially appropriate behaviors when going to the bathroom. Obviously, his ability to control his muscles and understand acceptable conduct regarding waste disposal depends on his age, intelligence, maturity and awareness of his own body.

Folklore dictates that somewhere in the ambiguous time frame of eighteen to twenty-four months, toddlers will start to show signs that they know something is going on down there in the engine room.

First, they gain an *awareness after the fact*. They produce a puddle, a full diaper or a steaming mound (or trail, if they're mobile at the time) and may stop to inspect it.

(Which brings me to the time we had guests over and a semi-naked eighteen-month-old Georgia toddled into the room. I heard one of my friends utter his now immortal words, "Where'd ya' get that pine cone from, Georgie?" There was a brief, uncertain silence and a heady stench in the air. It was not a pine cone.)

Second, after they realize that they actually produce various substances from various parts of their lower torso, they gradually gain *awareness before the fact*.

Many signals can indicate that something is about to happen. Your toddler may suddenly grab the front of his pants, make a face, turn red, shove his hands behind him as if he's trying to dig something out, look upset or look exceedingly happy. Some kids get all quiet and hide behind a large piece of furniture. Others do a squeezy-bottom dance, kind of like they've got chilies stuck up there.

Rachael used to stand stock-still with a determined look on her face. Georgia would suddenly disappear behind a door or into a corner or another room. Matilda would get the giggles and start chanting "Boohs . . . boohs." Your child will develop his own subtle signals, which you have to learn to read. If you don't, your carpet will pay the price.

Once toddlers reach the point when it becomes clear that they know something is happening, you can start training them.

(I remember as a seven-year-old watching my dad "train" our cat by burying its face deep into the spiral mousse it left for us under the television set. Something tells me that this approach probably won't go down too well with your child—or the authorities.)

When your toddler indicates to you that Mount St. Helens is about to blow—either by grunted word or anxious action—you have about two-point-five seconds to whip off his pants and get him to the drop zone.

The drop zone may be the toilet, although in reality, unless you have modified it with a toddler seat, that gaping porcelain void can be a frightening proposition to someone the size of a toddler. He may even think that you're trying to flush *him* down the S-bend.

> Your child will develop his own subtle signals, which you have to learn to read. If you don't, your carpet will pay the price.

Some use a sturdy "potty." These aren't just simple bowls as they were in our day, mind you. Now they come in a mind-numbing array of plastic shapes and colors. You can get cars, trucks, turtles, hippos, giraffes (especially good for boys!) . . . the list goes on.

You can even give the potty a name. The pride of our house is bright yellow Timmy the Tortoise. Friends of ours have a pink hippo affectionately known as Mrs. Gladys T. Burton (don't ask).

It takes a while to get used to the potty thing. Some kids hate it and get up one second after you put them on it. Others want to stay there all afternoon. Others bypass it altogether and graduate straight to "the big toilet."

Sometimes it's a false alarm and he will either sit there looking at you vacantly or scream bloody murder. This can be frustrating. If he does get upset, gently encourage him to sit patiently on the back of "Frank the Fire Truck" and try again. Refrain from *forcing* him to sit on the potty. He will only learn to dislike the experience.

After many failures, there will come a time when he produces the goods, right on target.

I'm quite embarrassed about this next part, but I'll tell you about it anyway.

I am a grown man with a college education. I consider myself to be a mature, well-adjusted adult, able to exist adequately in cultured surroundings. As such, I never would have believed the exhilaration and pride I experienced when each of my children learned to poop in Timmy's shell.

Recently, I have read that "going over the top" in celebration of potty victory is a parental no-no. The current advice is to stay calm.

Yeah, right.

I jumped up in the air, screamed like a maniac and, holding the potty turtle and its sacred contents proudly above my head, did a victory lap of the house. I danced a jig with Meredith and we called our parents. If I'd had one of those party thingamajigs that go "Wheee" when you blow them, no doubt I would have done that too.

Looking back, I'm just grateful there was no film in the camera at the time.

So much for staying calm.

However, the thought that my toilet-training days were over was short-lived. It is a long and laborious process, mixed with many successes and failures. Sometimes you will get him to the potty or toilet in time and he will go without trouble. Other times he will sit there for half an hour doing nothing, but ten seconds after he gets up, he'll poop under the kitchen table.

Try to remember that what he is doing is natural. He is not being dirty or vindictive by pooping on your floor (unless he's eight years old). He hasn't learned your cultural values about using the bathroom yet. Don't scold him for his failures. Be gently encouraging.

If he doesn't make it, say something like, "Hey Mark, I couldn't help but notice this massive pooey here in your toy box. Do you think the toilet might be a better place for that next time? Because then we can just flush it away instead of having to put all your Teddy bears in the washing machine . . . what do you think? Okay?"

This is better for your child's self-esteem than, "What the heck? You filthy little monster! Who is going to clean up all of this? Go in the bathroom next time, will you? Geez, you're eighteen months old! That's disgusting!"

After a while, the averages will improve. He can start wearing underwear around the house and you can start telling him how grown up he is.

Be prepared, however, for the mistakes.

Young children still poop their undies and even well-trained older children can wet their pants if they've left it too long or if they're tired or excited. Quite often I've found one of my girls standing in a puddle in the bathroom with a sad or anxious look on her face and her tights hopelessly tangled around her shoes. She just couldn't make it in time.

(This often happens when kids watch a video, because their brains switch off and they don't realize they need to go to the bathroom until it's too late. One of mine even went while watching a movie at the theater. The tragically funny part was that she was sitting on a friend's lap at the time.)

After a while, you can encourage your child onto the larger and now less ominous "big toilet." Providing a step may help. This could be a sturdy box of your own creation or a specially designed "toilet ladder" that has handrails and cutesy animals on it. Or you could buy a toilet frame, which is a miniature seat that locks inside the larger one. If you do use one of these, make sure you remove the kid's seat before your dinner party guests arrive. (That's one story I'm *definitely not* going to tell you!)

As your child gets older and gains confidence, you can encourage him to go to the bathroom by himself without having to be chaperoned by you. When this happens, it's fantastic. Open a bottle of champagne to celebrate the end of a fairly hideous era of your life.

There are three further things you will need to teach your toddler:

I. Bottom Wiping

At first, you're still going to have to provide the cleanup service afterward. Get long lengths of toilet paper and fold them and fold them and fold them again, so they're fairly thick. Then there is no way your fingers can . . . well, you know.

Right away, give your child the last piece of toilet paper to use on himself. This is a token gesture. He'll wave the paper behind him in the air. But after a while, his arms will grow and, little by little, he will be able to take on more of the role himself until you don't have to do it at all.

The larger and now less ominous toilet. . . .

2. Flushing

Teach him to flush after himself. Some kids enjoy this, others are put off by the noise, but they come around when they get used to it. This is a good habit to get into, particularly when your boss comes over for dinner and goes to use the toilet and . . . well, enough said.

Also, teach your toddler that flushing is for human waste, not for jewelry, Teddy bears, clothing or small pets.

> Teach your toddler that flushing is for human waste, not for jewelry, Teddy bears, clothing or small pets.

3. Hand Washing

From the very beginning, teach your child to wash his hands with soap. This is absolutely necessary for basic hygiene and the prevention of worms.

Even though your child has been showing control during the day, he is probably still wearing a diaper at night. After a while, however, you will start to notice that the diapers are dry in the morning or he will call for you in the middle of the night when he wants to go. When this pattern of day control/night awareness develops, you can start trying "no diapers" at night. This is a delicate game of bladder roulette. Explain to your child that tonight he won't be wearing a diaper and that if he has to go to the bathroom, he can get up or call for you. Strongly encourage him to go to the bathroom just before bed.

Don't give him three quarts of juice to drink just before bed, but whatever you do, don't dehydrate him from 4 P.M. onward in the hope that you can dry him up, either. If he's thirsty, let him drink water.

When this pattern of day control/ night awareness develops, you can start trying "no diapers" at night. This is a delicate game of bladder roulette.

There will be successes and failures. Success means a dry bed for him and a good night's sleep for you. Failure means getting up in the middle of the night, washing the young 'un and changing jammies and sheets. Once again, don't reprimand. Your child needs encouragement and comfort. Wetting the bed is common among two-year-olds, less common among five-year-olds.

Of course, some kids don't get the hang of it for a long time. Let's be honest: Most of us can remember having at least one luxurious dream about standing in a waterfall or whatever and then waking up in soaked pajamas. *All* kids will wet their beds to varying degrees, but if it's an unmanageable problem, ask your family doctor about it. She may reassure you or suggest you visit one of her specialist colleagues, who will ask you some questions and charge you a vast sum of money—doctors know that parents of bedwetters are desperate people.

There are two other things you need to consider when it comes to toilets, bowels and so forth:

1. The Size of Your Kid's Bladder

As you are finding out, your toddler's bladder is even smaller than the one your wife had when she was nine-months' pregnant. Toddlers' bladders take a few hours to fill up, but only seconds to empty. When they gotta go, they gotta go. There's no such thing as "hang on a minute" with little Craig who has just thrust his hands into his pants and is physically holding back the flow.

It's bad enough when you're at home. But after a while you grow confident and you take little Craig to the supermarket. Halfway through shopping, when you're near the frozen peas, he makes that face and starts that dance and says, "I wanna go weee." You say, "Just hang on a—" but he's already going. You had two-point-five seconds to act—and you blew it.

You must be prepared for these situations. And by "prepared," I don't mean that you can actually do anything about it. I mean prepared as in coping with the embarrassment you'll experience as you crouch with your two-year-old who is whizzing in the gutter in the middle of the city during lunch hour. (I learned this lesson the hard way when we took the kids into the city to watch fireworks. But that's another story.)

You always have to think ahead: Where is there a toilet that I can get to right now? In supermarkets and shopping centers, you have to know where you're going to go (toilet? potted plant? behind a display?)—that is, assuming you have the time.

Sometimes there will be no toilet. You'll be out walking, or stuck in a traffic jam or traveling down the highway at 60 miles per hour.

Improvise.

After a while, you'll get used to encouraging your child to urinate behind trees, in gutters or on the tire of someone else's car.

2. Vocabulary

Carefully consider the words you use to describe going to the bathroom, because your child will latch on to these words and use them in socially delicate situations. He will scream them out in supermarkets and will announce to your friends in proud detail what he just did in the bathroom. He will tell his baby-sitter, kindergarten teacher and the kids at the playground.

Embarrassment will be hiding around every corner.

Imagine having lunch with, say, six or seven cultured guests, and your three-year-old comes screaming up to the table.

"I JUST DID A POOEY!!!"

(Hysterical laughter.)

"Thank you for telling us that, darli—"

"It was two pieces!"

(Polite laughter.)

"That's enough, tha—"

"One was a big piece and it hurt, but the other was a little tiny one that came out after. It didn't hurt at all . . . and there was a big wee, too."

(Silence.)

"We don't really want to hear about all—"

"And I wiped my own butt . . . SEE!"

(Drops pants, turns around, bends over. Guests put knives and forks down and say they're full.)

For this reason, you need to figure out what kind of bathroom vocabulary you're going to use.

It shouldn't be too formal. Little kids sound pretentious saying stuff like, "I have to excrete," "I want to have a movement," "I would like to defecate," "Where can I urinate?" and "My lower colon needs evacuation." Statements like these will get them beat up at school.

Nor can they be too colloquial. It's just not nice hearing a child say, "Time to drop a load," "Where do I piss around here?" and so on.

But it shouldn't be too cute, either. It's just plain embarrassing hearing kids (or even worse, their parents) say stuff like, "It's woopsie time," "I have to go doo-doo," "Mr. Brownie wants to come out to say hello" and so on.

That doesn't leave you with much choice, does it?

There are of course the traditional favorites. Most of these have many varied permutations. For example, the conventionally accepted "poo" can also be "poos," "poo-poo," "poo-poos," "pooey," "poop," "poopies," and all these words can be prefixed by the word "Mister" to create a whole new set of combinations—"Mr. Poo," "Mr. Pooey," "Mr. Poos" and so on. In fact, you can create an entire fictional extended family out of human waste.

Then again, you could just teach them to say, "Excuse me, I have to go to the bathroom."

CHAPTER 5
Eating

PARENTS know that food is important. We digest a good deal of propaganda about staying "healthy," "growing big and strong," "eating up" and "having a balanced diet." We even vaguely remember something about the seven basic food groups: grains, meat, fruit and vegetables, fats, dairy, chocolate and beer.

We all know that small children need a healthful, balanced diet. The problem is that it's easy to become overzealous. This is not helped by books that say you have to have so many grams of this or this many servings of that per day or else your child will have sand kicked in his face at the beach.

Someone once gave us a magnetic refrigerator thingy proclaiming the approximate daily nutritional needs of a one- to three-year-old child. I tried to follow it fairly closely.

Rachael didn't mind the dairy (1/2 cup milk, 7 ounces yogurt, 2 ounces cheese, 1/2 cup pudding). Things went well with the fruit and vegetables (1/2 carrot, 1/2 potato, 1/2 cup juice, 1/4 cup mixed vegetables, 1 apple). She was even patient with the grains (2 slices of bread, 1/2 cup cereal, 1/2 cup spaghetti, 1 roll, 1/2 cup oatmeal). Things went awry, however, with the meat and meat-substitute part (2 ounces chicken, 1 egg, a big scoop of peanut butter, 1/2 cup baked beans, 1 fish stick). Maybe I shouldn't have cooked it into one big omelet.

I won't even mention the section that said, and I quote, "2 teaspoons of fat or oil."

I got fed up with creating little namby-pamby meals. I got fed up with weighing every little portion and reading the side of every package. Half the time I couldn't figure out the servings anyway. (I still don't know what "fl oz" means.) And I got sick of cooking just one fish stick.

So I gave up after a day.

There are two problems with following the perfectly balanced meal chart.

First, your toddler is already full and isn't interested in your food because she spends the whole day wandering around picking up anything that will fit into her mouth and trying to suck the nutrition out of it. She doesn't care what it is. Plastic blocks, moldy fruit, stuff out of the trash. All she knows is that if she shovels enough junk into her mouth, odds are that sooner or later she'll get something edible.

All she knows is that if she shovels enough junk into her mouth, odds are that sooner or later she'll get something edible.

Second, she doesn't touch half of what you give her anyway. And of the stuff she does touch, most goes into her hair or on her clothes. I've been making "kid sandwiches" for five years now and it's only just dawned on me that my kids don't eat bread. They open the sandwich, eat whatever is inside and then rip up the bread, mold it into shapes and stomp it into the grout of our tiled floor.

It's all well and good for us to have our basic food groups. But kids have their own. The five toddler basic food groups are from

- the lawn (snails, dirt, leaves, berries)
- the kitchen floor (crumbs, crusts, peels)
- the supermarket (chewing gum, cigarette butts, tissues)
- the car (moldy apples, oil-stained rags)
- their loose diaper (say no more)

Once they get a little older, they become more selective and their tastebuds grow more sophisticated. The five basic food groups for preschoolers are

- chips
- any drink that fizzes, especially red or green ones
- chocolate
- any takeout food, especially if it comes with a toy
- lollipops

Don't be too concerned about this seemingly unbalanced intake of vitamins, minerals, carbohydrates and fats. Human-kind has made it through several thousand years on far less substantial foodstuffs than we have at our disposal. When Jesus was walking the earth, people lived off locusts, honey and weeds blowing around in the wilderness; in China, rice and sweet 'n' sour pork; and in my father's hometown, gravel and engine oil.

We, on the other hand, have freezers and genetically engineered fruit and vegetables. We also live in the most cosmopolitan country on the planet and have in our local grocery stores all sorts of bizarre foodstuffs from exotic lands that our ancestors would have referred to as (in the words of my father) "foreign garbage."

Meredith and I have never bothered making special meals for our kids, with the exception of grilled-cheese sandwiches while we indulge in a particularly spicy or exotic meal. Basically, they've gone straight from breast milk to slushy cereal to whatever we're having.

To start, the whole meal (for example, roast beef, potato, squash) goes into a blender to form a slushy roast dinner. Once they get a little older and they have teeth, a little manual dexterity and understand the basic concept of putting the stuff from the bowl into their own mouths, we start making meals a little chunkier. Grabbable hunks of meat, cooked carrot sticks, cheese pieces, veggies, bread and, to finish the meal, some banana. It's important to make sure that whatever you give them can fit down their throats. Watch out for "hard" foods such as carrots, celery, nuts, apples and so on.

It is also around this time that they are quarantined at the other end of the table, away from the rest of the family, because we all have an aversion to being showered in scraps.

Of course, this all rests on the assumption that *your* diet is decent in the first place. I am assuming that somewhere amid all the canned junk and frozen stuff there is something reasonably fresh. If a cursory glance in your refrigerator reveals only a dozen frozen pizzas, your child is in big trouble.

Go and take a look in the mirror. If you look reasonably healthy, your diet does not consist solely of beer and microwave TV dinners, and you make it to the produce aisle at least once a week, then your toddler has a chance.

If not, consult your doctor—and a dietitian.

Getting Them to Eat

Just because you have a good supply of varied and nutritious foods does not mean that your child will immediately begin gratefully consuming every meal you serve . . . that is, unless every meal is soda, chips and a bag of candy, complete with plastic toy.

Some kids will take one look at the meal in front of them, pout, pronounce it "yucky," fold their arms in front of them and refuse to eat. Such children are called "fussy eaters," which is a euphemism for "pain in the behind." To be fair, kids have tastebuds just like we do, so you have to cut them some slack and realize that there are things they might find truly repulsive. Fair enough. I mean, does anybody like liver?

More often than not, however, their refusal has more to do with their mood at the time and the dawning realization that they can make your life a misery. Here are a few things that might help you get your child to eat:

- Buy her a set of special kid-sized silverware and a plastic cup and plate. If you are feeling extravagant, go to a novelty store and have a photo of her printed on the cup and plate.
- Psyche her up by telling her how yummy the dinner is. Lick your lips and gobble down yours.
- Make a game out of eating. Do the good old "here comes the airplane" routine. Make a surprised face every time she eats a mouthful, or yell out the number of mouthfuls she's eaten. Bury peas and carrots under the mashed potatoes and tell her to dig for buried treasure.
- Make deals and use bribery, such as, "There'll be no ice cream until you've had ten more mouthfuls" or "If we don't finish all the food on the table, the leftovers will attract rats that will roam the house while we sleep, looking for things to eat." Give her a stamp or a sticker every time she "eats up."
- Present the food in interesting ways. Cut sandwiches into shapes. Arrange vegetables into patterns. I have a friend whose son doesn't like to eat apples. So he cuts an apple into squares, puts them in a line on a plate and calls it

"choo-choo train apple." Then, his son can't eat it fast enough. A seasoned parent can even sculpt the Statue of Liberty out of mashed potatoes.

- Serve only food she likes. Of course, seven days of grilled-cheese sandwiches will give her scurvy, but at least you'll have some quiet at the table.
- Give meals interesting names. Georgia, for example, refuses to eat vegetarian lasagna. So instead we call it "Georgia Surprise" and she absolutely wolfs it down. The surprise, of course, is that she eats it just because we change its name! I reckon I could get her to eat compost on toast simply by calling it "super-duper chockie whiz-bangs."

In your attempts to encourage consumption, avoid saying these three things at all costs:

- Don't you know there are people starving in Africa?
- Well, we'll just sit here till you finish.
- What's the matter? Don't you like roadkill?

Snacking

Once upon a time in human history, people ate when they were hungry. Day or night, morning or afternoon, if they wanted to eat, they'd go out and kill a bison or take a drink from the river.

We, however, have developed a strict system commonly referred to as "three square meals a day." I find this to be kind of a joke, really. My first meal of the day is a hastily gulped glass of juice and a piece of toast as I run out the door. My second is a cup of coffee and a muffin. Not really what you'd call *square*.

In our culture, being hungry between these three square meals is a bad thing. It's called "snacking." It has overtones of being naughty and unhealthful.

Anyway, the point of all this is that little kids love to snack. Almost all day, you will have to deal with a whiny voice repeating, "I hungry" or "I wanna jink" over and over and over.

I have no problem with this. If they're hungry, let them eat. If they're thirsty, let them drink.

Your child is growing, growing, growing and burning up energy just by running around all day looking for stuff to smash.

Her body is smaller than yours, so a walk across the park is a marathon for her. Don't think that just because you can go all day on a cup of coffee and a bar of chocolate, she can too.

Of course, there are a few stipulations.

First, don't let your child snack on junk. This helps you see how hungry she really is.

When Rachael says to me, "Dad, I'm hungry," I give her an apple. Sometimes she looks at me, pouts and says, "No, I'm hungry for chocolate." In this situation, I know that her hunger is more related to her tastebuds than her stomach. "Apple or nothing," I say.

> Sometimes she looks at me, pouts and says, "No, I'm hungry for chocolate." In this situation, I know that her hunger is more related to her tastebuds than her stomach.

When Georgia tells me she is dying of thirst, I give her a glass of water. When she throws it on the floor and starts kicking her legs and screaming, "No, Dad, I'm thirsty for DR. FIZZY!" I say, "Drink water or be thirsty."

Keep the snacks half decent. Give your child dried apricots, a piece of cheese, a banana, juice, water or milk. Then occasionally give her a treat—sugary drink, some chips, a cracker or two.

Second, you need to learn the difference between *hungry* and *greedy*. If your child is starting to look as if she's training for toddler sumo, maybe you'd better ease off the ice cream sandwiches.

But remember, all toddlers have that swollen-belly pear-shape thing happening so they look as if they've swallowed a balloon. That doesn't mean your child is overweight. It just means her organs are waiting for the rest of her body to catch up. All toddlers look like that.

Third, a snack is a quick pick-me-up, not a meal. Don't let snacking replace proper meals. If she snacks all afternoon and then eats nothing at dinner, you've got the balance wrong. If snacking is becoming a problem in your house, give her soy milk and Brussels sprouts as a snack. That'll put her back on track.

Skills

Babies have appalling table manners. They slurp and burp and dribble when they eat and then spew afterward.

Then things get difficult.

They suddenly develop manual dexterity and want to grab the spoon. They spit the food back at you. They turn their heads at the last moment so you shove mushy spinach in their hair. They wrestle the bowl from you and tip it on their heads or in their laps.

With the onset of physical capability and dexterity, you can introduce your child to the concept of feeding herself. This won't happen overnight. It will take a long time to turn her from a baby with no eating skills into a child who can actually get most of the food into her mouth. It will take a long time for her to develop the necessary hand-eye-mouth coordination, to say nothing of the physical strength required to lift cups and cut steak. Take it one step at a time. Rome wasn't built in a day and a toddler will take a while to learn the fundamentals of eating techniques.

The first stage is the messiest and most frustrating.

Strap her in a highchair, put a bowl of food in front of her and then run for it. Take cover as quickly as possible, because when she dives into that food, it's like a grenade going off in a bucket of rotten fruit. Statistically, out of all the food that starts flying around, some of it will go down her throat.

Be prepared for carnage. You will soon discover that this is why most parents bathe their children *after* dinner, not before.

At first, everything will be fingers only. She'll grab handfuls of food and shovel it into her mouth or throw it on the floor. After a while, you'll be able to leave a spoon next to her bowl and she'll start experimenting with it. The first few times, she'll stick it up her nose or in her ear, but day by day she'll start to get the hang of it.

The problem at this stage, however, is that she will soon figure out that a spoon is like a slingshot, the purpose of which is to increase the ballistic range of thrown objects—in this case, the range of her high-velocity mashed potatoes. This puts all other people at the dinner table at considerable risk.

At the same time, you can start introducing drinking skills.

As a baby, her only form of intake is generally through a bottle or breast. If you jump straight to a cup, she'll just knock it over or pour it over her face and clothes, which introduces the problem of her drowning at the table.

It's best to go in stages. From the bottle, introduce the lidded cup with either a spout or a straw on the top. Once she's mastered that, upgrade to a two-handled plastic mug. Let her practice using it while she's in the bath, because then it doesn't matter when 90 percent of the contents miss her mouth.

By age two, she'll probably have the skill to manage a normal plastic cup. Most of the time.

By age three or four, she should be able to manage a knife and fork almost adequately, as long as she's not cutting or spearing anything too tough. Even a five-year-old can struggle trying to slice a sausage or cut through a pie crust.

By the time she starts kindergarten, the situation will have improved markedly. Your child should be able to sit at the table for an extended period and, on the whole, be able to consume food and liquid without too much trouble. But occasional spills and accidents will still occur. Cups will tip over and food will still find its way to the floor. There will often be enough food on the front of her shirt to feed a small Third World village. But as long as she's not being deliberately messy or silly, remember that she's still learning. (Even *I* drop food on the table at times, especially at my favorite Thai restaurant.) I constantly have to remind myself that they are little children and I have to have realistic expectations. Obviously, some days are better than others.

I like the idea of family time around the table.

Dinnertime: The Last Bastion

I'm kind of an old-fashioned guy. I grew up in a family where no matter what else happened, dinner was eaten at the table with conversation for entertainment rather than TV. This was the one time when we could catch up on the day's events and meet together as a family. The only exception was Sunday night soup with toast in front of "The Wonderful World of Disney." (This was my parents' attempt to stay in touch with their son.)

I like the idea of family time around the table. I rush out the door in the morning, and I'm at work all day. Having dinner together reminds me that I have a family. It is a little haven at the end of a busy day where I can enjoy a meal and engage in calm conversation.

But when dinnertime goes sour, it goes *really* sour.

Rachael sits in Georgia's chair—tantrum. Georgia touches Rachael's cup—tantrum. Matilda won't sit in her chair—I have a tantrum. There's a brawl over whose turn it is to say grace. Someone kicks someone else under the table. Georgia is screaming. Matilda throws her plate. Rachael tastes her dinner and pronounces it yucky. Georgia agrees with her older sibling, even though she hasn't tasted it. Georgia spills my drink. Rachael falls off her chair. Matilda ruins her clean jammies by pouring gravy down the front. I start to raise my voice and get angry. The table settles down to conversations about the politics of sandbox domination by the boys at preschool. Georgia mushes her entire meal into a soft goulash that she then smears all over the placemat. Another drink tips over. When I go to get a dishtowel, all the girls shove celery down their undies.

> Tell her every day that spitting food across the table is not an acceptable way of saying that you don't like the taste.

Yep, it's certainly not as peaceful and relaxing as it used to be.

But that's life at the table with kids.

Struggle on. Do your best. Teach your child about the right kinds of food to eat. Ensure she has a half-decent and balanced diet. Show her how to hold her knife, fork and spoon. Tell her every day that spitting food across the table is not an acceptable way of saying that you don't like the taste.

Because one day she'll have to go to an important work dinner or to a romantic restaurant on a hot date—and if she still eats like a toddler, she's in big trouble.

CHAPTER 6
Baths

MEREDITH says we bathe our kids for hygienic reasons.

I think it's just so we can identify them.

Kids get dirty. Very dirty. Their little bodies whiz around the house and garden, building up a static charge that turns them into dirt magnets. All the filth in the neighborhood—mud, earthworms, dough, paint, crumbs, crayons, chocolate, fluff, tree sap, sandwich spreads, mucus, meconium from their newborn baby sister—is sucked into their toddler vortex. They wind up at the end of each day plastered in a thick paste of unidentifiable muck and with a forest of caked-on, crunchy crumbs around their noses and mouths.

This is bad because you have to wash them.

Bathing a baby is supposedly one of those meaningful parental joys that is often depicted in slow motion in TV commercials. I mean, it's kind of cute holding your baby in one hand while he gurgles and his arms and legs splash about.

Of course, they never tell you about the trouble of setting up the bath, the bad back caused by the bathing stool and that most disgusting of all jobs—cleaning the creamy crud out of their Shar Pei–like folds of skin.

But bathing a baby is a picnic compared with bathing a toddler. At least a baby just stays there and takes it, whether he likes it or not. A toddler, on the other hand, can actually fight you off. You see, he either loves it or hates it—and this can change from day to day.

The bath is one of the many places where he can start exerting his tenacious, bulldoglike individuality, manifested in his refusal to cooperate. You say "Bathtime" and he says, "No." He'll scream and holler and throw a tantrum at the sound of the running water. You'll have to fight him in the name of basic cleanliness, or call it quits and attack him with a washcloth when he's not looking.

The next day he'll be trying to get in the bath before he's even out of his clothes. He will laugh and splash and then throw a tantrum when you try to take him out.

Have Fun in the Bath

I really enjoy taking a bath with my kids . . . well, for the first five minutes, anyway. I mean, I get wet when I crouch down next to the bath, so I might as well get in there with them. It's fun to pile in and sing songs and play games and splash each other. It's a good place to talk and laugh. We also play some great games—my favorite is a three-player game called "Abandon Bath." Here's how you play:

> The bath is one of the many places where he can start exerting his tenacious, bulldoglike individuality, manifested in his refusal to cooperate.

Get into the bath with your wife and child and splash around and generally have good family time together.

Soon, your toddler will get a strained expression on his face and will "launch a torpedo." Either you or your wife will need to be "the spotter." When you spot the torpedo, yell out either "Depth charge!" or "Torpedo!" depending on whether it sinks or floats. The object of the game is for everybody to get out of the bath without touching the torpedo. If you touch it, you die and lose the game. There are bonus points if you can also get all the bath toys out without contamination.

Another beauty is the "Hair-Washing Game." This is how it works:

Wash your toddler's hair.

If he doesn't scream, you win.

If he has a tantrum, you lose. But as a runner-up prize, you get a headache! Congratulations. Thanks for playing. Better luck next time.

This game is most notable for its unpredictability. Sometimes, your child will love it. He will gurgle and splash and, when you wash his hair, he'll say, "More!" Other times, his head will spin around and his eyes will roll back in their sockets as if he is trying to take a peek at his brain.

In relation to hair, it seems that most kids don't like getting water on their faces. You can try tilting his head back and covering his eyes with your hand. You can try doing it gradually. You can try using a cup to wet the back of his head. You can try making a game or a song out of it. You can try explaining to him beforehand what you are going to do. You can try bribery. You can try special kiddie shampoo, which is just normal shampoo inside a plastic figurine of a cartoon character at twice the price.

Or you can just get fed up and pour a whole bucket of water over his head and get the whole painful experience over in half a second. I admit to having done this, but it doesn't do a lot to promote the experience of future baths or to engender paternal trust.

Sometimes, you just have to wash him whether he likes it or not, especially if he is thickly matted with potatoes and gravy. Other times, however, if it's going to be too much fuss, just don't bother.

It took me a while to learn this. Once I went into battle with Matilda. I had said I was going to wash her hair and, because I had spoken, I got into one of those parental paradoxes where I would not back down.

It was an epic struggle between the immovable object and the unstoppable force.

In the end, I won. Matilda had something vaguely resembling washed hair and I had a headache. It only occurred to me later that she probably hadn't needed her hair washed anyway, and so I was left to consider whether my stance had been worth it.

Many parents try to distract their children by investing in the bath-toy market. At our place, the bathroom walls are lined with sponge dinosaurs and foam zoo animals. The bath is filled to overflowing with plastic boats, ducks, fish, windup subs, squirty things, cups, building blocks and so forth. In fact, if we fill it up enough, we don't have room to bathe our youngsters anymore.

Bubble bath can also make bathtime lots of fun. My kids *love* bubble bath, which is good because every birthday they get about five Disney cartoon figurines with screw-top heads, filled with bubble bath.

But don't relax or be lulled into a false sense of victory.

Because after the bath comes the nightmare of drying. If worst comes to worst, they can just drip-dry, but hair often needs more attention.

My kids hated having their hair dried until we introduced the "Magical Hair-Drying Machine!" This is simply a gimmick where I pretend to be a machine. They call out instructions such as "Slow" and consequently get a slow hair rub accompanied by low-volume mechanical noises. Then they yell out "FAST!" (this is my chance) and I rapidly lay into their scalp while screaming like a banshee. They think it's a great game.

Their hair gets dry but unfortunately looks like they've swallowed a grenade. This makes it difficult to brush, but the kids put up with it because we told them that if hair-brushing was going to be a hassle, we'd shave their heads.

Safety

But while cleanliness and fun are both important, several safety factors relating to bathtime need to be taken into consideration.

Don't Leave a Child Alone in the Bath

Toddlers may be able to sit up, but they are also good at falling over. And it takes only a few inches of water for a child to drown.

Bathtubs tend to be quite slippery, and one of the only handholds in the area happens to be the faucet, which is aimed straight at them. Parental folklore recommends that you don't leave a child alone in a bath until he's at least seven years old.

Be Vigilant

No doubt, as the father of a baby you are sharp-eyed and attentive. But remember that toddlers are more mobile, more inquisitive and more upright. Kids have little understanding of the dangers of drowning or scalding, so keep in mind the following tips:

- Keep the door shut when you're running a bath.
- Test the temperature of the water before he gets in.

- Buy a nonslip mat for the bathtub.
- Teach him that the faucets are off-limits.
- Teach him that the floor in the bathroom can be slippery.
- Teach him not to stand up or jump around in the bathtub.
- Be aware of the dangers of the bathroom, even if you're in there, too.
- Teach him not to put soap in his eyes.
- Teach him not to say, "I went pee-pee, Dad," when you're sitting in there with him.

When newborn Matilda had just come home from the hospital, I was undressing her for her bath and squatting down on the bathroom floor. Not three feet away, Georgia was slouching on the edge of the bathtub, watching the plastic boats swirl around in the tap stream. Then she was in the water—just like that. In the blink of an eye, she flipped in, head first, fully dressed.

It was fortunate that I was there and could grab her immediately. And it was fortunate that, for once, I had actually run a bath that wasn't too hot, so she wasn't scalded. I lay awake that night wondering what might have happened if I had just stepped out to make a quick phone call or if I'd run a characteristically boiling-hot bath.

Another time, an almost-toddling Matilda was getting a late-night bath after vomiting over everything in her bed. I was actually holding her and trying to rinse her hair when she reached out and turned the hot tap right onto herself. Fortunately, the water in the pipe had cooled and I turned it off immediately. But she still got a shock and so did I.

So be very careful. The bath should be a place of fun—and a place of hygiene—but most of all it should be a place of safety.

Don't Let Your Child Put in the Bubble Bath

I let Georgia do this once and she poured it *all* in. The six-foot wall of bubbles almost made it to the carpet in the hallway before we were able to get the situation under control. One or two capfuls is plenty.

Remember, too, that bubble bath obscures your view of what's under the water. Your child could let one loose in there and you wouldn't realize till a gap in the bubbles revealed a Loch Ness monster sliding around under the surface.

You also need to be careful getting into the bath. I once sat down in the bath rather heavily without checking to see what toys were already in there.

So be very careful. The bath should be a place of fun—and a place of hygiene—but most of all it should be a place of safety.

The proctologist was very professional about the whole unfortunate situation. He didn't even smile.

The whole unfortunate situation

CHAPTER 7
Playtime

TODDLERS have graduated from rattles and dangly things on elastic and are at a stage where they like to be engaged actively: picking things up; slamming things together; cramming things in their mouths. Their curiosity is exploding, as is their potential to do damage.

As far as a toddler is concerned, your entire body is one fantastic theme park full of fun activities. Your hair is good for yanking out; your eyes are good for gouging; your lips are good for stretching down over your chin; your nose is good for sticking fingers up; your stomach is good for blowing raspberries on; your testicles are good as a trampoline; your forehead is a great spot to press out cookie-cutter shapes.

> As far as a toddler is concerned, your entire body is one fantastic theme park full of fun activities.

Lie down on the ground and let your toddler jump on you. Throw her around in the air and onto furniture. Play peek-a-boo, hide-and-seek and tickles. Laugh a lot. Have a good time! Enjoy yourself. Enjoy your child. This is what being a dad is all about.

As your toddler grows, she doesn't lose this desire to engage in physical play. (I hope I can still roughhouse with my daughters when they're thirty years old . . . hang on a second, make that . . . um, ten.) Their level of play, however, will become more sophisticated, which is just as well because you'd get tired of jingly rattles and raspberries after ten years. (I get tired after ten minutes!)

When I grew up, *play* meant toy cars, kicking a ball, climbing trees, fistfights and burning defenseless insects with a magnifying glass. Despite my best efforts, my girls do not enjoy these things. They much prefer tea parties, dressing up, fashion parades and pushing dolls around in toy strollers.

I don't know about you, but I can only last so long at passing the sugar and chomping on imaginary crackers. And I look lousy in a dress. To be honest with you, sometimes—well, often—I find it plain hard work to play with my daughters, particularly when I have something pressing to do. But it has to be done.

There's a limitless world of play to engage in:

- physical play, such as wrestling, tickling, running, jumping and dancing
- creative play, such as molding and decorating modeling clay
- intellectual play, such as books, computer games and puzzles
- imaginative play, such as dressing up and pretending to be other people and having adventures on the high seas or in the jungle
- industrial play, such as building towers
- messy play, such as making mudpies and jumping through the sprinkler
- destructive play, such as ripping the heads off every flower in the garden
- TV play, such as sitting immobile with a glazed expression and an open mouth, staring straight ahead.

The list is endless.

It's important to play with your child. In fact, if she had her way, she would play with you all the time. Unfortunately, she doesn't realize that in the real world, you *can't* play all the time. You have to go to work. Repairs need to be made. Lawns need to be mowed. Shopping, cooking, cleaning . . . obviously you are not going to be at her beck and call for every play experience.

Sometimes I have to say to my children, "Sorry, guys. I have to write a book on how to be a good dad, so I'm not going to play with you right now."

> I just can't get the idea out of my head that when they're all teenagers, it'll be *them* saying, "Not now, Dad."

But even if I do have work to do, at times I'll succumb to the earnest look on their faces. I just can't get the idea out of my head that when they're all teenagers, it'll be *them* saying, "Not now, Dad."

Deadlines can wait. My kids won't.

Toys, Toys and More Toys

Toddlers are curious. As such, in their eyes, your entire home is a playground, built entirely for their pleasure. They just can't wait to get their hands on your compact discs, videotapes, remote controls, computer disks, power tools, cupboards with childproof locks, wallet and credit cards, jelly jars and the telephone.

This is why parents buy toys—to distract their toddlers from all the valuable stuff they don't want touched. Sooner or later, you'll find yourself buying a few little playthings and then a birthday or two will pass by and before you know it, your house will start to look like a bomb went off in Santa's workshop.

You are much better off having a few really good toys than a room full of garbage.

But beware! There are many bad toys on the market. Toys that are ridiculously expensive. Toys that don't do anything. Toys that are gimmicky or too complex. Toys that have a thousand pieces. Toys that only last five minutes or break too easily. Toys that are dangerous.

You are much better off having a few really good toys than a room full of garbage. Of course, choosing a toy is another matter. When you buy a toy, there are several things you should keep in mind.

Don't Get Fooled into Equating Cost with the Real Value of a Toy

When I was a kid, there was a toy store in our local shopping center. It was small but brimming with treasure. Now, toy stores are giant warehouses that contain literally thousands of toys. The treasure is still there. It's just hidden amid all the garbage. These places are designed to make kids throw tantrums and give adults wallet hernias. Don't get sucked into all the glitz and gloss and advertising.

Product marketing is a billion-dollar business. They take a product worth five dollars, slap a sticker of a cartoon character on it and suddenly it's worth twenty bucks! Incredible! There are lunchboxes, hairbrushes, toothbrushes, drink bottles, rubber balls, shoes, socks, underwear, T-shirts, plates, cups, coloring books . . . the list is endless, as will be your debt if you succumb to such product manipulation.

Sometimes the best toys are the simplest ones: a red ball, a toy car, a hat or a patch of dirt and a plastic shovel.

Once I got a huge department-store box that was previously home to a refrigerator.

I took it home.

I put it on the floor.

The kids climbed in and never wanted to get out. It was the best toy they'd ever had. In the end I had to throw it out because it got wet and collapsed into a mushy pancake.

The same principle applies to toys for the bath. Forget all the complex waterwheels and squirty doodads that do all sorts of wonderful things in the water. By far the most popular items in our bathroom are plastic cups, a plastic ice-cream container and washcloths.

My kids also love to play on my computer (not in the bath, though). Obviously this is a more expensive option, for both hardware and software. But if you already have a computer in your house, a lot of the kids' software on the market is high quality and not too pricey. You can get stuff for all ages. For younger kids, there are games that teach mouse and keyboard skills with lots of color, fun and noise. For older kids, there are literally hundreds of letter- and number-recognition activities, spelling and reading games, puzzles, pictures, sounds . . . great stuff! Matilda, for example, loves a game in which she smashes the keyboard with both hands and the screen makes funny noises and changes colors. (As you can imagine, this is not my favorite game.) Georgia loves a particular interactive CD storybook in which she makes characters do tricks on the screen. Rachael enjoys a creativity program with which she makes up her own adventure picture books. And Dad just loves to turn on his computer and find that all the keys are sticky.

Remember that Some Toys Need More Adult Supervision than Others

There's not too much damage you can do with a giant, soft ball, but a toddler with a pack of crayons or a handful of clay can reduce the market value of your home by several thousand dollars. For this reason, such implements of destruction should be kept up high where they can be accessed only with adult permission and supervision . . . and a stepladder.

There's not too much damage you can do with a giant, soft ball, but a toddler with a pack of crayons or a handful of clay can reduce the market value of your home by several thousand dollars.

Also watch out for toys with lots of little parts, which are potentially dangerous for younger children. When Rachael turned five, I bought her a two-hundred-piece zoo set. What I forgot, however, was that Georgia was three and Matilda was a toy-hungry toddler. Within minutes, the two hundred pieces were spread everywhere. There were lions in the toilet (and I do mean *in* the toilet), giraffes in our bed, rhinos in my sock drawer and little pieces of fencing in the toaster. We ended up with a sixty-five-piece zoo set. I suppose we were lucky, though. Matilda could have choked on a giraffe quite easily. So keep choky-sized toys out of reach as well.

Exert Control over the Toy Situation

Soon you will realize that toys have a mind of their own, because they will take over your house. They will spread into every room and every nook and cranny. When you stumble into your child's room in the middle of the night to see why she's crying, your bare feet will encounter an obstacle course of sharp blocks, rolling balls and things that crack when you tread on them. Toys will mysteriously disappear and then reappear three weeks later. Sometimes you will wake up to scampering noises and find a Teddy bear at the foot of your bed—that wasn't there when you went to bed.

Ooohhh . . . spooky.

(I have a recurring nightmare that I'll wake up one morning to find Barbie next to me in bed. Then again, maybe that wouldn't be so bad . . .)

You must make a place for the toys. If you have the luxury of a spare bedroom, turn it into a toy room. Heck, it'll look like a nuclear holocaust but it's better to have one incredibly messy room than to have the entire floor area of your home covered in a thin layer of toys. At least you can shut the door. If you don't have a toy room, the bottom of a closet or a laundry basket will do. (Be warned, however. There is a dimensional law of physics that dictates that toys will fill whatever space you assign to them.)

One of the best moves I ever made was to buy a couple of stackable plastic crates for toy storage. You can shovel everything into them and simply stack them in the corner. (Of course, you should buy these crates rather than snatch them from behind the grocery store where they've been left outside for the last three weeks. That would be illegal. And I certainly wouldn't want you to do anything illegal.)

Once you've got this massive stockpile of toys and a place to store them, you must teach your child toy-management skills. If you start when she's three, she should just about have the hang of it by the time she's fifteen.

When my kids play, they do it with a ravenous hunger. They don't sit quietly with one toy and then put it away nicely, like the kids on the box. No, they go into a frenzy, empty out all the boxes and crates and play with them all simultaneously. Five minutes into playtime and the carpet is no longer visible.

Your child should learn a sense of responsibility from an early age, and there's no reason why she can't pick up after herself.

With a toddler, you'll need to show her how to put things away, and you'll end up doing most of the work. She might start off picking up her play set or doll and handing it to you. Her version of putting it away might be throwing it *near* the toy box.

> She might start off picking up her play set or doll and handing it to you. Her version of putting it away might be throwing it *near* the toy box.

When she's three or four, however, she should be able to do it by herself. But sometimes you will encounter that obstinate refusal to pick things up that young, tired children are so good at. Logic won't work. You know what I'm talking about.

"Pick up your toys, please, and put them in this box."

"No."

"Who made this mess?"

"Me."

"Well, you clean it up, then."

"Doan wonnuu!" (Translation: "I don't want to.")

If this happens, use the old "There'll be no (dinner/TV/other various favorite things) till *all* your toys are put away." Rachael only made it without four meals until she gave in and put Barbie back in bed.

Another thing that helps keep the mess down is to throw toys away. After a few years, you'll have an entire room filled with boxes of toys, most of which aren't used anymore. (What self-respecting five-year-old would play with a baby's rattle?) But for some bizarre reason, parents hate to throw stuff out. Maybe those moldy half-chewed teething rings bring back too many happy memories.

If you're going to have more babies, then it's worth keeping the baby toys; that is, the ones that are still intact. Some will be almost beyond the point of recognition. Some will have soaked up so much saliva that they have long spindly mold colonies growing on them.

C'mon . . . throw 'em out. You know you're going to get a zillion presents anyway when the new baby arrives.

Also, toss out all the toys that are missing integral parts. I used to think that we had hundreds of great toys, until the day Meredith ventured into the toy room (leaving a trail of breadcrumbs so she could find her way out again) and sorted everything into little piles. She discovered that we had only seven intact toys; the other sixty-eight were only partial toys. I suspect the missing pieces are stuck in the S-bend of the toilet, in the garden, behind the piano or in Matilda's lower colon.

Don't Tell Anyone that You Buy Toy Guns for Your Son and Dolls for Your Daughter

Look, I took Psychology 101 in college. I read the study that showed men consider their sons to be alert, muscular and well-coordinated and their daughters to be delicate, fine-featured and soft. I saw that film where the dads hand little trucks to their sons and cookie cutters to their daughters. And that survey that indicates dads are rougher and more physical and active with their sons. So I promised myself that my kids would not be gender stereotyped.

As it turned out, I had daughters, so I adopted the old "girls can do anything" routine, which worked fine—until Rachael launched herself off our balcony, flapping her arms madly. As we drove to the emergency room, I heard her mumble to Meredith between sobs, "Dad said . . . that . . . I could do . . . anything."

Anyway, I was not going to fall victim to forcing dolls and kitchen utensils upon my girls. I was going to give them tanks, toy soldiers, bows and arrows, old kegs of beer, footballs.

It didn't work. There's nothing they love better than dressing up as princesses, wearing lip gloss and making cakes.

It doesn't matter how open you try to be with your kids. It doesn't matter how much you try to shield them from stereotyping, it's in their blood. It's hormonal. You can't argue with thousands of years of genetic programming.

Boys like cars, toy guns and mud. They like to smash, yell, run and destroy.

Girls like dresses, dolls and playing nurse. They like to sing, dance, dress up and develop relationships.

I know it's not politically correct but that's all there is to it. I even heard some professor from UCLA say on the radio, and I quote, "There is a lot of hormonal evidence to suggest that children, males and females, have inherent dispositions to different types of play."

So there you have it.

You just can't beat unsubstantiated thirdhand anecdotal evidence.

Don't try to argue with me. I've spoken to my friends and they all agree.

I read one book that said if your son wants to dress up as a princess, why not let him?

Yeah? Well, I'll tell you why not.

The author obviously didn't go to my old school where, during recess, it was either marbles or cars for the boys and skipping or that hand-clapping jump-rope thing for the girls.

I can just imagine walking out of the boys' restroom dressed as Priscilla, Queen of the Playground. Within seconds, I would have been inspecting the toilet bowl from the inside.

Do these books seriously expect dads to go to the toy store and buy dolls for their sons?

Yeah, right.

So when it comes to gender stereotyping, I say go for it.

CHAPTER 8
Bedtime

Cribs and Beds

CRIBS are fine for babies, but sooner or later your child will have to move to a bed. This can present some problems.

First, a toddler starts out imprisoned in his crib by bars, often against his will. Eventually, he will give up his wailing, lie down and fall asleep; that's if the sides of his crib are more than six feet high and lined with barbed wire so he can't climb out. If you suddenly throw him in a bed, obviously without bars, he will shoot straight out again as if he's attached to rubber bands.

Second, some kids spend their nights with their heads down and their bottoms up in the air, pushing around like a pig searching for goodies in the sheets. The surrounding bars of the old crib acted like the walls of a bumper-car rink and kept him from free-falling to the carpet. If you're concerned about your toddler falling out of his new bed, put a couple of pillows or a mattress on the floor next to the bed.

Third, while some may love the idea of moving to a bed, others may not take to it so readily. Some kids actually *like* their cribs. After all, it's all they've ever known and they may like all the toys in there and the security of the bars. They may even be fond of the view of the ceiling or the wall decorations in the vicinity. Beds, on the other hand, may seem foreign and coldly enormous to them. You can't really move a child into a bed until he's old enough to understand the concept that you want him to stay there.

Rachael moved to a bed sometime around the age of two. We talked to her a few days before the big changeover and psyched her up for it. We made it sound like a big, exciting and special event. We spoke about how, now that she was no longer a baby, it was time for her to sleep in a big girl's bed. (Georgia and Matilda got the "just like your big sister" routine.)

Then, on the day the bed was delivered, it was done with much fanfare. She helped put it up. We jumped on it, climbed under it and wrestled on it. We transferred her favorite pillow, rug, bears and dolls from crib to bed.

Going to bed that first night was accomplished with a minimum of fuss and not too much falling out. The next morning, there was a lot of "aren't you a big girl?" talk.

We have friends whose son wasn't at all happy about making the change, so they put him back in his crib and took one of the sides down for a few weeks. At the same time they left the bed in his room so he could get used to it. This was a good transitional step and he was soon happy about the move.

If your toddler is anxious or upset about abandoning his crib, there's no point in forcing the issue. Maybe he's not ready for it yet. Hold off a while longer. As long as he's out by his eighteenth birthday, he should be okay.

But before you get cocky, if you thought making the switch from a crib to a bed was hard, you haven't seen anything yet. Just wait till you encounter all the nonsense that goes on every night as you try to get him to *stay* there.

The Battle of the Bed

Every night as bedtime draws near, you can taste it in the back of your throat, that deep foreboding that something bad is approaching, something not nice. The full moon appears in the sky as the cold night wraps its icy fingers around your house. And outside, up and down your street, the howling begins. It is the sound of children everywhere being put to bed.

When Samuel Taylor Coleridge wrote in "The Rime of the Ancient Mariner,"

> *Oh Sleep! it is a gentle thing,*
> *Beloved from Pole to Pole!*

he obviously had not tried putting a three-year-old to bed. There is certainly nothing "gentle" about it and it is certainly not a "beloved" part of their day.

The worst thing about bedtime is the unpredictability.

Sometimes our three get into bed enthusiastically and fall asleep right away and don't wake until morning. (Well, by "sometimes" I mean "twice.") Other times they whine and cry and fuss and scream and keep getting up despite our escalating tempers.

And then, just to keep us on our toes during the night, they throw in a few nightmares, a couple of vomits, a thirst attack and some bedwetting at one, three and five in the morning.

There are no rules carved in stone, so basically it's up to you to find out what works for your child. Every family and every child is different.

I know a couple whose toddler screams for an hour at the very *thought* of going to bed, but their four-year-old falls asleep within minutes. "We just can't keep Louise up after five-thirty!" they confess, as if it's a real burden. (Of course, Louise was swimming at three months, talking at one and using the toilet like a professional by the tender age of eighteen months.)

Most kids aren't like Louise. Going to bed can be a real drama. Toddler Matilda sometimes puts herself to bed. She grabs her juice bottle and her blanky and heads into the bedroom. Rachael and Georgia, however, are older, stronger, less tired, more stubborn and generally not eager to miss out on whatever action happens to be going on in the house at the time.

Experiment with a few procedures. Find something— anything—that will work on your child to get him to crash more easily. For a toddler, it might be a special blanket, a bottle of juice, a long snuggle or a windup music box. For a two- to five-year-old, it might be a Teddy bear or a doll or being read a (short) favorite book before bed. Some friends of ours have a tape player in their son's room that they use to play either soothing music or one of those read-along stories. This works well for them, as long as they don't play "Hakuna Matata" or anything from *Aladdin*, both of which send him into a frenzy.

But no matter what, remember that the nightly *Battle of the Bed* is a struggle for supremacy of the house. In one corner, the reigning champions: Mom and Dad. In the other corner, the challenger: Timmy the Cantankerous Preschooler.

It is, in short, him versus you.

Kid versus adults.

Offspring versus parents.

All good battles need good battle strategies and the *Battle of the Bed* is no different. You should hold a council of war with your wife to make plans. For starters, you need attack strategies that will break his will and put the odds on your side right from the very beginning. You need to know your enemy and be alert for his countermeasures. Solid follow-up defense strategies are also required.

With strong leadership and teamwork, you will defeat your foe . . . most of the time. Sometimes you will fail and the victory will be his, but remember that many battles are lost in the winning of a war.

Let's look at some of the classic parental bedding tactics.

Attack Strategy One: Consistency

The most important thing is to establish a consistent pattern every night. Toddlers like consistency because it lets them know where they stand. If they go to bed at five one night and at ten the next, they'll be confused. If they are allowed to watch three hours of TV one night but none the next, they'll be upset. They'll want TV and late bed *every* night.

Decide on a reasonable bedtime for your child. It's probably going to be in the vicinity of 6 to 8 P.M. Don't create problems for yourself by picking a time that's too early, because he won't be tired and the sun will be beaming through his window and you'll spend several hours trying to keep him in there. On the other hand, don't pick a time that's too late because kids can get overtired and then it's almost impossible to put them down. I know a couple who let their toddler decide when he wanted to go to bed. Their reasoning was that he would go when he was tired. Of course, he stayed up all hours, got grumpy and made their lives miserable. You can imagine the catastrophic results of this folly. Don't do this. Besides, you want and need some time to yourself!

For us, 7 P.M. has always been the magic time. I don't know why exactly. It just turned out that way and seems to strike the right balance between too early and too late.

Once you've established a consistent time, stick to it. This should be a prime factor in your consideration of evening activities and social planning. Don't go changing the routine because of every whim that comes along.

Having said that, however, occasional flexibility is okay. If, for example, the girls have had a decent afternoon nap and we are having guests over for dinner, we might let them stay up to say hello and have a quick chat. But we make it clear that this is a treat and that when the time comes, they are to go to bed with—what has become a slogan in our house—*no fuss*.

And then, just when you get it right, daylight saving kicks in and really messes things up.

Attack Strategy Two: Structure

Along with consistency, a nightly routine gives you a psychological edge. Your child will soon associate the structure of the routine with the inevitable bedtime that follows.

Make a list of all those activities you want or need to pack in during that final hour or two and then create a timetable for each night. Work backward from the set bedtime so that all activities will meet the deadline.

Theoretically, our nightly routine is

    6:00 P.M. dinner

    6:20 P.M. bath

    6:35 P.M. jammies and stories

    6:50 P.M. teeth-brushing and going to the bathroom

    6:55 P.M. hugs, kisses, prayers, "I love you," lights out

    7:00 P.M. tucking in

    7:05 P.M. asleep

The one time this actually happened was really terrific. But in reality, it's more like this:

    6:15 P.M. late dinner

    6:35 P.M. I realize I forgot to run the bath

    6:40 P.M. fights about getting into the bath

    6:41 P.M. bath

    6:50 P.M. fights about getting out of the bath

    6:51 P.M. fights about what jammies to wear

    7:05 P.M. fights about what stories we're going to read

7:07 P.M. stories

7:15 P.M. teeth-brushing and going to the bathroom

7:30 P.M. I yell at whoever has been on the toilet for ten minutes

7:31 P.M. I clean toothpaste off the floor and change Matilda's pajamas

7:35 P.M. hugs, kisses, prayers, "I love you," lights out

7:40 P.M. I psyche up in preparation for kids' first antibed assault

7:41 P.M. kids' first antibed assault

7:50 P.M. Matilda dirties diaper and needs changing

8:00 P.M. Georgia comes out to ask about the meaning of Easter

8:25 P.M. Matilda wants a drink

8:30 P.M. Rachael comes out to ask about Native American history

8:40 P.M. the sing-a-long begins

8:41 P.M. I go in and yell at them to be quiet

8:51 P.M. Meredith goes in and yells at them to be quiet

9:01 P.M. I go in and lie on their floor and fall asleep

9:03 P.M. kids fall asleep

11:48 P.M. I wake up freezing cold with a stiff neck.

Attack Strategy Three: Calm Down

Going to bed is boring. It is dark, quiet and still—everything most toddlers hate. Staying up, on the other hand, is action, noise, light, food, company and possibly even television. No wonder they don't want to go to bed.

You need to turn the psychological battle odds another inch in your favor. The whole house needs to calm down to lull your toddler into a nocturnal state of quiet. When they get into bed, you want their brain waves and heartbeat set almost at "comatose." You don't want them hyped up for a big battle.

Loud music, the television blaring, lights ablaze, lots of laughter and voices everywhere, roughhousing, and running around before bed are simply going to charge them up and give them more power to battle you later on.

In our house, after the kids have had a bath we dim all the lights and read stories in quiet tones. The house is still. We keep the TV in the closet with the doors closed, so it's not distracting them and they don't feel like they're missing out on anything. We dim the light in their room or leave the door open a little with the hall light on. This tends to pacify them a little. And we keep things quiet for about half an hour after they've gone to bed. This approach won't work every time, but it's a head start.

Attack Strategy Four: Storytelling

An integral part of the calming-down process is storytelling. This is one of those cutesy parent-and-child things that you will look back on fondly in years to come. But you can't just blab out any old tale. It has to be carefully constructed. It has to have the right amount of engaging content without exciting them too much. There are many different approaches you can take in your quest to be a master storyteller.

Classics

You can always rely on the Brothers Grimm or Hans Christian Andersen to get you out of trouble—if you can remember them properly, that is. On many an occasion I have found my memory lacking and only my shabby ad-libbing has saved the day.

I know one couple who doesn't tell these stories because their kids are "sensitive." They get upset easily and are quickly scared by some of the tales. Which is understandable when you think about it. *Hansel and Gretel,* for example, is a story of child abuse, witchcraft, cannibalism and murder. *Little Red Riding Hood* stars a giant slobbering carnivore and blood-covered axes. *The Pied Piper* is about a rat plague and child kidnapping. In *The Red Shoes,* the little girl has her feet chopped off by a woodsman.

Some kids won't be phased by this at all.

Others will spend the night huddled beneath the covers.

The Cliché Fantasy Story

The old ad-libbed "Once upon a time . . ." stories are pretty hard to beat. You can say pretty much anything as long as there's mention of a princess, a prince, a frog, a ring, a castle, a dragon, knights, maidens, old women, a treasure, a pirate, a magic pond or tree and, of course, a happy ending where the "bad people" have justice unleashed on them and the "good people" get married.

This is an old favorite that rarely fails to satisfy.

Moral Tales

This is your chance to indoctrinate your child without her knowing:

> *There was once a little girl who worked hard at school and always did what her dad said. She kept her room tidy and ate her vegetables. As a teenager, she didn't experiment with drugs and she always came home by ten. When she finished college, she became a loving mother and a lawyer earning a good salary and she had her dad over for dinner once a week, and all because she never smoked as a child or stayed up after her bedtime.*

The Never-Ending Inane Story

This is a useful one if your child is a little charged up and you need that extra-long knockout. This story goes on and on and on and ultimately has no real plot or direction. It is just a rambling narrative. The more boring the better.

I often tell the story of a boy or a girl and what happens to them in the course of their day. Behold:

> *Once a little boy woke up in his bed. It was a warm bed with a big checkered blanket and two fluffy pillows. The boy got up and decided to put on some socks, because his feet were cold. He walked over to his sock drawer and opened it and do you know what was inside? Yes, socks. He had red socks and blue socks, a pair of green-striped socks, lots of odd socks and some thick socks. . . .*

Your story is off to a good start and nothing has happened yet. By the time he's put on his undies, shorts, shirt and shoes, half an hour has passed.

A decent breakfast description can take a seasoned father up to forty-five minutes.

Retelling Their Day

This is my kids' favorite. It works like this: Make your child the protagonist and retell what he did that day. For example, if we had been to the zoo:

Once there were three girls: Rachael—she was the big sister; Georgia—she was the middle sister; and Matilda—she was the youngest sister. One day, they decided to go to the zoo. So Mommy and Daddy packed a picnic lunch with some juice and some ham sandwiches and then they all jumped in the car.

On the way they sang silly songs like "I'm a Crocodile," "Doopee Woopee Do" and "Touch Your Nose." It was lots of fun. Once, a silly man in another car drove through a red light and Daddy almost crashed, so he chased after him and yelled that the silly man was a "stupid, blind idiot." Mommy told Daddy that he was being immature and was endangering the lives of the three girls.

When they arrived at the zoo, they went in and saw the kangaroos. Daddy was late because he was still complaining to the management about the price of the kids' tickets . . .

And so on. Include lots of detail (with creative license) about your child. Children just love to hear about themselves in stories. I'm sure it also helps develop their memory as well, though I have no research basis whatsoever for that statement.

Family History
Tell your child stories about when you were a kid: your old school, his grandparents and so on. Tell him the romantic story of how you and your wife met and married and got pregnant. Leave out the naughty parts.

Stories to Avoid
Don't tell your child stories that will scare him witless:

- Once there was a boy who had a goblin under his bed and every night when his dad tucked him in and turned the lights out, he could hear it breathing and sharpening its knife . . .
- But little did the boy know that both his parents were *werewolves* . . .
- And then the ninety-year-old woman slipped off her negligee, revealing her alabaster . . .

And then the princess developed an eating disorder.

Don't tell your child stories that will make him cry:

- But the little boy never got up again. The parents cried and cried and cried and were sad for the rest of their lives.
- The hunter's bullet hit Bambi's mom just behind the ear and it came out her right nostril. Her limp corpse slapped heavily onto the forest floor . . .

Stories are best told with your child in bed and you near the door. That way, there's a chance he'll nod off. But more often than not, five minutes after you've sneaked out of the room, he'll yell out, "AND THEN WHAT HAPPENED?"

Know Your Enemy

Military tacticians say that half the battle is knowing the enemy; their weapons, their training, their limits of endurance. You need to know what countermeasures, tricks and ploys your child will use against you in his quest for nocturnal domination.

Don't be deceived. Your toddler might look innocent and may at times seem as dumb as a post, but he's an expert in adult psychology. He figured you out long ago and will use every trick in the book to wear you down. He will aim for your weak spots, which you have stupidly revealed to him on many occasions.

> Your toddler might look innocent and may at times seem as dumb as a post, but he's an expert in adult psychology.

Not only do children invent their own terrorist tactics, they also get information from other toddlers. What do you think

they talk about at the playground and in kindergarten? It's a
Council of War. I've even heard rumors of a toddler internet
bulletin board where a worldwide fraternity of toddlers post
their nocturnal battle plans for all to see and share.

Children have a whole arsenal of tactics and ploys at their
disposal, a few of which are listed below.

Delay Tactics

Every extra second that they can eke out before they go to bed is
worth it. They will use any means in their power to stretch it
out. They'll ask for more time in the bath. They'll sit on the
toilet for half an hour. They'll ask for "just one more story." If
you're really unlucky, they will interrupt and ask questions
during the story, like so:

"Once there was a little boy—"

"Why?"

"Be quiet. The little boy lived in a house—"

"No, he lived in a rabbit hole."

"Warren. Now, the little boy, whose name was Jack—"

"Warren!"

"No, that was the hole."

"The hole was Warren?"

"Exactly!"

"Why?"

Don't be fooled into thinking they give a hoot about your
story. This tactic won't work for long. As its name suggests, it is
only delaying the inevitable.

Defiance

Despite the fact that Georgia has gone to bed at seven almost
every night of her life, on 50 percent of the occasions when we
tell her it's bedtime she says, "I don't want to." Other favorites
are "I'm not tired," "That's boring for me," "I want to stay" and
the universal statement of defiance, "No." If that fails, there's
the good old "limp body" routine that makes it difficult to pick
her up. She slides out of bed, kicks off the covers, wriggles,
screams and so forth.

Amnesia

You've put your child in bed and he's been quiet for a few minutes. Then the little voice starts up with all the things he forgot:

"I forgot to clean my teeth."

"No, you didn't. I saw you. Be quiet."

"I didn't go to the bathroom."

"Yes, you did. Go to sleep."

"I don't remember taking a bath."

"You took a bath. Be quiet."

"I didn't get a bear."

"I don't care. Go to sleep."

or the reverse amnesia twist, about all the things *you* forgot:

"You forgot to give me a kiss and a hug."

"Trust me, it happened. Be quiet."

"You forgot to give me dinner."

"No, I didn't. We had a roast. Go to sleep."

"You forgot to read me a story."

"We had three stories. Be quiet!"

Stupid Questions and Statements

Children know that once they've been put to bed, if they wander out without a good excuse, they're in big trouble. So they start coming up with earth-shatteringly important ideas that just cannot wait a moment longer.

The following scenario is common in our house:

We are having a dinner party. The girls have been in bed for an hour. Suddenly amid the riotous laughter (which usually accompanies our dinner parties) there is a movement in the shadows behind the doorjamb. Little fingers and a slice of face appear in the shaft of light.

Then the stupid questions and comments begin:

" 'Scuse me . . . I was just wondering: When's Christmas?"

"Daaaahhhddd? If an orange is orange, why isn't a banana called a yellow?"

"You know that girl at my preschool called Anne? Well, she has a brother and do you know his name? It's Mark."

And then there is the most entertaining strategy of all. Younger children are particularly adept at this. It's the one where they start talking before they've actually figured out anything to say:

"Daaaahhhddd? I was in my, in my, in my roooommm . . . and I . . . um well, you know I was at the dinner . . . at dinnertime, I, I, I, I, I, I, I, Rachael said and, and, and Matilda was then and . . . what you . . . um . . . um . . .. Dad . . . well, I was . . ." (and as their eyes meet with a plant in the corner) "Is that plant still alive?"

Playing on Your Emotions

This is my greatest weakness. My children play on my desire to be a good dad, a loving dad, a caring dad. It can come in many forms; little voices calling out from the darkness:

"I want a hug."
"I want to give you a kiss, Dad."
"I want to spend more time with you, Dad."
"I am not an animal."
"I miss you, Dad."
"I'm (insert appropriate word here) lonely/scared/sad/sick."
"I want to go back to Kansas."
"I got a tummy ache."
"You only care about your book."
"You promised."
"But I haven't seen you all day."

I find myself standing outside their door, listening to their pathetic pleas for love and attention, torn between my desire to be a loving father and my desire to play computer golf in the study. Sometimes I am strong. I can pick up the vibes in their voices and know they're just bluffing. I walk away.

Other times, I ignore what the books say and go in and lie on the floor and tell another story or hug them or hold their hands. Heck, I love that stuff, but it doesn't happen every night.

Persistence

When all the cute tricks fail, they bring out the big guns. This is the "if at first you don't succeed" maneuver. You put them in bed. They come out. You put them back. They come out. You put them back. They come out. You start getting angry. You put them back. They come out. You start making threats and giving warnings. You put them back. They come out. You give final warnings. You put them back. They come out. You give final warnings again. You put them back. They come out. You give final warnings again. You put them back. They come out. You get angry. They cry. You put them back. You feel angry and frustrated, as if you're the only man in the world suffering this torment.

When I'm engaged in this nightly struggle, I sometimes look out my daughters' bedroom window at the lights of the city and think, "Out there somewhere, at this very moment, there are thousands of guys doing exactly the same thing." I have even entertained thoughts of starting up a party line for nocturnal dads:

"Hi, I'm Rob and my kids just won't shut up."

"Hey there, Chris here, my four-year-old just kicked me out of my own bed."

"Hi, I'm Lance and my daughter just upchucked."

And then, when all their tactics have failed, they start screaming. They figure if they can't get you through skill, they'll fight dirty: Wailing, choking, banging things . . . and then sudden and total silence so you run in to see if they're okay— and they've got you right where they want you.

Covert Operations

This one can catch you by surprise.

One night, I put the girls to bed. We got our TV out of the closet and Meredith and I watched a video. Close to the end of the movie, I went out to make popcorn and almost tripped over the three prostrate bodies who'd set up base camp (complete with pillows, blankets and bears) on the other side of the glass door and were silently watching the movie.

My girls would make excellent assassins. They could sneak up on anyone. You see, kids can be silent and stealthy when they want to be, and even though you think they're asleep, they're out in your study surfing the internet with other members of the toddler army of the night.

Defense Strategy

Once the battle is underway, you will need to fight their countermeasures.

The Green Berets have a motto: *Strike swiftly*.

This is a good motto for parents, too.

There are two time zones in which you need to be wary of the toddler assault: at bedtime and in the middle of the night.

After you put them to bed, they'll start up with all the tricks (mentioned above) and you have to strike swiftly and firmly. You also have to figure out the difference between game playing and genuine distress. You don't want to be a sap, but you don't want to be cruel, either. Sometimes their cry will be a tired whine, but sometimes it will be a bona fide scream because they think there are spiders crawling all over them. (Heck, I think that sometimes, too.)

On occasion, the path of least resistance with my three has been to lie on their floor or bed and tell them a story. This usually puts them to sleep. Unfortunately, it usually puts me to sleep as well.

Yep, there's nothing like waking at 2 A.M., totally disoriented, hungry, wearing rumpled work clothes, with a sore back, cold feet, a mouth that feels like the bottom of an elevator and a face with carpet patterns stenciled into it.

Sometimes they'll cry a little before nodding off, and sometimes they'll just keep crying. Depending on the intensity of their distress, you should pop in after a set time and calm them down (hair-stroking, back-patting, a quiet song or two, a few words) and then leave again—and repeat the process if necessary, but with a longer time allowance before action.

With older children who are a little more aware (say, three or four years old), read them the riot act so they know where they stand:

"You are in bed now because it is your bedtime. You are to stay in your bed. No fuss. It's time for sleep. Do not call out. Do not come out. Do not collect $200. I love you. See you in the morning. Goodnight."

Some may come straight after you like a shot, whereas others will probably start with some calling out, just to test the water. Then they'll start with the questions and protests.

Don't engage them in a ten-minute debate. Put them back to bed immediately and firmly explain that they are not to come out again. A quick hug may be in order for younger ones to settle them down again.

Then read them the riot act, part two:

"You are not to come out. We've been very fair and have had stories and hugs, but soon I will get angry. If you keep coming out, I will shut the door. Stay in bed and we'll keep the door open. Good night. See you in the morning."

The next time they emerge, carry out your threat.

"I said you were not to come out. Now I'm going to shut the door. I will come back in one minute and if there's no fuss, we'll open the door again!"

(Of course, you leave the light dimmer on or the night-light plugged in.)

Then you fulfill your promise, and either open the door again ("You are doing the right thing, so I will open the door. Good night!") or, if they're ready in the shadows to leap out through the crack, you repeat the process.

A tall three-year-old, however, may be able to open the door himself. Some parenting books advise roping the door closed: Maybe that works, but it doesn't really appeal to me so I've never done it.

You have to keep being firm and acting immediately. When the assault is particularly savage, and they keep coming out and keep coming out, you have to be strong.

On a few occasions I've been involved in a ridiculous standoff. Georgia is out of bed and approaches her bedroom door while I am standing there.

"Go back to bed!"

She takes a step toward me.

"Go back to bed—now—or there'll be trouble."

Her determined gaze meets mine.

It's a battle of wills.

Another step.

"I mean it."

Another step.

(Strangely, I think back to that police drama I saw on TV the other night where the storekeeper pointed a gun at a robber who was walking slowly toward him. The storekeeper kept making threats, but the bad guy kept coming. "Shoot! Shoot!" I cried from the safety of my easy chair—but he didn't. The bad guy got the gun and blew the storekeeper away.)

"The question you gotta ask yourself, punk, is *how far do you think you can push me?*"

Another step.

I draw an imaginary line on the carpet with my finger.

"Don't cross that line."

She stops at the line, raises her eyes to meet mine and then slowly, almost imperceptibly, her toes start to nudge forward . . . a toenail . . . two toes, three, four, five . . . still coming.

With a sigh, I pick her up and put her in bed, lie on the floor and begin the story. "Once there was a dad who didn't get enough sleep and he had to start seeing a shrink . . ."

All this tough-guy talk about being firm and rigid is one thing. Putting it into practice is another.

As Clint says, "A man's gotta know his limitations."

On occasion, for one reason or another, you'll be outgunned by the enemy and you have to know when to surrender for the sake of all involved. For example, if you're having a cocktail party and your child is excited about all the guests, let him stay up for half an hour to meet everyone and get the excitement out of his system. Or if he has just had a long and late afternoon nap and isn't tired, compensate by letting him go to bed a little later.

Even now, with all three kids, there is the occasional day when Meredith and I, both exhausted from work, look at each other and wonder, "How much do we really want to win today's battle?"

Sometimes, and by this I mean rarely, we cut our losses and let the kids win. They stay up and sit quietly and draw while we work (they know they're treading on eggshells and that the first murmur from them and it's off to bed) or we'll get the TV out of the closet and let them watch part of a video.

But, a word of warning: If you cut some slack, set clear parameters. Don't cut slack on your slack on your slack, or you'll pay for it for years to come.

But wait . . . there's more!

Don't think that just because he's fallen asleep you can start the ticker-tape parade. The second assault comes when you least expect it and when you're least able put up a good fight—at random intervals during the night.

Part of the battle has already been won, given that the sleep patterns you used to have as a childless man disappeared the night the baby came home. Now your baby has become a toddler, you're probably used to stumbling down the hallway in the middle of the night, freezing your butt off and banging your toes on those blasted toys left in the hall. It's just a part of life.

Night waking can occur for a number of reasons.

Your child might just be whimpering and whining because he wants you to hold his hand for the next seven hours. If you live in the real world and have to go to work the next morning, options like this aren't advisable. Kids have to learn that nighttime is for sleeping and that Mom and Dad go to bed in a different room and prefer to sleep without interruption.

The controlled crying method is a widespread favorite. Let him cry for five minutes before you go in, then hug, soothe, sing and bail. You know from experience that as soon as you take that step away from the crib or bed, he'll start up again, but this time you don't go back in for *ten* minutes. The next time, fifteen. And so on. He'll learn after a while, but it will take perseverance on your end.

Obviously, if your child has a cold and is feeling miserable, you'll need to modify your plan. If worst comes to worst, give him some medicine, wrap him in a blanket, put him on your lap and watch some late-night TV. (Be warned, though, late-night TV is addictive.)

You may also need to modify your plan if your child gets so wound up that he's hysterical; you know, choking, real screaming, hyperventilating, vomiting and so forth.

Aside from just being whiny or sick, he might wake up because he's had a bad dream or is cold or thirsty or has just wet the bed. These things need to be dealt with. A wet bed needs to be changed, a cold child needs to be covered, an upset child needs to be calmed down. Sometimes a kid's imagination goes wild and he thinks there are nasty creatures or whatever under his bed or on the wall.

Rachael went berserk one night about a snake under her bed. I came heroically to the rescue and knelt down next to the bed to calm her down.

"Sshh . . . there's nothing under the bed . . . it's okay . . ." (and so on and so forth).

"You haven't (sniff) even looked, Dad (sniff). Please look, Dad (sob) . . . please . . ."

"Okay, sweetie, I'll look. See? There's nothing und— AAARGGGHHHH!!!"

The 6-foot-long python curled up just inches away from my face made me choke out those final words.

Surprised?

Ha, ha. Only kidding. Nothing of the sort happened at all. Let's try that again.

Rachael went berserk one night about a snake under her bed. I came heroically to the rescue and knelt down next to the bed to calm her down.

"Sshhh . . . there's nothing under the bed . . . it's okay . . ." (and so on and so forth).

"You haven't (sniff) even looked, Dad (sniff). Please look, Dad (sob) . . . please . . ."

"Okay, sweetie, I'll look. See? There's nothing under the bed. There's no snakes . . . no spiders . . . no lions or bears . . . no gigantic savage dogs . . . no nocturnal monsters with ridiculously bulbous eyes . . . no festering corpses covered in maggots— nothing! Good night."

The next morning, Meredith said to me, "I just don't understand it! I went in to Rachael about five times last night. She was raving about dogs and spiders and lions and who knows what! I wonder what triggered all that?"

"Hmm, I wonder," I mumbled, looking off into the distance.

Often a night-light will partially solve the problem of being scared of the dark, but it also creates a new problem: He can see to get out of the bedroom and head down the hallway to his target—your bed.

(Someone should market a night-light with a motion sensor that, when activated, declares in a military voice: "WARNING!! You have five seconds to get back into bed. Then the monsters will be released. You have been warned. I repeat, the MONSTERS will come if you do not go right back to bed. Five-four-three. . . ." They'd make a fortune.)

Your bed is a nice place. It's big and warm and has two protective adults in there for company. Without a doubt, it's the best place to be at 2 A.M. Most parents and authors say that as soon as your child hits your bed, you should take him back to his own room, quickly and firmly. Explain to him that his bed is his bed and that is where he sleeps.

As I said before, if he's wet or scared or sick, he deserves a different kind of attention. If he's really upset, he might pop into your bed for a hug or until he falls asleep, at which point you promptly return him to his own bed. That protective closeness—snuggling or holding hands—is quite nice on occasion. But don't let it become a habit.

If he just wants to hang out with you some more, strike swiftly.

This quick-and-firm-return method works well—if you actually wake up enough do it. Our kids come down the hallway in stealth mode, avoiding my parental radar. They just appear between the sheets as if beamed there from the *Starship Enterprise*. More often than not, I remain in a semicomatose state in which I am vaguely aware that there's an infant invader in the bed and that I'm uncomfortable as a result, but I'm not awake enough to organize my faculties into getting up and carrying her back to bed. And so I remain in an exhausted delirium for four or five hours.

Some parents actually encourage the practice of kids and parents all in the same bed. After all, the Neanderthals back in the cave didn't separate their kids. (Yeah, but they also ate uncooked meat.)

Well, if that's what you aspire to or if you find it works well for you, fine. Do your own thing. Personally, I can think of nothing worse. This is for three reasons:

1. I have an aversion to being covered in urine, especially if it's not mine. (Though it's better than a guy at work whose child actually pooped on his pillow. I kid you not.)

2. I like to sleep. Toddlers are the worst bed companions. They steal covers, wriggle, poke, kick, slobber, cry, whine, talk, snore, pinch and clamber. And they smell. I would rather lie next to a Saint Bernard with dysentery. With toddlers, you end up with a ten-inch strip of bed, no covers and cold feet at the base of your spine.

   And it's even worse if all three get in en masse. When I was a teenager, the idea of being in bed with four females appealed, but this wasn't quite how I pictured it.

3. I'll sum this up in two words and let you work it out: *morning stiffy*. Enough said.

For these reasons, we have barbed wire, electrified doorknobs, a giant inflatable alien, an obstacle course and landmines under the carpet in the hall.

The kids *never* bother us anymore.

Reinforcements

In any battle between warring factions, there may come a time when you need to call in for backup. Usually this is supplied in the husband-wife partnership. It's always easier to face the foe with another soldier by your side.

However, if you ever get out of your depth, you may need to bring in the big guns and form an alliance with one of the excellent miracle-working organizations that are seasoned veterans in this type of warfare. We have used them on occasion, as have several friends.

If you need help, don't be afraid to ask for it. Talk to your friends and other parents. Look in the phone book under community health and services. Contact your doctor or local hospital for a recommendation.

And always remember the words of Churchill, that great parental educator:

> *We will fight them in their bedrooms,*
> *We will fight them in the hallways,*
> *We will fight them in our own beds.*
> *We will nevah surrender.*

CHAPTER 9

Vomit, Snot and Lice

*This chapter is about medical stuff, in which I have
absolutely no training whatsoever.*

I RECENTLY became Dr. Downey, but that is a doctorate in
education, not medicine. I'm one of those guys you see on TV
shows where, on a flight over the Pacific, a flight attendant asks,
"Is there a doctor on board?" and he puts his hand up and has to
go to the back of the plane to deliver a baby despite trying to
explain the mistake, but they can't hear him over the woman's
screams, and it's only after he's conducted the Cesarean with
nothing but plastic airline cutlery and a sewing kit that the
confusion is explained amid tears of joy, and then he gets his
face in the paper and the parents name their child after him,
even though it's a girl. And his name is Kevin.

Still with me?

The point is that I'm an ace in the field of education but my
qualification in medicine is a merit badge from my old scout
troop for tying tourniquets.

Toddlers and little kids get sick. But this is no surprise when
you think of all the horrible things they do. They mistake dog
poop for dough and mold it into shapes. They eat anything they
pick up off the ground at the grocery store. They suck and then
swap toys at the playground and preschool that are coated in
bubonic plague from that kid whose house was sealed in plastic
by the Centers for Disease Control and Prevention. Given the
chance, they'll drink from puddles on the road. They go to day
care, the playground, Sunday school and kindergarten, which
are infectious hothouses of infant disease. To make things worse,
their immune systems are not quite ready to cope with all the
germs and garbage floating around in the air.

Obviously, they are going to get sick.

There are zillions of illnesses that can strike your child. Horrifying diseases and medical conditions, from the quickly fixed to the tragically fatal, from the common to the rare.

Some can be prevented or healed. Some cannot.

It is not my intention here to deal with "extraordinary" illnesses. I don't have the background or personal skills to do it sensitively. Instead, I discuss some of the more everyday medical things you might encounter.

Food Allergies

An allergy isn't really an illness, but a negative reaction of some sort to a stimulus, usually a certain food.

I have several allergies. If I eat rhubarb, parsnip or soy milk, I vomit. Not because my body rejects them, but because they just taste disgusting.

Allergies are kind of a hit-or-miss affair. You don't know your child has an allergy until you feed her something and she breaks out in a rash. And that's if you're lucky. If your child is extremely allergic, she can do stuff like stop breathing.

Some allergies are relatively insignificant. Matilda, for example, gets a few hives when she drinks milk. Georgia has a slight reaction to peanut butter. Rachael starts crying if we serve Brussels sprouts for dinner.

> Keep your eye on your child when she first starts eating real food. Introduce new foods one at a time.

Others are much nastier. Some friends of ours have a daughter who is allergic to most everything. She has spent many weeks in the hospital and can only eat rice, chicken, pears and, on occasion, potatoes and bananas. I know another guy who almost dies if he so much as smells seafood.

Keep your eye on your child when she first starts eating real food. Introduce new foods one at a time. Watch out for nasty reactions and don't make the problem food a regular part of her diet.

If she has a really bad reaction to something, see your doctor who, once again, will send you to see one of her specialist pals who'll charge you large amounts of cash.

Vaccinations

Vaccinating your child against certain diseases is not compulsory, but it is widely and strongly recommended. Most schools will require detailed vaccination records before they will let you enroll your child. In the United States, contact your state Health Services Department or school district office to find out which vaccinations are required. Many schools and states follow the immunization program recommended by the American Academy of Pediatrics.

> It's up to you to make the final decision about vaccination. But at least do yourself and your child the favor of making an *informed* decision. Speak to a health professional.

Some parents are vocally opposed to vaccination and the risks involved. Others don't have their children vaccinated due to ignorance (they might mistakenly believe that a certain vaccination is no longer necessary) and due to laziness (parents who couldn't be bothered with the inconvenience of making an appointment).

Hey, it's a free country and you can do what you like. My three kids have had their full vaccinations to date. They're protected from polio, whooping cough, measles, onomatopoeia, mumps, diphtheria, halitosis, meningitis, tetanus, rubella, hepatitis B and apotheosis. If there were a vaccination against whining, they'd have that one, too.

There are risks involved. Some children react badly to the vaccinations. There have been cases of reported brain damage and even death. Statistics and scientific research, however, suggest that the protective advantages far outweigh the minuscule risks. As far as I'm concerned, kids are also at risk when you strap them into a car or let them climb a tree—they're at risk in almost everything they do.

It's up to you to make the final decision. But at least do yourself and your child the favor of making an *informed* decision. Speak to a health professional. Contact your doctor, hospital, local health services or mother-in-law.

Common Illnesses

There is an array of standard illnesses you are likely to encounter, including chickenpox, colds, allergies, fevers, ear/eye/nose/throat infections, tummy aches, diarrhea and a kid-style leprosy called *impetigo*. However, *all* kids suffer from the three recurring small-child sicknesses: vomit, snot and head lice.

Vomit

When adults vomit, they usually do it behind closed doors in the bathroom. Little children, however, are not yet skilled in vomit etiquette. That's why they'll let loose in the car or at the dinner table without any warning whatsoever.

The worst is when they vomit during the night and it dries in their hair and sticks them to their sheets like plaster. (On this matter, I only have this to say: Keep a towel and a small bucket in the back of your car. You'll soon find out why.)

Snot

Don't worry about snot. All toddlers and little kids are full of snot. Sometimes it runs in viscous rivulets. Other times it sets like concrete from their upper lips to their chins and only laser therapy will get it off. Mucus forests are perfectly normal.

Head Lice

Have you ever seen chimpanzees at the zoo picking through each other's hairs and inspecting their findings? You will soon know how that feels, because your child will come home one day with lice in her hair.

Lice are highly infectious little crawly things that you remove with a mixture of parental picking and a napalmlike shampoo that really, really stinks. You will spend torturous hours cleaning up your toddler and the next day she'll sit next to some kid who's running a refuge for homeless head lice in her own scalp—and you're back at square one.

Unfortunately, all schools and daycares have one head-lice version of Typhoid Mary, a toddler whose parents don't seem to notice or do anything about it. Don't let your child play at this kid's house. You can try to give the parents a hint by ringing a bell and calling out "unclean! unclean!" any time you see them in public.

To Worry or Not to Worry

A lot of toddler sicknesses you will learn to take in stride. A good sleep or a dose of kids' cough syrup should take care of a sniffle or cough. An enormous projectile vomit may clear the system and bring quick recovery if a temperamental stomach is in action.

However, if in doubt or if you're anxious; if your child has a prolonged illness or symptoms out of the ordinary; if she's listless, floppy, has a high temperature or is obviously uncomfortable or in pain, take her to the doctor. You will soon learn to read the signs and know the difference between a passing sniffle and something worse.

Medicine

At some point, your child will have to take medicine, which is often a "terrific flavor!" like tangy orange or super-sweet strawberry.

Sometimes, she'll go for it, maybe enjoy it or even ask for it! Lucky you.

Other times, her jaw will clamp shut like a bull terrier's and not even those special police-rescue pliers for ripping off car doors will do any good.

With a toddler, you may be able to conceal the medicine in her meal or drink. Or you can make happy faces and tell her how yummy it is. With older children, reason has been known to work. "Do you want to get better? Take this then, please. I know you don't like it, but you're going to take it, so let's get it over and done with."

A bribe will often bring a favorable response. "Quick, drink this down and then we'll read this book and have some ice cream."

Any method that gets the medicine into her system is fine, though obviously it's better if you have the child's cooperation. But on occasion, you may have to force the issue.

I'm kind of a pragmatist in this regard. If the medicine is necessary for her welfare, then she's going to take it.

Dad has spoken.

End of story.

Sometimes you have to be cruel to be kind.

I think it's better to strike swiftly and put up with ten seconds of dramatics than to prolong the agony and have half an hour of anger, frustration and hysterics . . . usually ending in failure anyway.

Get her before she knows what's going on. You'll need another person for this method to be truly effective.

Tell her that she's about to have medicine. Then move fast. Immobilize the arms. Put a finger in the side of her mouth. Tilt her head back. Then the other person dumps it in with a spoon or syringe. Close her mouth. Give her a treat and a hug and tell her that it's all over and it wasn't that bad. When she's settled down, explain what you did and why you did it.

Then go and shower off the cough syrup she spat all over your face.

CHAPTER 10

Mess

MY HOUSE is always messy. That's no reflection on my wife
or on my kids or, for that matter, on me. It's just the way it is.
Being a dad is messy. Having a child in your house is messy. You
can't have fire without smoke, you can't have a cat without
hairballs, and you can't have a child without a messy house.

When you first became a dad, you probably noticed a change
in the mess level of your house. You know what I mean by mess:
general disarray, things not where they should be, piles of
laundry scattered here and there,
dishes in the sink, clothes on the
floor, mold in the refrigerator,
diapers underfoot and CDs put
away in the wrong cases. Here's the
bad news: *Things just get worse*.

> As children get older,
> they get messier. Not only that,
> they demand more of your
> time, which makes you
> messy as well.

As children get older, they get messier. Not only that, they
demand more of your time, which makes you messy as well. On
top of this, they bring home helium balloons from the shopping
center, fast-food chain or birthday party and these just hang
around, breeding in the skylight until they lose their zing and
flop around on the floor.

But mainly the mess is due to the fact that most people have
several children within a few years of each other. In your house
you might have a baby, a toddler and a small child. The
potential destructive force of such a combination is frightening.

Here's a typical Saturday morning in many homes:

You get up and find the kids have already emptied out every
toy box. Your toddler—no longer satisfied by a fluffy toy with a
jingly bell—has found a container of talcum powder, has twisted
the lid open and is making "snow" in the kitchen. You don't
worry about making the bed, and you start breakfast. The
breakfast table is now a wasteland. There are plastic bowls,
spilled milk, pieces of cereal and toast crusts underfoot with

every step you take. Just as you consider cleaning up, the baby wakes up and needs changing. You enter the bathroom and wade through the knee-deep drift of bath toys that you were too tired to pick up last night. In the minute *that* takes, your toddler has emptied and shredded a tissue box and has pulled all the books off the lower shelves in the living room. There are jammies and pieces of clothing everywhere. Your oldest child has just emptied a box of building blocks in the middle of the floor. The baby is screaming for mushy rice cereal. Somewhere you can hear crayons scraping on a wall. The toddler has unrolled an entire spool of toilet paper and is stuffing dirty laundry down the toilet.

The house is chaos. And it's only eight in the morning.

You'll be pleased to know, however, that there is a way to have a tidy house. Tie up your children, never go anywhere with them and don't let them touch anything. Let them have one Teddy bear and one book apiece and never allow them to come out into the "adult part" of the house (which is everywhere except their bedrooms). Spend all your time tidying and cleaning and never spend any time with them.

But you'd have to ask yourself this question: "What's the point, then, of being a parent?"

There is hope, however. Here are a few methods for dealing with damage control.

Realistic Expectations

Don't compare your house with those of your childless friends, with photos in glossy magazines or with those of anyone who has paid help. Accept mess as a part of parental fate and wallow in it. Give in to the chaos. Let it consume you. Get sloppy. Whatever takes you four hours to clean takes your child one minute to destroy. The mathematical odds are not in your favor.

> Whatever takes you four hours to clean takes your child one minute to destroy. The mathematical odds are not in your favor.

Your house will never be tidy all at once, except maybe on those special occasions when you stay up till 3 A.M. straightening up because your parents are coming

Give in to the chaos.

for lunch the next day. At best, you can clean one room at a time, moving around in a circular pattern.

Last-Minute Whirlwind Shovel Method

Some friends of mine have three young children, but their house is always immaculate. Spotless. Pristine. Everything in its place. Dust-free.

This used to be a source of frustration for me. How could they do this? It just didn't seem fair that my place looked like a nuclear test site and theirs looked like the Brady house.

That was before I discovered their secret.

I was on my way to their bathroom when I turned left instead of right. I turned the handle of the door.

Ten minutes later, as they were pulling the last vestiges of clothing and toys off me, they embarrassingly admitted that whenever people come to visit, they literally shovel, push, kick and throw any offending mess into the spare room.

By the time I opened that door, they had not cleaned it out for three weeks. And they were worried because Grandma had come to lunch two days ago and they hadn't seen her since.

Still, there is a point that can be learned here. A plastic garden rake is effective on a variety of flooring surfaces and makes light work of most living rooms and bedrooms.

Divide and Conquer

Sometimes we just get fed up and, when the kids have gone to bed or to a neighbor's to play, Meredith and I attack the mess. Or one of us takes the kids out so the other can get the house in order. We go at it frantically, passionately, in an ordered, controlled sweep. We move with swift determination, heaving toys, clothes and books out of our path.

Of course, order is destroyed several minutes later, but at least we know there are no rats or mushroom colonies germinating under the mess.

Constancy

This takes effort and an obsessive personality.

Always clean up as you go, never relying on the idea that you will get back to it. Because you never will. So after a bath, make sure all the toys are put away and all clothes disposed of before moving on to something else. When cooking, put things away and clean as you go. After dinner, clear the table, do all the dishes and wipe the kitchen counters before going to watch television.

This is a good approach, but it assumes you have lots of free time and the iron-will to stick to any one task for longer than a few seconds. It also ignores the possibility that while you are tidying up in one room, your child is somewhere else making even more mess.

Child Labor

The law says you can't send your child down into the coal mines anymore . . . but it doesn't say anything about putting their toys away.

> Don't wait for him to turn ten before you reveal that you are not, in actual fact, the hired help whose job it is to clean up after him.

As your child grows, teach him to clean up after himself. It's good for his development and will help him not to grow up expecting everything to be done for him. Don't wait for him to turn ten before you reveal that you are not, in actual fact, the hired help whose job it is to clean up after him.

I'm not talking about getting your toddler to do three hours of vacuuming every Saturday morning. Start small.

After a bath, get him to put his bath toys away. Train him to put his dirty clothes in the laundry basket instead of on the floor. When he empties a crate of toys, tell him no TV till they've been put away. Ask him to carry his bowl to the kitchen after breakfast. Encourage him to put away his shoes when he takes them off. Teach him that the house is where everybody has to live, not just him.

Start as soon as possible. With a three-year-old, you'll need to help him and show him what to do, and you'll end up doing most of the work. By the time he's eighteen, he should be quite capable of operating mostly on his own, with only minimal yelling and nagging on your part. If you're lucky.

Throw Things Out!

Children grow up so fast, both physically and intellectually, when they are young. They outgrow their clothes, toys and books with frightening regularity.

If you are planning on having more children, have a clean-out day and pack unnecessary things in a box or bag. If not, give them to friends or to a charity or toss them in the garbage can.

If you are going to dispose of anything, however, make like Harry Potter under his Invisibility Cloak and do it at midnight. Because whatever you choose to get rid of will suddenly become the most beloved object in your child's stash, even if it hasn't been glanced at in years.

"Dad, don't throw that out! It's mine!" he will say.

"Come on. . . you're five years old," you will respond.

"But it's my faaaavooorite!"

"It's a teething ring, for goodness sake!"

"DAAHHDDD!!!!"

Don't Bother

Another alternative is not to clean up at all. The mess will only come back again, so don't waste your time.

CHAPTER 11

Accidents

ACCIDENTS will happen. It's a fact of life. It doesn't matter
how hard you try to avoid them, they'll happen anyway,
especially when you don't expect it—which is, of course, why
they are called accidents.

Kids have lots of accidents. They
are accident magnets. Accidents
cruise around in the atmosphere just
waiting for a toddler to appear. Large
hospitals deal with thousands of
injured children every year.

> Kids have lots of accidents.
> They are accident magnets.
> Accidents cruise around in the
> atmosphere just waiting for a
> toddler to appear.

Furthermore, many of the children who are hospitalized and
many of those who die as a result of their injuries are under the
age of five—an important fact for parents to think about.

Toddlers have lots of accidents because:

- They don't understand how the world works and have a
  poor grasp of the concepts of danger and safety. As adults,
  we have learned tons of everyday things that keep us alive
  and healthy. Scissors are sharp. Hot water scalds. Concrete
  is hard. Cars travel fast. Glass cuts. Rottweilers bite. Disco
  music rots your brain. Stripes and polka dots don't go
  together. Toddlers *don't* know these things.

- They are not only naturally curious but stupid as well. If a
  baby sees a cord dangling from an ironing board, she will
  think, "Mmm, I wonder what that is?" and will pull it. A
  toddler, on the other hand, will see a cord dangling from an
  ironing board and think, "Mmm, I hypothesize that there is
  an iron on the other end of this cord . . . I wonder if it will
  fall on my head if I pull it?" and will pull it.

- They have recently learned to stand and walk, so they can
  get to danger areas much more easily and much more
  quickly. They can reach up above their heads to pull things
  down on themselves. They can get to the stairs or the

fireplace or the pond or the road a lot faster than before. And their wobbly, uncertain stumbling just makes things worse.

- They do not possess the same physical and mental skills as adults. Their sense of balance is not terrific. Their perception of distance, speed and size is flawed. They are overconfident and do not have a sense of "healthy fear."

Combine a toddler's curiosity with her ignorance, instability and poor mobility, and the result is lots of accidents.

Many accidents are minor, everyday occurrences: Tanya falls over and scrapes her knee. Others are bad: George falls off the swing and breaks his arm. Some are worse: Steve pulls a pot full of boiling water onto his head.

And then there are the real nightmares: Christa runs behind the car when Dad is backing out of the driveway.

It's not nice to hear. Children's hospitals and emergency rooms are filled with kids just like yours every day of the year. All those parents you read about in the paper, whose kids have been burned or hit by cars or whatever, didn't plan for those things to happen.

Sure, some parents almost seem to ask for it. The idiots in big cars you see driving around on Saturday mornings with all the kids climbing around in the back without seatbelts. The jerks who lock their kids in the house while they run out to shop.

My hope is that *most* dads are sensible, caring, concerned, cautious and protective guys, just like you and me. The problem is that it doesn't matter how good our intentions are. It takes only *one* moment of distraction—count it, one—to find yourself biting your fingernails while you wait in the emergency room. Your child only needs to be in the wrong place at the wrong time once for an accident to occur.

> It takes only *one* moment of distraction—count it, one— to find yourself biting your fingernails while you wait in the emergency room.

It's happened to me several times.

Once, I was clowning around with Georgia in a shopping cart. I hit a bump. The shopping cart stopped. She didn't. It was a beautifully executed one-and-a-half somersault before her skull hit the concrete. (The judge gave her a ten.)

Another time I left a library bag on the dresser next to Matilda's crib. When we went in to check on her before bed, she had wrapped the cord of the bag around her neck—not once, but twice.

When Rachael was a newly mobile walker, I left a door open and she crawled up a steep and precarious flight of steps. She made it to the top before being accidentally found by another family member.

The thought of Rachael plummeting down the steps or Georgia having brain surgery or Matilda slowly choking in her sleep ties my stomach in knots.

Parents have a natural and desirable tendency to be protective. I don't want anything to happen to my kids. I don't want them to be hurt at all. I don't want to be one of those dads on the news.

The only problem is that life doesn't work like that.

When they are newborn, they are 100 percent dependent on you. They come out and say, "Hello, I'm your baby. I can't do anything for myself. My life is totally in your hands!"

But they can't stay that way. As your child grows up, you can't watch her twenty-four hours a day. Nor can you strap her down and leave her in a padded room till she reaches adulthood just so she has absolutely no chance of hurting herself. You simply can't spend your entire life following your child around, ready to catch her if she shows the first sign of bumping into something or falling over. Not only will you ruin your life, but your kid will end up with no survival skills. You can't hold her hand through every experience or she'll never learn anything for herself.

As she gets older, you have to let go. She has to learn to stand on her own two feet, avoid danger and survive in her environment. At some stage, you have to take off the training wheels. There has to be a point when you let her go down the back steps by herself; when you trust her around hot coffee; when you let her use a knife; when she crosses the road for the first time by herself; when you let her go to a party. And there will come a time when you have to let your daughter go out with a guy named Spike who has tattoos and drives a van. (For me, that'll be when my daughters are thirty.)

Like reeling in a fish, the trick is knowing how much to let go and at what time.

There are no rulebooks about this, so you have to use your PD, depending on the personality, intelligence, skills and commonsense of your offspring.

"What is PD?" I hear you cry.

Glad you asked.

At high school, during boring geography lessons (weren't they all?), my friends and I used to think up two-word nicknames using our initials. And so I was Pregnant Dog, Police Department, Private Detective, Pineapple Donut and my friends' favorite, still raised at informal dinner parties, Pubic Deficiency. (Thanks, guys.)

But the PD I'm talking about here is not one of these. Pubic deficiency, for example, will not help you be a better dad. No indeed. What I'm talking about is "parental discretion."

You have to use your parental discretion to work out where to draw the line between coddling and carelessness.

And that's a fine line.

A good starting point is to accept the everyday accidents. You might as well, since you simply can't stop them from occurring unless you hold your child's hand twenty-four hours a day. And just because your child bumps her head or cuts her foot or falls out of bed does not mean that you are a bad parent. The odd bump, scratch and bruise is all part of growing up.

But you have to find the balance between pampering your child on the one hand and being callous on the other. For example, on a bike trail.

The bike trail in our local park is a great place for little kids to gather. It is a concrete circuit, complete with miniature stop signs and pedestrian crossings—which is laughable considering the kids have no idea what they are anyway. Consequently, it's more like a demolition derby with kids on scooters and bikes with training wheels traveling at high speeds in random directions. As you can imagine, the "road" surface is thick with bits and pieces of kids' knees and elbows, and aside from the sound of little metal bikes crashing into other little metal bikes, the air is heavy with the sound of bones knocking together.

Now, the first thing that kids do when they fall over is look up to see if anybody is watching. If not, they go back to what they were doing. If they have an audience, however, let the tears flood forth!

Some parents are over-protective. Their child falls over so they drop everything and pick her up and hug her and soothe her ("Oh, my poooor baaayby . . . oh my daaaarling . . ." and so on). The kid loves the attention but ends up being a whining wuss who runs screaming to Mom or Dad over every little bump.

Other parents are overly casual. Their child falls nine feet backward off a slide and lands on his head. He lies there motionless in the sand, with the wind knocked out of him, while Dad calls out from his barbecue pit, "Get up, Phil—and stop acting like a girl!"

A friend of mine has exactly the right approach. When his son falls off his bike and is lying prone in those initial seconds, he quickly picks him up, brushes him off, checks him over and says something like, "There . . . you're okay now," puts him back on the bike and shoves him off on his merry way. The kid never even has time to suck in enough breath for a scream. But he is sensitive to those times when his son has really hurt himself, and he gives him adequate amounts of comfort and Band-Aids before putting him back on the bike trail to face Mad Max again.

These everyday bumps and bruises are one thing. While we accept that all kids will fall off bikes and trip on doormats and cut their hands on something or other (trust me . . . they'll find something), it's important that you remove as much danger as possible from the equation. Think safety all the time and reduce the chance of extraordinary accidents.

The problem is that the mobility that comes with toddlerdom can catch you by surprise. She can walk and climb and reach up above her head. And when she falls, which will be often, she's got farther to go before her head makes that sickening thud on the tiles.

Prevention

The way I see it, it's better to be proactive than reactive in dealing with toddler accidents. In other words, prevention is better than cure. You need to think like a toddler and figure out all the ways you could harm yourself—then think like an adult and figure out all the ways you can stop your toddler thinking like a toddler and harming yourself . . . I mean herself . . . I think.

You have to establish patterns and personal habits that may be new to you. You have to develop a mindset that says many accidents can be prevented, and you have to think ahead and figure out how.

I'm assuming that you already made some changes in your house when your baby started to crawl. But you have to keep searching for danger areas. Here are a few things to keep in mind.

Hot Beverage Awareness

Be careful with hot coffee and tea, which account for half of all scalds to children. A cup on the edge of your kitchen counter, or on a table with a tempting long tablecloth or on the floor at your feet, just invites disaster. Be careful particularly with small coffee tables, which a toddler might crash into for support. Watch out for your idiot friends, who hold a cup of hot coffee in one hand and your child in the other arm.

Danger in the Kitchen

Adapt your kitchen to prevent contact with hot surfaces and electrical appliances. When cooking, keep the pot, pan or wok handles away from the edge. Get into the habit of using the back burner on the stove top. Make sure there is no access to cords attached to toasters or food processors. If you have a floor-level oven, fence off the kitchen altogether. It's not too difficult to rig up a piece of playpen in the doorway to serve as a barricade. Also remember that electric stove tops retain heat for a long time after they've been turned off.

Doggy Alert

When at the park, keep an eye out for dogs. Most dogs I have encountered have been well behaved around the kids, but I don't want to be fifteen feet away when one decides to be the exception to the rule.

Shut the Darn Door!

Close access doors to potential danger areas: kitchen, garage, bathroom, disco record collection, stairways and outside. If you have to, write a note on the door saying "Don't forget to shut me."

> And remember that one day soon you will discover that not only can your toddler walk, she can also climb.

And remember that one day soon you will discover that not only can your toddler walk, she can also climb.

It's chilling to walk into a room and see her halfway up a bookshelf, hanging on with one hand while leaning out into space trying to open the door with the other. So you may need to make sure there is nothing near doors that a toddler can climb up or onto in an escape attempt.

Be Car-Smart

When getting into a car, account for all your kids. When I say goodbye in the morning, I kiss them all and close the door behind me so I know they're inside.

If they come outside to wave goodbye, I don't even touch the emergency brake till I actually have all of them in my field of vision and know they're nowhere near me.

Kids can move fast. It's no good spotting them, then putting on your seatbelt, adjusting your sunglasses, tuning the radio and then moving off. By that time, they could all be behind the car, thinking they're playing some funny hiding game.

Once Meredith was going out and I was waving goodbye on the front lawn with the kids. Rachael was distraught at not being able to go with her mom. As Meredith backed out of the driveway, Rachael broke into a teary run toward the car to try to stop her. Fortunately, there was no danger; first, because Meredith was watching and second, because I tackled Rachael on the gravel before she got too close.

(For hints on teaching your child road awareness, see "Cars" on page 138.)

Securely Lock All Dangerous Windows

I once read about a toddler who pushed his bedroom window open and fell out. Unfortunately, he was five stories up and tumbled out onto a concrete driveway. Miraculously, he survived, but his survival must be considered the exception rather than the rule.

Knives and Other Sharp Things

Don't give your toddler fine china, glassware or sharp eating implements. Plastic will do until she has convinced you that she is able to handle cutlery without attempting her own eye surgery. Go through the second drawer in the kitchen, which no doubt is crammed with cooking utensils that resemble medieval instruments of torture, and move all sharp objects out of your toddler's reach.

If They Don't Need a Head, They Don't Need a Helmet

The moment your child gets on a bike, scooter or skateboard, she should wear a helmet, even in the sanctity of the backyard. (In most communities, children are required by law to wear an approved helmet when bike riding.) It might cost a few bucks, but it's a lot cheaper than brain surgery. Shoes and tough protective clothing that covers elbows and knees is also a good idea.

The moment your child gets on a bike, scooter or skateboard, she should wear a helmet, even in the sanctity of the backyard. It might cost a few bucks, but it's a lot cheaper than brain surgery.

UV or Not UV, That Is the Question

Protect your child from the sun. When outside, she should wear a hat, proper clothing and sunglasses. At the beach, she's better off in an American Cancer Society full-body swimsuit rather than skinny-dipping like you did as a kid. Sunscreen (that's at least SPF 15, not that oil-based junk you used to put on when you were a teenager) should be worn and reapplied every hour or so. Kids should avoid being in the sun between 10 A.M. and 2 P.M. This is the peak danger period when the sun's radiation is at its strongest.

Protect from Poison

Establish toxic areas in your house where poisons, dangerous chemicals, fluids, powders and flammable materials are kept. For example, you might use a high kitchen cupboard for all your cleaning stuff (not under the sink, as most families do), a locked bathroom cabinet for all your medicines and a locked cupboard in the garage for all your paints and cleansers. I bought a lockable steel cabinet at a garage sale that is now full of motor oil, paint, sprays, solvents, acids and so forth.

Remember that just because a product doesn't have a skull and crossbones on it doesn't mean that it's not potentially dangerous. One spoonful of eucalyptus oil, for example, can kill a child. Keep matches and lighters out of reach also. Children can and do start fires by playing with matches.

Beware of Stranglers

Make sure there are no dangling cords from curtains or blinds, especially near your child's crib or bed. These can easily get wrapped and tangled around a child's throat.

Water Hazard

Drowning is a major cause of death among children aged one to four. If you have a swimming pool, spend an incredible amount of time and money making sure that no child has even the slightest hope of getting near it. If I had a pool, I'd build a thirty-foot-high electric fence around it and I'd take out all the water and instead fill it with Rottweilers.

Be careful not only with the six-foot-deep adult backyard pools but also with those little blow-up wading pools. A child can drown in just one inch of water. Never leave a wading pool with water in it and never leave your child unsupervised. Deflate the pool after every use. Even rainwater could fill it enough to create a hazard. Ensure that fish ponds and other standing bodies of water are also off-limits.

Beware the Bath

Don't ever leave the door open when you're running the bath. And never leave your child alone in the bath. Not only can she drown but she can scald herself in a fraction of a second— literally. Once when I was washing Matilda, she grabbed the nearby tap and wrenched it on. The water hit her in a solid stream. Fortunately it was cold, but I was surprised at how quickly it happened.

Watch Out for Objects that Choke

As you already know, children like to put things in their
mouths. The problem comes when this blocks the flow of air
to their lungs. Keep coins, beads, plastic farm animals and pen
caps, among other tiny items, out of reach. Also watch out for
"hard foods" that can be responsible for choking: peanuts,
carrots, celery and apples. (Hospitals report a massive increase
in choking on nuts every Christmas.)

Be Careful with Glass

In an average house there may be a shower screen and a few
glass doors. You should replace old glass with safety glass or add
a safety film (like the ones used in some window tinting) that
will prevent it from splintering when broken. The back part of
our house has five floor-to-ceiling glass panels. Even though it's
safety glass, we have decorated it with stickers at both kid and
adult eye-level to prevent anyone from thinking it's an open
space and trying to pass through it. (Then we went to our
summer cabin and Matilda ran through a glass door. She now
has fifteen stitches testifying to how careful us parents must be!)

Secure the Hot Things

Make sure the heating system in your house is secure. Gas,
electric, kerosene, slow-combustion and open fireplaces all offer
their own hazards. Ensure that they are off-limits, perhaps with
a screen or fireguard.

Most kids seem to be sensible about not grabbing a flaming
log. However, the sides of a grill or heater sometimes look like
cold black enamel, even though you could fry an egg on them.
It only takes a blink of an eye for all the skin on their hands to
burn off.

Buy Safe Sleepwear

Be sure to buy flame-retardant pajamas for your children. If the
tag doesn't say that it is flame-retardant, then it isn't. Kids don't
care what it says—they are only interested in the cartoon
character on the front. However, you should read the labels and
make sure you aren't dressing your kid in some sort of flammable
stunt-suit.

Also watch out for long cords, ribbon and lace. These dangle down and can easily ignite over a flame, acting like the fuse of a bomb.

Install Some Fire Alarms

Fire alarms cost less than fast-food for the entire family. Sure, the alarms will go off every time you burn the toast, but this is nothing compared with the protection they provide.

Be Prepared

It's well worth your while to take an accredited first-aid course. This may come in handy and perhaps ward off injury or even death. You'll learn things such as resuscitation, how to wrap bandages, stop bleeding, deal with poisons and prevent your children from doing "The Macarena."

Go to the Local Pharmacy

Bring $200, get a large basket and tell them that you have a toddler. They'll help you.

If you have any spare cash, get your broker to invest in a company that manufactures Band-Aids. Band-Aids are great. They have incredible magical healing properties for both real and imagined hurts. Colorful Band-Aids with cartoon characters on them are more powerful and tend to ease the pain more quickly. Which must be why they are more expensive.

Teach Your Children Well

When it comes to safety, perhaps the best thing you can do is teach your child what is and what is not dangerous; what is allowed and what is not. This will help her to protect herself from harm. It is also extra insurance for those times when you have the circular saw plugged in and lying on the floor while you answer the phone.

Of course, the way you teach her needs to be appropriate for her age.

For a young toddler, your teaching might take the form of pretending to touch something and going "Ow! Ow!" or "Hot!" and making a face that indicates extreme pain. Then when she tries to touch it, say quite firmly "No!" Even then, don't assume that she's got the idea. Watch her like a hawk and keep reinforcing the "no" message.

With young children, however, you can use reason and explanation: "See this coffee here? It is very hot. It will burn you. Don't come near it. Do you understand? Hot. Danger. Stay away from here."

Or my personal favorite: "If you touch that, I'm going to send you to your room and I won't let you out till you're eighteen years old."

That never fails.

Remember that prevention is better than cure. Learning by experience might be okay if she wants to eat a lemon, but not when she's playing with one of those knives you see on TV that cuts through old boots and cans and then slices a tomato with the ease of a surgeon's scalpel.

In summary (for all of you who got through school by reading Cliffs Notes™):

- Accept everyday scrapes and bumps as a normal part of growing up.
- Find the balance between caring and coddling.
- Establish personal habits and routines with safety in mind.
- Think prevention.
- Teach them about danger, safety and common sense.
- Pray.

I hope you'll enjoy many accident-free days and will have to go to the emergency room only once or twice . . . a year.

CHAPTER 12
Birthdays

RON HOWARD'S film *Parenthood* is one of my favorites. It contains a great scene in which the Buckman parents (Steve Martin and Mary Steenburgen) put on a birthday party for their son Kevin.

But, at the last minute, disaster strikes. Cowboy Dan, the gunfighting balloon man, fails to arrive. In a desperate attempt to save the day, Dad fills in. He chops up a bath mat as a pair of chaps and dons his son's gun belt before appearing in front of the entertainment-hungry throng as Cowboy Gil.

The party is a complete success. The kids love him. There is laughter, merriment and whimsy. Cowboy Gil enters local mythology. And best of all, as Kevin gets into bed at night, he thanks his dad and tells him he loves him. He tells him he is the best.

I have always wanted to be Cowboy Gil.

Something appeals to me about coming to the rescue, about saving the party and being a hero in the eyes of my children.

When Rachael turned five, I got my chance. She was having a "dress-up" party and, as the first guest arrived, she declared hysterically that she wanted a grownup to dress up as well.

With seconds to spare, I headed into the bedroom to transform myself into Pirate Pete, Terror of the High Seas. Baggy pants, motorcycle boots, a silk shirt left over from the seventies, a make-up scar, an eye patch from the first-aid kit, a sword from the kids' toy box, a bent coat hanger as a hook and a hanky that Grandma gave me for Christmas as a bandanna—I was in business.

It was with great excitement that I burst in on the dozen or so assembled guests, all under the age of five. And when I say burst, I do mean "burst." I leapt up on the table, called out "AARRGGH, M' HEARTIES!!! YO HO HO!!" and swished my hook menacingly through the air.

The next few moments are blurry.

I vaguely remember a brief, stunned silence before the tears and screams began. Peter Pan and Robin Hood immediately took it upon themselves to defend the group by hitting me over the head and pounding my crotch with their swords. Wendy, the Little Mermaid and the entire contingent of fairies broke down and began to howl. Cinderella ran screaming from the room.

We were able to calm down most of the kids within a few moments, but Princess Jasmine's dad had to come back to the party and stay with her for the entire time. He was less than thrilled.

That night as Rachael got into bed, there were no warm declarations of love or appreciation. Only a surly pout and words to the effect that I had wrecked her party. And the kindergarten parents still give me funny stares.

When I was in college, I did a study on the stress levels of major life experiences. The biggies were things like death of a spouse, divorce, changing jobs, moving, getting married and, of course, having children. (As if you didn't know that already.)

> Hosting a kid's party is a big deal. It takes a lot of planning and work. You can't just lock the kids in the backyard and toss bags of chips at them.

Whoever wrote this list obviously didn't have kids, because if they did, birthday parties would have been close to the top as a major cause of stomach ulcers in young dads and moms.

Hosting a kid's party is a big deal. It takes a lot of planning and work. You can't just lock the kids in the backyard and toss bags of chips at them.

So as you enter the realm of hosting parties, here are a few ideas that might help you out.

Don't Go Overboard

Most parents get excited at the prospect of their first child's first birthday. It has little to do with the child's accomplishment of turning one and a lot to do with the parents saying to the world, "Hey everybody, we've been parents for twelve months now and we're still alive—and sane!"

It is a parental rite of passage, a graduation. It is a public declaration (read, "boast") that you have faced the foe, walked in the valley of diapers and have emerged relatively unscathed.

When Rachael turned one it was a momentous occasion of epic proportions. As far as I was concerned, the twentieth century would be remembered for World War II, space exploration, Elvis, microwave popcorn and Rachael Downey's first birthday. It truly was a great occasion, so we decided to hold a celebration.

We planned a mammoth party.

My parents tried to warn me.

"Don't go overboard," they said.

"Keep it simple," they said.

But with the arrogance of youth, I ignored their advice. I mean, how can I trust people who refer to my CDs as "those tiny silver records?"

Being one, Rachael didn't have any real friends, so we did the honorable thing and invited all *our* friends so she didn't feel unpopular. It had all the makings of a Gatsbyesque bash: a guest list like the credits of *Titanic*, cheese platters, sausage rolls, wine, beer, juice, enough food to make even the Galloping Gourmet salivate, a huge cake lovingly crafted by my gorgeous wife and, of course, the token kids' food—cupcakes. There were balloons, party hats and those things that go *wheee* when you blow them.

That experience got birthdays out of my system. As we crawled into bed that night, I could tell Meredith would rather be dead than have another extravaganza like that . . . primarily because she said, "I would rather be dead than have another extravaganza like that."

As a consequence, Georgia didn't fare as well. For her first birthday, a few hastily contacted close family members gathered together for drinks, hot dogs and a cheesecake from the local twenty-four-hour service station.

And then there was Matilda.

Poor, poor Matilda.

A doughnut with a candle shoved in the top really was a pathetic effort now that I think about it.

As my parents said, don't go overboard with your child's parties, especially since to be fair and equal you will have to repeat them for any other children you may be careless enough to have. So if you, like us, have three kids, by the time they're ten you will have hosted more than thirty—that's right, count 'em—*thirty* birthday parties. That's a lot of cakes . . . and a lot of carpet shampoo.

The other reason for keeping things relatively low-key is that it is unwise to break the unspoken parental code relating to party one-upmanship. All parties must remain at the same level of extravagance, otherwise the snowball syndrome comes into effect and financial ruin is inevitable.

Once someone breaks from the pack and employs the Balloon Man, the next person will get Jack the Pony Man. Next it'll be the Kite Man, the Face-Painting Man, the magician, the petting zoo and before you know it you'll have a jumping castle and live bands performing in your backyard.

And all the other parents will hate you.

Choosing a Venue

You have two choices. You can either have the party at home . . . or not at home.

If at home, you don't have to worry about packing the car or setting up somewhere else. You have the convenience of the kitchen on hand and probably a fence and a gate to keep all the infant partygoers trapped like a slide of amoebas. If it's on the lawn, you can use a rake, shovel and hose to clean up. If it's raining, you simply move the kids from the lawn into the living room (assuming you're insured). You also have a bathroom and toilet, which is helpful.

> In a competition between your antique vase collection and an excited horde of kids hyped up on red punch and cupcakes, I wouldn't put my money on the pottery.

On the down side, however, your house will be destroyed. In a competition between your antique vase collection and an excited horde of kids hyped up on red punch and cupcakes, I wouldn't put my money on the pottery.

For these reasons, many choose to have their parties away from home. It doesn't really matter where—as long as it's nowhere near your expensive home entertainment system.

A popular spot is the local park. It takes a little preparation in terms of packing a few baskets full of birthday goodies but, at the end of the day, the paper plates go into the trash cans and you go home to a house that looks exactly the same as before the party.

When you are selecting an outdoor venue, you need to make sure that there is shade and shelter from the elements, as parents of sunburned children tend to get pretty nasty. Toilets, tables and decent parking are also an advantage.

Parks are a good choice because there's plenty of space for games and running around and kicking balls. Most also have enormous play areas with ladders and swings and tunnels that you couldn't possibly compete with in your backyard.

However, you need to be careful if it's on the beach, near a cliff, a main road or a kennel for rabid pit bull terriers—especially if there's a hole in the fence.

Another option is to go to a place that caters for kids and, more specifically, kids' parties. A wide variety of these places have sprung up in recent years, probably the result of the astute business observation that parents of young children are desperate when it comes to parties.

There are indoor gymnasiums full of slides, ball pits and tunnels; fairy castles with resident fairy queens; and, of course, the ever popular family fast-food chains.

Some people think that parties like this are a cop-out; that parents who take their kids to such places are taking the easy and convenient option. But you can see the appeal. You don't have to worry about shopping beforehand. You pay a few bucks per person that, depending on the deal, gives you invitations, food, entertainment and junk like balloons and party hats. And the main advantage is that when the animals have finished their feeding frenzy, you just walk on out of there and leave the underpaid teenagers to clean up the mess.

Now *that's* a good deal.

Who to Invite

Parties require guests, because without them there are no presents. But keep in mind a couple of things when deciding who to invite.

For first and second birthdays this is usually not an issue. You just invite your own friends; some of them will probably have kids of their own. But when it comes to the third, fourth and subsequent parties, your child will spoil it all by wanting *his* friends to come along. That's when the following tips really come in handy.

KISS (Keep It Small, Stupid!)

Only invite as many children as you can handle without destruction of property, threat to life or having to call any of the emergency services. Keep it small and manageable.

For a two- or three-year-old, a few friends are fine. For a four- or five-year-old, five to ten friends, tops. I know one couple who had nineteen kids to their four-year-old's birthday. Too late did they discover the destructive powers of such a swarm.

You must ensure that you can adequately supervise all the children. Invite helpful friends or let the parents know that you expect them to stay. It all depends on the number of kids you ask, their ages and where you are.

Be mentally and physically prepared for the fact that these other kids, who are going to invade your space and who are your legal responsibility, may not be as well behaved as your own well-balanced offspring.

Don't Invite Kids Named Chester

Kids named Chester always cheat in the games, blow out the candles on the cake, pull somebody's hair, spill their drinks in the chips and break the guest of honor's toys before he's even had a chance to read the assembly instructions.

Your alarm bells should start ringing when Chester's parents enthusiastically drop him off "just a little early." And you can bet they'll always be the last to pick him up.

Don't Ask Your Child, "Who Would You Like to Invite to Your Party?"

This is a catastrophic mistake. I know, because I made it.

When Rachael turned four, in a grandiose parental gesture, I reluctantly gave up my guest list for her party and said she could invite *her* friends for a change.

Don't invite kids named Chester

The conversation went like this:

"Rachael, who are your very special friends?"

She pondered carefully for a moment and in that cute little-kid voice that stretches out each syllable and goes up at the end of every sentence, she said,

"Jo-o-o-hn . . . aaaaaaaaand . . . um . . . Paaa-scaaale . . . aaaaaaand . . . Maathyoooooo . . . and . . . Kiiiir-stun. Um, dat's all Dad."

"Okay, we're set," I thought to myself. I wrote down the names: John, Pascale, Matthew, Kirsten. Great.

The next day, I checked to make sure no one had been left off the list, so I asked about the special friends again.

"Um . . . Joo-deee . . . and Saa-aandeee . . . and Siiiiiiimon . . . and um, um and . . . Aaaaanjee."

So I scribbled out John, Pascale, Matthew, Kirsten and wrote down Jodi, Sandy, Simon, Angie.

"Okay, darling, here's who's coming to your party: Jodi, Sandy, Simon, Angie. Is that right?"

"No, Dad. Not them. I don't want them!" And then, with a hint of hysteria, "NOT THEM!"

"Who then?"

"Kaaaren . . . and . . . Niiiicki . . . aaaaaaand, um, Richard."

This went on for a few days.

Tuesday: Matthew, Sarah, Trevor, Carolyn.

Wednesday: John, Chrissie, Cathy, Wayne.

Thursday: Bill, Brittany, Grant, Linda.

You get the picture?

In the end I realized sadly that my daughter had the brain of a houseplant and decided to invite my friends again after all.

Meredith, however, didn't go for this. So she asked the preschool teacher who Rachael played with, and we invited them instead.

Invitations

Once you've settled on who's coming, you need to invite them. Invitations are an important communication to the parents of the guests.

It's pretty obvious that you say who the party's for, where it's going to be and when its going to start. If it's an outdoor party, you might like to include a brief contingency statement in case of rain, hail or hurricane.

The most important part of the invitation, however, is when the party is going to end. Two hours is plenty of time for a kids' party. A lot of parents (quite sensibly) use the time to catch up on some chores or shopping—but if you don't tell them when it ends, they might try to squeeze in a quick trip to Hawaii.

Food

You can't have a party without food. Kids love food. They expect food. If you don't feed them, they will turn on you and kill you.

But what should you feed them?

When I was a little kid, my parents put on parties modeled on Willy Wonka's chocolate factory. There were sparkling bottles of fizzy drinks in several flavors and strong cocktails of red and green cordials, bowls overflowing with chips and toffees and brightly wrapped taffy, mountains of lollipops and landscapes of cupcakes; plates strewn with chocolate cake, chocolate cookies, chocolate ice cream covered in chocolate sauce and, of course, chocolate candies.

Checklist

Depending on where the party's going to be and what you intend to do, write a checklist of all the things you'll need. Here are a few ideas:

✓ headache pills
✓ tablecloth/picnic blanket
✓ plastic cups and utensils
✓ paper plates and napkins
✓ party hats
✓ tetanus shots
✓ Band-Aids and sunscreen
✓ towels
✓ tissues

✓ fire-extinguisher
✓ balloons
✓ games
✓ food and drink
✓ cake
✓ party horns
✓ party bags
✓ garbage bags
✓ earplugs

If you don't mind spending a few dollars, toy stores and supermarkets stock "party packs" that contain all the essentials. They're worth about a dime but sell for about six bucks because they're covered in characters from kids' TV shows.

The disadvantage is that they cost money and because they are disposable, you are not helping the environment.

The advantage is that at the end of the party, you throw everything away.

My infant comrades would attack like a plague of locusts, leaving only crumbs and shredded tablecloth as evidence of their collective appetite.

But after a while my parents got tired of all my guests going wild, running around, hitting each other and smashing furniture.

To say nothing of the vomit.

I don't suppose you could blame the kids. They had enough garbage in their stomachs to make a junkyard goat feel queasy, and then my dad would throw us all around in what he referred to as "party games."

Then again, don't overreact and do a health-food party. Once, instead of her usual chocolate-face cookies, Meredith made alfalfa men, using cream cheese and savory crackers as a base. I'm sure I don't need to elaborate on what an abysmal failure these were. Heck, one day of pigging out on total junk isn't going to hurt them.

Hot dogs and ketchup are an old favorite. Little pizza slices or miniburgers also go down well. Cut-up sandwiches. Chips and dip. A fruit platter. Juice or punch to wash it all down. A simple cake with a few candles.

Fantastic.

The kids are happy.

The parents are happy.

Also, if you are having parents at the party, make sure you cater to them too. Some parents don't take kindly to being served cupcakes and happy-face chocolate-chip cookies. A cheese platter with some deli meat and dip, a loaf of bread, a few bottles of champagne, juice . . . and you're in business.

Games

Even in the current politically correct climate, at most parties I've been to, the moms do the food and the cake and the dads do the games and the videotaping.

If you contain a horde of toddlers and children in a confined space for two hours, they'll only be amused by food for so long. And if you don't keep them occupied, they'll start destroying stuff.

You have to have a stash of good games up your sleeve. Here are a few favorites.

> If you contain a horde of toddlers and children in a confined space for two hours, they'll only be amused by food for so long.

Candy Hunt

Hide hard candies on the ground and in low branches for the kids to find. Keep a few in your pockets for those who haven't quite got the knack yet and are looking up at the sky. Make sure you put adults on the perimeters of the lawn or park to prevent enthusiastic hunters from traveling too far in their quest. Also, keep your eyes open for kids who are picking up garbage, dog droppings and hypodermic needles.

Pin the Tail on the Donkey

This is a classic. Of course, you don't have to use a tail or a donkey. You can pin anything to anything. Let your creativity run wild. All you need is some sort of picture or poster and something to stick on it. Try *Pin the nose on the Mona Lisa, Pin the breast on the centerfold, Pin the allegation to the politician.*

Pass the Package

This takes a little preparation. Buy a decent big prize, like an action figure or tradable cards, and wrap it in sheets of newspaper. Between each layer, put some stickers, candies or little gimmicky toys. Make sure you have as many layers as there are guests at the party. Sit the kids in a circle while you play a tape or sing a song. They pass the package around like a hot potato and whoever has it when the music stops gets to rip off a layer and keep what's inside. Make sure that you stop at least once on every child so everyone "wins" something. That way you avoid tears.

If you want to give the party that extra pizzazz, make the final prize a dead rabbit or a pig's head. This will ensure your place in the local parenting mythology for many years to come.

Balloon Frenzy

This is a great game for tiring out even the most energetic youngsters. Blow up a balloon and let it go—the kids have to chase after it. Whoever gets it wins a prize!

A caution, however: Don't play this game near a cliff, major road or large body of water.

Statues

Play a tape or sing a song. While the music is on, the kids leap around energetically—kick their legs, swing their arms, jump, hop, whatever. When the music stops, they have to freeze into a statue. Round by round, eliminate those who move after the music stops. When they get good at it, stop the music and leave it off for an hour. That way, you'll get some peace and quiet.

Potato Roll

This is a great game that kids really love. You need a flat, hard surface, like the floor of a garage or a deck. Draw a giant target in chalk on the ground. It should look like an archery board, with points in each concentric circle—say, 100, 50, 25, 10. The kids have to take turns standing a few feet away and bowling a potato into the target. It is surprisingly hard, especially if you use oblong potatoes.

Find Dad

Tell the kids that you're going to hide. They shut their eyes and count to twenty. While they're doing that, sneak off to your car. Drive to a friend's place and watch the TV for an hour. Come back at the end of the party shouting, "I won! I won!"

There are also some games that are best avoided.

Hide and Seek

Cover your eyes and count to twenty very slowly, "...nineteen... twenty. Here I come!"

You look up. There are no kids anywhere. Twenty seconds ago there were thirty children. Now there are none. You are alone in the middle of a park stretching off into the distance, mile after mile. You realize that in theory this game is good, but in reality . . .

You spend the next six hours (along with the local police) hauling kids out of trees, rabbit burrows and drains.

Don't do it.

Food Fight

Self-explanatory.

Archery

Self-explanatory.

Tease the Rottweiler

Self-explanatory.

Simon Says

This may be a good game for older kids, but it's too complex for young 'uns. I found this out at one of Georgia's parties.

This is how it went:

"Simon says, hands on heads."

(All hands go on heads.)

"Hands down!"

(All hands go down.)

"Ah-hah! You're all out!"

(Confused looks from the kids.)

"Okay, another round . . . Simon says touch your toes."

(All kids touch their toes.)

"Touch your ears!"

(All kids touch their ears.)

"Ah-hah! You're all out!"

(Confused looks from the kids again. Some start to cry.)

This went on for a while before Meredith pointed out to me that the kids didn't have any idea what was going on and I was the only one enjoying myself.

Party Bags

The United Nations Bill of Rights for the Child ensures that all children, regardless of race, color or creed, have the right to food, shelter, education and party bags.

I have never been a great supporter of the party bag. It just doesn't make much sense to me that you put on a party and feed the kids . . . and then you're expected to provide them with party stuff to take home as well.

Always hand the party bags out as the kids are leaving. That way, their parents have to put up with the sticky fingers and the sugar overdose.

Unfortunately, it's one of those "this is what everybody else does, so I'll have to do it, too" situations. You'll soon see what I mean. The party comes to an end and all the kids start lining up expectantly for their party bags. And the parents are just as bad. They probably wolf down the goodies themselves when they're driving home. I know I do.

Always hand the party bags out as the kids are leaving. That way, their parents have to put up with the sticky fingers and the sugar overdose.

And if a kid was rude to you at the party, hide a hot pepper in his bag.

Other People's Parties

Not only do you have to face the nightmare of your child's
birthday party once a year, but increasingly you will notice an
endless stream of cute cards announcing a party almost every
weekend.

Make no mistake. You cannot escape them. Birthday parties
are a major feature of the small-child annual social calendar.

If your child goes to day care, Sunday school or kindergarten,
he'll have a huge network of friends who will all, quite
inconveniently, have a birthday sometime during the year. If
you're about to enter into the birthday-party-guest era, here are
a few tips that might help you out.

Supervision

I remember the first "real" birthday party Rachael went to. She
was really excited about it, and to be honest, so was I. She was
dressed up in her "party dress" with little white frilly socks, shiny
shoes and a complicated ribbon thing (something that I've still
failed to master after five years).

We drove to the house, clearly identifiable by the two limp
balloons dangling on the mailbox. Upon entering the backyard,
however, alarm bells started going off in my head.

In the middle of twenty frenzied children was a barbecue . . .
at least that's what I think it was supposed to be. The raging
inferno looked more like a sacrificial altar for burnt offerings to
some infant deity.

I also was not impressed by the fact that there were only two
adults present as well as a backyard pool and a cliff.

When dropping off your precious child at little Sarah's
birthday party, remind yourself that anyone with the necessary
functioning biological parts can be a parent. And this "anyone"
might be in charge of the party.

At most parties your youngster goes to, you will already
know the parents from the neighborhood or school. You have
probably checked them out and know what they're like. You will
know whether you trust them and accept their methods of
dealing with children.

But what about when your child gets an invitation to Billy McConnell's party, to be held next Saturday down at the park? You ask your wife who this kid is and she doesn't know. So you ask your little one who Billy is and he doesn't really know either.

You don't know Billy's parents from a bar of soap. They might be wonderful citizens, fine upstanding humanitarians, leaders of our community and the best parents in the world . . . or they could be mindless morons who are planning to drink beer while the kids go for a swim.

> The point is, you wouldn't lend your car to people you didn't know. May I suggest, therefore, that you might want to be a tad cautious before leaving your child in the care of a stranger?

The point is, you wouldn't lend your car to people you didn't know. May I suggest, therefore, that you might want to be a tad cautious before leaving your child in the care of a stranger?

Don't be embarrassed about checking out the situation. I'm not talking about pulling out a clipboard and interviewing the parents about their family history, criminal records and views on nuclear testing. But if you don't know them, call them up and ask about the arrangements for the party. If you hear a banjo playing in the background, RSVP in the negative. Or, when you do drop off your kid, go and meet the other parents and check out the situation. Assure yourself that all is well and that your child is in good hands.

If not, don't be afraid to stay for the duration or simply come up with some lame excuse for having to leave with your child in fifteen minutes. After all, it's your job to ensure the welfare of the fruit of your loins.

Presents

Tradition dictates that when you go to a party, you take a present. I know several parents who buy birthday-type presents in bulk and keep them stored till needed. This means they don't have to make a special trip to the toy store every weekend.

If you're a real schmuck, you can always select a few dud presents from your own child's birthday party to palm off on someone else. Just make sure you don't give it back to the original giver.

For little kids, you should be able to buy something small at your local drugstore, bookstore or supermarket.

When purchasing, consider the following factors.

How Old Is the Recipient?

For example, a one-year-old will love one of those smash-the-ball-with-the-hammer contraptions. A five-year-old will not. A five-year-old will love a book. A one-year-old will suck the pages.

How Much Do You Want to Spend?

This often depends on who the recipient is. If it's your nephew or niece, you may feel more inclined to spend a few extra bucks and get something a tad more extravagant than if it's some snotty-nosed kid down the road who you don't like all that much anyway.

You don't have to spend a huge amount. A few dollars will get you something decent in a supermarket, such as a bucket and shovel set. A couple hundred dollars will get you something decent, such as a mini-scale Formula One race car with disc brakes and an air bag.

In my years of anecdotal observation, I have come to the conclusion that there is little correlation between the price tag on a present and the enjoyment a child will get from it. I have seen plenty of kids ignore the expensive present and play with the box that it came in instead.

Also, consider the cumulative financial impact of many birthdays per year multiplied by the number of children you're going to have, multiplied by several years. If you have three kids who go to ten parties each per year for ten years and you spend ten dollars per present, that will add up to three thousand dollars. Which is a lot of money to spend on plastic.

Do You Like the Parents?

If you happen to like the parents, there are plenty of good presents available. After monitoring the present-giving protocol at kids' parties for a few years now, I have come up with a list.

For little kids
- balls
- dolls
- dump trucks
- bath toys (boats and squirty things)
- books made out of cardboard
- plastic knives, forks, spoons, plates, bowls, cups

For not-so-little kids
- umbrellas
- kites
- stickers
- bubble bath
- lunch boxes
- drink bottles
- bubble blowers
- bucket and shovel sets
- bat and ball sets
- sketchy boards
- books
- cassettes
- modems

If you don't like the parents, however, here's your chance for revenge. You can get some really good stuff to make their lives more miserable. Plastic musical instruments such as drums, whistles and trumpets will drive them insane within days. Paints, crayons and modeling clay will eventually find their way onto the walls and into the Persian rug, no matter how careful the parents are. A cute Rottweiler puppy will no doubt be a present for which they will never forget you.

My personal favorite, however, is any present that has thousands of tiny pieces: jigsaw puzzles, do-it-yourself jewelry kits, small building blocks. Presents like these will spread out like the plague into the darkest corners of every room, and for years to come little pieces will emerge from time to time in sock drawers, linen closets, picnic baskets and in the tread of their shoes.

But the best anti-present of all is the sandbox. A backyard sandbox does two things only.

First, it brings buckets of sand into the house hidden in the creases of the child's clothing. Second, it sends out a message to all the cats in the neighborhood: "Attention. Public toilet. All welcome. No waiting."

CHAPTER 13
Baby-Sitting

THERE will come a time when you and your wife need to go somewhere and it won't be appropriate for your child to go with you—say, a wedding or an afternoon of whitewater rafting. If such events do not arise of their own accord, you should make something up, because if you never get away from your child, you will go nuts. In these circumstances, you need a baby-sitter.

There is not much actual sitting of babies going on in parentland. Most parents take their babies with them wherever they go. In reality, most baby-sitting involves young children. But they keep the word "baby" in the title because if it were called "toddler-sitting," no one would do it. They'd run away with great haste.

Anyway, there will come times when you need the services of some ~~sucker~~ person to mind your child when you're out. Common sense, the law and your child all dictate that simply leaving her alone to explore your house is not such a good idea.

But who do you ask?

Who can you trust?

Who will do a good job?

Who will cost you the least?

If you're lucky, you might have a few friends or relatives who don't have a child of their own and who still think that minding yours for a couple of hours is a novelty. If they're sensible, trustworthy, partially deaf and have the guts to change a toddler's diaper or face a preschooler's "I don't want to go to bed" tantrum, milk them for everything you can get. Because the moment they have a child of their own, they won't want to borrow yours.

If you're lucky, you might have grandparents nearby who would love to spend some time with your offspring. They no doubt will use it as an opportunity to spoil their grandchild with love, attention and lollipops—and to make a mental list of all the things you are doing wrong as a parent.

Aside from being free (unless your folks are real misers, who charge you!), grandparents are a good value because they allow your child to experience her extended family, something that is sadly lacking in modern western society.

They've been there and done that all before, though you may need to update them on some modern parenting skills, such as how to operate a disposable diaper and the remote control on your VCR. Also, you can trust most grandparents to do a good job, as long as

- They did a good job as your parents.
- They are still in possession of all their faculties.
- Grandpa thinks the wooden spoon and the belt are respectively for stirring cake mix and holding up pants, not tools of discipline.
- Grandma doesn't serve that rhubarb thing she used to give you when you were a boy.

If you are lacking in gracious friends or willing relatives, you will have to enlist external assistance.

Many areas have baby-sitting clubs that operate out of churches, synagogues, preschools or clubs and are made up of a small group of local parents. Often, instead of money being involved, a credit-point system is used: If you baby-sit, you *accumulate* points per hour; if you use a baby-sitter from the club, you *spend* points per hour. The supervision of the central roster is passed from member to member every few weeks.

These clubs have the benefit of being small, local and made up of people in a similar situation as yourself. They cost nothing, although for every hour your child is baby-sat, you'll have to baby-sit someone else's child in return. This is a ripoff if your child is an angel and you end up baby-sitting a kid named Damien with a weird glint in his eyes. But it's a great opportunity to check out their refrigerator, their cable television and, if they have a computer, to log a few hours looking for nudie pictures on the internet, then laugh knowing the spam e-mail that will plague their household for generations to come.

If you are new to an area or there's no club nearby, you may have to utilize the services of a total stranger to look after your children—an odd concept considering most of us wouldn't even trust our lawnmowers to a total stranger. In this regard, you don't want someone who has a police ID number underneath her photo, a pierced nose or a chainsaw under his arm. You want someone who wears horn-rimmed glasses and a cardigan, has excellent references and knows all the words to *The Sound of Music*.

> You want someone who wears horn-rimmed glasses and a cardigan, has excellent references and knows all the words to *The Sound of Music*.

You want someone you can trust, someone with brains and, preferably, someone who has had some vague connection with children before. You're much better off getting a mom or dad who are baby-sitting on the side to make a little extra cash than a twelve-year-old who's sick of washing cars. Some parents use sitters who advertise in the local paper or phonebook. With this comes a sense of it being an organized and legitimate business.

Other parents rely on word of mouth. They ask their neighbors and friends. Some even call up a local church or school to ask for a recommendation.

No matter who you get, it's a good idea to meet them beforehand so you can see whether you like them. On the day, you could even ask them to come an hour early so your child can get used to them before you leave.

And don't forget two extremely important things: Leave a contact phone number, and convey your expectations to them clearly. You may have a specific code of discipline, food regulations, bed times, video censorship and so forth. You don't, for example, want to come home at midnight to find your four-year-old still up watching *Scream* with an empty gallon-tub of ice cream on her lap. So it is important for your rules and routines to be clearly spelled out.

Except for grandparents. They'll do anything they damn well please. And there's not a thing you can do about it.

CHAPTER 14
Television

IT ALL STARTED with some cardboard, knitting needles, string, wax, glue, an empty bread box, motorcycle headlights, an old motor and a piece of piano wire. In 1925, John Logie Baird put these together and gave the world the first electric baby-sitter—television.

Television certainly played an important role in my development. As a kid, I liked nothing better than Saturday morning cartoons. Later in life, I tried to be cool by imitating the Fonz. I learned my fashion sense from Dr. Who. My taste in music is largely the result of Sunday nights in front of *Soul Train*. I couldn't have gotten through college without *The Streets of San Francisco*. And all I know about sex I learned from *Charlie's Angels*.

There is no possible way that Baird could have imagined the incredible universal consequences of his humble apparatus. It has become our chief means of domestic entertainment and information. Nearly every home has one set, or two or three or four or five. Television shows come into our homes every day and stay around for hours, keeping us up way after we intended to go to bed. It often goes on first thing in the morning and stays on at the dinner table, late at night and even when we're in bed.

Amazingly, the single biggest television audience is preschool children. They spend most of their time at home but don't have the skills to go off and do lots of other things by themselves. No wonder most children learn to operate the contrast control on the remote before they can speak.

The situation has not been helped by the VCR. In previous decades, when the "kids' shows" finished and the bad soap operas began, the TV was switched off (hopefully). Now, however, when the kids' shows run out you simply pop in a tape from your own library or from your stack of rented films. That way, you *never* have to turn it off.

Cable television has also made a considerable impact. There are ten times as many stations as there were when you and I were growing up, which translates into ten times as much garbage to select from. There are multiple channels devoted exclusively to kids' shows. It's like Saturday morning cartoons, twenty-four hours a day, seven days a week.

Anyway, the point is that television is a central part of modern living for children and we're stuck with it. But it's important to think about exactly *how* you want the television to be used in your house.

Why You Should Turn It *On*

First, let me say that I think television is a good thing. There are four reasons for this:

1. It is a terrific baby-sitter, especially if it's hooked up to a VCR. It's perfect for those times when you need to have a few moments to yourself to do something: to clean up or complete a job or take a nap or get a few minutes of peace and quiet in the bathroom or write a book or when you can no longer tolerate lifting up the flap on their favorite picture book.

2. It can be educational. There are many high-quality interactive shows made specifically for young children. They are colorful, bright and entertaining. They teach numbers, letters, songs, actions, words, violence, sex and how to swear.

3. It can sometimes serve as a springboard to talking about issues raised: to learn about communication, conflict, right and wrong, relationships, how the world works, ethical and moral issues, current affairs, life, death and so forth.

4. It can be a fun thing to do as a family. I enjoy getting under a blanket with the wife and kids and watching Disney's latest offering.

Why You Should Turn It *Off*

Like all marvels of science, there is a flip side to the miracle of television. It's important to teach your child responsible patterns of TV viewing. In the words of Von Feilitzen (whoever he is):

> [The] *parents' example is one of the strongest factors explaining children's viewing habits. The more one's parents watch TV, the more the child watches. The more positive parents' attitude to TV, the more the child watches. And the more parents feel they derive from TV viewing, the more the child watches. In other words, the child learns . . . by observing the rest of the family's behavior.*

Unfortunately, many people are slaves to the television. They walk in the door and turn it on and it often stays on until they leave the house or go to bed. In this regard, you need to be the master of the TV, not vice versa.

Show your child that TV doesn't rule your life. Instead of watching it while sitting at the dinner table, switch the darn thing off and talk about something interesting, like how many poo-poos your child did today. Don't spend all weekend watching sports shows. Don't let your child eat breakfast in front of it. Don't have the TV on in the background all the time.

Meredith and I found that TV was dominating our domestic life. The kids were watching too much of it ("Can we watch that video again please, Dad?" "No, kids, six times is enough for one day.") and whenever they were watching, they became oblivious to outside influence, such as me telling them to wash up for dinner.

Meredith and I were watching TV every night for a few hours, only to declare the night's viewing "a waste of time." I also have the bad habit of getting hooked by infomercials or bad seventies science fiction films at around midnight. Too often did I go to bed in the wee hours, regretting my lack of self-control.

So, in a valiant move, we put our TV in a closet and it no longer dominates our routine. It comes out on holidays and on the occasional Friday when there's nothing better than getting some takeout Chinese food and watching a new Disney release with the kids.

If I had the guts, I'd simply put a hammer through the screen and shut the whole thing down forever. But my lofty theoretical ideals don't seem so important at six-thirty on Saturday morning when the cartoons start and I want to sleep for another hour.

As they grow up in this environment, I hope my kids will see TV as a means of entertainment that can be turned on and off at will. It does not have to be on all the time.

How Much Should They Watch?

Once your child starts expressing the desire to watch the TV, it is up to you to control the *quantity* of his viewing. If given the opportunity, he will just watch show after show after show, including the test pattern for hour after hour after hour. He'll end up with a leather behind and, as our mothers used to say, "square eyes."

Some parents allow TV only on the weekends; others, half an hour a day. Various reports state that there are children who watch as much as eleven hours a day. You need to figure out how much TV you think is okay for your child to watch.

In some cases, overexposure to television at an early age can have a detrimental effect on a child's speech development. One report I read concluded that children under the age of one should not be exposed to television at all and that children aged two to three should see no more than an hour a day.

Massive exposure is not good for preschool children either. It can have a negative effect on their creativity, speech, vision, attentiveness and social capability. You see, if they sit and watch long enough, they'll never have to do anything for themselves.

They'll watch other kids climbing trees instead of being out there themselves stuck up an oak. They'll never learn to bake or skip or splash in puddles because they can watch someone else do it in glorious 2-D.

What Should They Watch?

The other thing to keep an eye on is the *quality* of their viewing.

Children pick up a lot from TV, both deliberately and subconsciously. They imitate behavior they see, which is why many schools discourage play related to *Pokemon* and have written to parents expressing their concerns.

Children can also be confused by TV. They have no concept of the characters as actors or of the production process, and they often think that what they see is real and in the present. Up to the age of five, children have trouble discerning whether cartoons and puppets are real. Even children of six sometimes cannot readily distinguish between fantasy and reality. They can be confused by talking animals, scared by monsters, sucked in by soap operas and think that supernatural powers and stunts are at the disposal of normal mortals.

This confusion is at its worst when it induces fears or bad dreams, which are common. I was thirteen when I saw *Alien* and I wouldn't go into a dark room for three months afterward. Imagine how much worse it is for a four-year-old who finds characters or scenes deathly frightening, even though we might find them laughable.

Anyone with the brain of a potato should instinctively know that a three-year-old is not going to enjoy *Terminator* or *Chainsaw Killers from Mars*. Yet every so often I talk to parents whose values are markedly different from mine. They let their kids watch shows that mine won't see till they are much older.

So be careful when it comes to things like "going to a friend's place to play and watch a video," and make sure that you are happy with what's going to be seen. Some parents might think that *Jurassic Park* is a great kids' film. It is unless your child is five. If you don't like it, tell them so and make other arrangements. Don't let any other parent dictate your own values and fast-talk you into making compromises. *You're* going to be the one getting up at 2 A.M. when your son thinks there's a T-Rex in his closet.

The problem of censorship also comes from less obvious areas.

Be careful about having the news on in the background, for example. The evening news is like a horror movie. It's full of war footage, widows weeping over their husbands' bodies, tear-jerker funerals, murders, fires, drought, suicides, famine, riots, plane crashes and celebrity weddings.

> Be careful about having the news on in the background. The evening news is like a horror movie.

Often Rachael or Georgia have asked me a question about a news item I was watching while they were drawing or playing on the other side of the room. I had no idea they even heard, let alone understood. And while I don't want to be overprotective and shield my children from the realities of the world, I find it difficult to explain to a three-year-old why a man with a rifle killed a class of kindergarten children.

And then there are commercials. Advertising campaigns directed at kids are a gillion-goggle dollar business. Kids' commercials are flashy, jingly, fast-paced, action-packed extravaganzas of light and sound. They promote an abundance of junk, especially sugary foods and cheaply made plastic toys.

You'd probably never let a door-to-door salesman into your house to brainwash your kids, so don't let the TV do it, either.

Off to the Movies

The movies need to be treated with care and caution. There's the battle of trying to get into the movie theater without succumbing to your child's pathetic pleas for sticky gummy worms or melty chocolate. Then you take him to the restroom but he doesn't want to go . . . until half an hour after the movie has started and he changes his mind. Then he wants to sit on your lap and ask you nonsensical questions about the plot.

But the main problem at the movies is the G rating. It took me a long time to figure this out. I used to have faith that everything in a G-rated film would be okay for a child.

Big mistake.

This was brought home to me when I took the girls to see one of those matinee-style boy-and-his-dog kids' films (adults at children's prices). I should have realized when I noticed that all the other "G" kids were twelve or thirteen. At one point, the boy was lost in the wilds in a thunderstorm and was being chased by savage wolves. It was dark, the boy was crying and the music was in a minor key. Several screaming young children were soon being carried out of the theater. Later in the movie, the dog got washed down the river. That did it. Another wave of screaming children were hauled out by their parents.

On reflection, I am amazed that a film like that could have the same rating as one of those dopey toddler shows on TV. The G rating could probably be broken up a little more to provide us parents with more information, as the following examples illustrate.

G rating: MNI (Mind-Numbingly Innocuous)

This could be applied to those totally harmless kids' shows in which even the most timid and paranoid toddler could not possibly find anything vaguely scary or nasty.

This would be most children's programs (*Blue's Clues*, *Sesame Street*, *Barney*), puppet shows (*Gumby*, *Thomas the Tank Engine*), cartoons (*Spot*, *The Little Prince*) and that weird French show with the little animated men who speak in funny voices. If your child is frightened by these, you have a serious problem.

G rating: CWB (Cartoons with Baddies)

This is a step up from the previous category. The cartoons are wholesome, fun entertainment with good moral values but slightly scary villains. Disney's offerings are a good example of this: *Aladdin*, *101 Dalmatians*, *Tarzan*, *Dinosaur*, *Beauty and the Beast*, *The Little Mermaid* and *The Lion King* all have baddies who will have some preschoolers diving for pillows.

G rating: PRWCFCHTPBSTK (Psuedo-Reality with Cute Furry Critters; Harmless to Parents but Scary to Kids)

At this level, you take a step away from cartoons and hand puppets to real actors and special effects. These are shows like *The Neverending Story, Ewok Adventure, Star Wars, Phantom Menace, The Polar Bear King, Labyrinth* and *Power Rangers.*

To adults, the friendly critters and giant talking animals are cute, perhaps even ridiculous. To kids, however, the shaggy manes, bulging eyes and sharp teeth can be a source of pure terror. To say nothing of the fact that in proportion to them, the creatures are enormous.

G rating: FTYSWYWYARTBGSFKBWYSTYRYFACIS (Films that You Saw When You Were Young and Remember to Be Great Shows for Kids but When You Show Them You Realize You Forgot about Certain Inappropriate Scenes)

Yeah sure, *The Wizard of Oz* is a great kids' film . . . right up to the moment the flying monkeys appear.

Even with my classification system, the main problem comes when you take your child to a G-rated movie or rent a G-rated video that you haven't actually seen yourself.

There is an unspoken rule among teachers that you never show a film to a class unless you've watched it first. (A teacher friend of mine from a Christian school once took a class of young boys to see *Jesus of Montreal,* believing it to be a biblical epic. He hadn't counted on the excerpt from a porno movie in the opening minutes of the film.)

The same principle should be applied to parenting.

If you can, watch a show first or get a recommendation from a like-minded parent. If can't do this, at least be around so that you can cover your child's eyes or put your hands over his ears.

Oh, and by the way, *The Silence of the Lambs* is not a children's film about sheep with laryngitis.

CHAPTER 15
Childspeak

CHILDREN learn to talk by mimicking us and gradually developing awareness and control over the sounds that come out of their mouths.

Talk to your child all the time, from the day she is born. Obviously she won't respond with a witty retort, but the sound will stimulate her and establish a framework for a system of communication. Talk to her while you change her diaper, make dinner, walk down the aisle of the grocery store, play in the bath, drive in the car and take her for a stroll.

As her language skills evolve, ask her questions, tell her the names of things, sing songs with her, teach her new words, tell her stories and engage her in conversation, however simple it may seem. This is one of the fun parts of fathering. This is what it's all about—communicating, explaining, discussing life, the universe and everything.

When you come home from work, ask your child about her day. Her conversation skills will not be great at first. You may have to be satisfied with a "I dun a poo-poos' day, Dad." But when she gets older you can talk about more intellectually stimulating stuff, such as finger-painting.

> Don't watch TV at the dinner table. Tell her what you did all day. Make up stories. Tell her stories from your past. Tell her you love her.

Don't watch TV at the dinner table. Tell her what you did all day. Make up stories. Tell her stories from your past (only wholesome ones, please). Tell her you love her. Talk to her.

Because one day when she's eighteen, you're going to say, "Come and sit down and have a chat with your old dad . . ."

And she's going to say, "Not now, Dad, gotta go."

After a few years of being babbled at by adults, a child slowly picks up words and phrases and starts to put them into meaningful utterances—that is, until she becomes a teenager, at which point her language skills will actually regress.

It's usually at this juncture, the beginning of verbal communication, that parenting books start telling you what you can expect at what age.

I'm going to avoid this for two reasons.

First, I don't know any kids who fit the mold (including mine), and so generations of parents go by with parenting books in one hand and calendars in the other, either distraught that their beloved offspring are mentally challenged or elated that they are turning out to be gifted and talented.

Second, it gets me out of doing any sort of reliable research and I can fall back (again) on my own anecdotal observations and homespun truths.

It happens like this.

When a baby is born, she doesn't know that she has a mouth. She probably doesn't even realize that the screaming she hears in her crib at night is coming from her. But after a while she figures out that she has a mouth and pretty soon she starts associating the giggles and other strange sounds she hears with that particular orifice. She still has no control over the sounds she makes, but you start to hear her experimenting while she plays or lies in her crib. Sometimes she grunts ("pah," "bah," "dup") and sometimes she sings ("laa-laa-loo-loo," "Canoo ere da jrums Fernanno?")

She is slowly figuring out how to use her mouth, teeth, lips, tongue and vocal chords. Her burgeoning skills are stimulated when parents join in and react to the sounds and mimic them back to her—often, for some bizarre reason, with exaggerated yelps of delight, contorted facial expressions and tummy tickling.

(It is a little-known fact that toddlers can actually talk. They don't, however, because it's so entertaining making us adults carry on like verbose idiots. I overheard Matilda in day care one morning saying to the other one-year-olds, "Yeah, my parents are pretty funny, too. All I gotta do is say 'whee' and they go absolutely nuts.")

Anyway, in the general vicinity of the first year, give or take several months, your toddler will put words together into sentences. But when I say sentences, I mean *toddler* sentences, not *adult* sentences. So, while sitting in the bath, she will look at you and say, "Ahdee-daa-daa-daaAAAAAA-bub-bub-bub."

"Oh really?" you'll say.

"Nyah-ya-ya," she'll reply.

"Is that right?"

"Dup-dup-ba-ba-pppppphhhhhtttttt."

"Well, isn't that just terrific!"

I don't know what's going on in their heads, but it strikes me as remarkable that even at such a young age, toddlers understand the conventions of conversation; that you communicate using a pattern of sounds and that you take turns talking to each other.

You will start to notice that she understands some of what you are saying well before she can vocalize the sounds herself. You can ask her to point out the tractor or sheep or flower in a book and she will. You can tell her to pick up her socks or come to you for a cracker and she will. You can do all that stuff like, "Where's your nose?" "Where's Dad?" "Where's the birdie?" and so on.

This audio comprehension is the vital ingredient in the preparation for her first words.

She will also start attempting to communicate with you when she wants something. She will point to the refrigerator and say, "Nar-duh bup bup." In the bath she will point at something and say, "Woh dob dobbuh." This can be frustrating for her because it will take you a long time to figure anything out. But she will struggle on, trying to hit the nail on the head.

And eventually she will. It'll probably be a word like "Djugh." Most dads will say, "Did you hear that? Did you hear that? She said *Dad*."

And the moms will say, "No . . . no, I think she said *Mom*." This disagreement will go on for weeks, until they realize that the standard toddler first word is actually "*No.*"

This is a multipurpose word that can be used in all situations:

"Time for bed."

"No."

"Bathtime."

"No."

"Eat your food."

"No."

Then follows a few months during which your toddler assembles a collection of functional commands that she uses to get what she wants. This is a survival mechanism.

A Toddler Glossary

At first, her words tend to be monosyllabic grunts with specific meanings:

- **da**   Dad
- **ma**   Mom
- **ahp**   apple
- **boohs**   I've pooped myself
- **jink**   more juice
- **yuk**   I'm going to vomit
- **loll**   give me that lollipop or I'll throw a tantrum
- **boohg**   read to me
- **elv**   No, Dad, actually I think it was Elvis Presley who starred in *Girls! Girls! Girls!*

More complex words, such as "astrophysics," "cappuccino," "xylophone" and "combine harvester," don't come till much later.

There'll be a few months of high jinks when your guests will be thrilled by your toddler's vocabulary stunts. For some reason, around this time parents develop a bizarre fascination with animal noises and are proud of the fact that little Scott knows all the sounds from the average farm. But you can stay amused

by a toddler chanting "Moooo" for only so long. The novelty
will wear off and you'll be back to your old boring self again.

From then on, it's just a matter of building.

One-word units become two-word units:

"Gor-gor tuhn." (It's Georgia's turn.)

Three-word units:

"Ra-ra wahn da." (Rachael wants that.)

Four-word units:

"Tihda jus go poos." (Matilda has pooped all over the rug.)

And beyond:

"Da, I carn ge ee ardry eeyor poota." (Dad, I can't get into
the hard drive on your computer.)

Don't expect too much too soon. Even after she's picked up a
little vocabulary, her mouth still has to learn how to pronounce
the words so that others can
understand them.

But you will learn your toddler's
unique way of speaking. This is
often quite amusing because, for a
while, parents are the only ones who
understand their own child. Likewise, you will find yourself not
having a clue what other kids are saying, and their parents will
look at you as if you're a moron.

> Even after she's picked up a
> little vocabulary, her mouth still
> has to learn how to pronounce
> the words so that others can
> understand them.

"Hello, Jim. How was your day, darling?"

"I ayda na."

"What'd he say?"

"He said, 'I ate a banana.' "

"Oh. And was it a good banana?"

"Yub a num wenow."

"What'd he say?"

"He said, 'The banana was overripe but no pesticides were
used in its growth.' "

"Oh."

It is important that you don't fall into the trap I have fallen
into three times now.

After a while, in an attempt to communicate more easily
with each of my children, I slip into toddlerspeak without

realizing. Meredith pointed this out to me one day when I was standing in the kitchen saying to Matilda, "Bubba wanna tudder ackie?"(Would you like that other type of cracker?). Meredith asked me if I was trying to teach Matilda some sort of perverse pidgin English.

The problem is that if parents only speak to toddlers using their own language, it is hard for the kids to learn how to speak in an adult code.

For a long time, your toddler will tend to respond to you rather than initiate a conversation. She will be able to name objects that she wants and say "no" and "why" to your requests, but you won't often find her starting an in-depth conversation.

There will come a day, however, when your child crosses the line. She will have vocabulary, she will have grammar, she will have content, she will have confidence, she will have curiosity. She will be a fully qualified user of childspeak . . . and then there'll be nothing you can do to shut her up.

There are two main types of childspeak.

The Ten-Minute Ramble

Her vocabulary is limited and she thinks and feels at a more advanced level than she is able to express herself. One of the consequences of this is that her *desire* to converse is not matched by her *ability* to converse. And so you will experience the joy of listening to endlessly meaningless sentences:

"Dad?"

"Yeah?"

"Um . . . I, I, I . . . um, Dad?"

"Yeah?"

"I . . . we, we, we . . . um . . . you know that, that, that thing of . . ."

"Yes."

"Well, I know . . . I know that . . . um, um . . . hey! I, I, I want . . . I want to see and the . . . and then . . . and then, then, um, then we all are going . . . Dad?"

"Yep."

" 'Cause I know . . . I, I, I, I know and want . . . I want that . . . and you with you too?"

"Yep."

"And . . . and . . . and . . . and . . . and . . . and . . . (long pause) . . . and then I saw . . . and then he walk . . . and then you know? Like and we did the other day . . . and um?"

"Yep."

I could write pages of this stuff.

It's even worse if you call home from work and you've got only a minute to tell your wife an important message and you make the mistake of getting your youngster on the phone and she starts rambling on about something, half of which you can't understand anyway, so you go and make a cup of coffee and come back and she's still raving, so you sit in your office yelling "PUT MOMMY BACK ON THE PHONE!" and eventually hang up in frustration.

Be patient with your toddler as she learns to speak. She can only get better. Don't let her know that you're not listening or are frustrated by her inability to articulate. Don't tell her to be quiet or to get to the point. Give her the freedom to explore her vocabulary and experiment with communication.

Questions

A toddler's poor brain is so empty that she is just dying to find out the reason for everything—even things that don't have a reason. Consequently, you end up having long but limited conversations about a small range of subjects. It's hard to discuss anything complex or abstract with a person who has a fifty-word vocabulary, half of which are words to describe human waste.

The current record holder for inane conversation in our family is Georgia, who managed to respond with the word "why" eighteen times in succession during my explanation of why some cats are black and some cats are white.

It's hard to discuss anything complex or abstract with a person who has a fifty-word vocabulary, half of which are words to describe human waste.

Still, it's really important not to put your child off. Don't tell her to shut up. Her infant brain is craving your attention and only through interaction will she learn and develop. She needs to know that she can talk to you and that you're interested in what she has to say, even if it is only about puking the previous night.

Having said that, however, I would like to qualify myself. Everybody's got a limit.

We are only human, so we cannot be expected to engage in two-hour conversations trying to come up with reasons why Thomas the Tank Engine is blue rather than red. After all, there are lawns to be mowed and laundry to be washed.

You need to have some strategies for shutting her up and getting on with your life. I have four procedures for terminating inane conversations that show no sign of natural cessation.

Talk Nonsense

You've been trying to explain why birds can fly and humans can't. The conversation has been circular for at least fifteen minutes . . .

"Because they have wings and we don't."

"Why?"

"Because we are not born with wings. It is not part of our design."

"Why not?"

"It's just not."

"How do wings work?"

"They push up on the air."

"Why?"

You face the fact that resolution is not in the cards and decide to resort to the nonsense answer.

"They push up on the air because gobbi dundar pootep morendi. Okay? Are you satisfied now?"

While I'm not sure if that look you receive in return is one of satisfaction or confusion, at least it puts an end to your aeronautical theorizing so you can get back to the crossword.

Standard Answer

Instead of talking nonsense, have a phrase up your sleeve that is your standard answer to all possible questions.

For me, the phrase is, "Because the dinosaurs became extinct." Observe:

"Why are you my dad?"

"Because Mom and I made you. I'm your dad and you're my daughter."

"Why aren't I a boy?"

"Because that's the way you came out. Only God decides stuff like that. We just get you as you are."

"Why?"

"Because the dinosaurs became extinct."

"Oh."

This little phrase has got me out of many lengthy discussions and has satisfied the girls' curiosity on numerous occasions. The only problem is that I fear I may have created some misconceptions. I won't be surprised when one of them fails a college genetics exam because she has attributed hereditary gene defects to the extinction of *Tyrannosaurus rex*.

Bluff

I'm usually forced to bluff my way when one of my girls does that thing where she just answers "why?" to every one of my responses, or when her question actually has no answer (How is Santa going to get through the vent of our heater?) or requires a university degree in astrophysics to answer (How does gravity work?), or if I simply don't know the answer (How come they keep re-running *Brady Bunch* on TV?).

And so we get scenes like

"Dad, why is a banana bent?"

"I don't know."

"Oh Dad, you know everything. Why isn't it straight?"

"That's just the way it is."

"Why?"

"Because."

"Because why?"

"Well, they're bent because . . . if they were straight they wouldn't fit in the fruit bowl."

Keeps me sane.

And amused.

Lie

One morning I took the girls to see *Bambi*. I love going to the movies with my kids. Their wide-eyed wonder reminds me of when I was young and my aunt took me to "the big city" to see films like *The Wizard of Oz*.

Anyway, the movie started and they all climbed up on my lap and we ate popcorn.

Then the questions started. "Where's Bambi's mom gone?"

"I don't know. Sshhh . . . watch the movie."

"Bambi gone?"

"Stop fooling, Dad. You know. Where Bambi's mom?"

"She's gone away."

"Where? Where's she gone?"

"Where gone Bambi's mom, Dad?"

"Well . . . she died. She's dead. Now, be quiet."

"Is she in heaven? Why is she dead?"

"Yes, she's in heaven because . . . the hunters shot her. Now be quiet."

"Are dey de bad men are dey, Da?"

"Yes. They're the bad men. Hey c'mon, sweetie, don't cry. It's all right. It's just a cartoon. Georgia . . . come back here."

"Why is it a (sniff) . . . why is it a (sniff) . . . why is it a (sniff) . . . cartoon?"

Then, from the row behind, a deep voice.

"Hey, pipe down . . . we can't hear the movie."

"Why can't that man hear the movie Dad? Dad? What are you doing hiding under the seat Dad? Dad?"

"Daaaddd . . ."

"DAD!"

It went on like this for a while until I lied and told the kids that Bambi's mom had gone to the Rockies on vacation and would be back in the sequel. At least it got us to the end of the film.

The Next Level

All this is well and good. Your child learns words and starts asking questions and everything is fine and dandy. But as she gets older and her speaking and listening skills become more sophisticated, there are some things you need to remember. Here are a few important things to keep in mind.

Political Correctness

We live in an age in which a spade is a "challenged shovel." Our language is littered with euphemisms and ambiguous names and titles that don't sound as offensive as their predecessors. Kids haven't yet learned our delicate social constraints, so they can sometimes put you in awkward situations. Kids do not know the word "subtlety." In real terms, that means your child is going to point out to you in a loud voice anything that she considers to be out of the ordinary.

> Kids do not know the word "subtlety."

So when you are standing in the supermarket checkout line behind a woman with a dark complexion, you can trust her to say in a loud voice, "Look, Dad, there's a chocolate lady."

You visit a friend and your toddler says, "You have a funny nose, like an elephant."

At a barbecue, "Why do you have blue hair?"

At the library, "That man has only one arm."

At the mechanic's shop, "Where's your hair gone?"

At the park, "That man did a smell."

At a picnic, "That lady has no boosies."

While addressing her question or comment (and clamping your hand over her mouth), you need to teach her socially appropriate ways of speaking. For example, explain about different skin colors, different body shapes and sizes, how everybody is an individual.

And then explain to her that if she says stuff like that again, you'll phone Santa and cancel her Christmas presents.

Sarcasm

When talking to your child, remember that sarcasm is not part of their world. It is a complex system that is difficult to comprehend. Kids take what we say at face value and are not as sensitive to the nuances of tone and exaggerated expression as we are.

For this reason, don't be sarcastic. It took me a while to figure this out. Let's look at the following scenario.

Matilda has a chocolate bar. I ask her if I can please have a piece—a request that I don't consider to be unreasonable, especially considering it happens to be *mine*. (My kids were born with an instinctive knowledge of the old adage, "What's yours is mine, Dad." They're good at sharing—that is, when it's *me* sharing with *them*.)

She breaks off some and puts it in my hand. At first I think she has dropped it, because my hand is empty. Then I notice a meager brown smear that has fallen down into the crease that runs across the palm of my hand. ("What's mine is mine, Dad.")

At times like this, my rapier wit is at its best:

"Well, I just want to say *thank you*, Matilda, for your generosity. Sharing is such an important part of being in a family, don't you think? I'm *really grateful* and will certainly remember this occasion the next time *you* want to share something with *me*."

I wanted a change of heart.

I wanted self-awareness.

I wanted embarrassment.

I wanted more chocolate.

What I got was a proud chocolatey smile and a sincere, "Thanks, Dad."

I wondered where I went wrong.

Where I went wrong was using sarcasm on a child who takes my words at face value.

Secrets

Just as it takes a few years before the concept of sarcasm is clear in a child's head, so too does it take a while for them to understand the social processes involved in the telling and keeping of secrets.

To you and me, a secret is something that by definition you are supposed to keep to yourself. To a child, however, a secret is an important piece of information that needs to be told to *everybody she knows*.

Consider the following scenario:

Your wife is in the backyard mixing cement. (I originally wrote "doing the laundry," but my editor said that was sexist.) You are upstairs roughhousing on the carpet with the kids. In a fit of excitement, you smash your wife's favorite vase.

Oh no! Tragedy! You know that you will not hear the end of this. So you say to little Neil, "Neil, listen very carefully. This will upset Mommy very much. She doesn't *need* to know about this. She doesn't *want* to know about this. This will be *our little secret*. Okay?"

"Okay, Dad."

You turn to little Debbie. "Debbie, darling. Listen to Daddy. Sometimes we just keep things to ourselves and don't tell anybody. This is one of those times. Mommy will come in soon and you and Neil and Daddy are not going to say anything about the broken vase. Okay?"

"Uh-huh."

You hear footsteps coming up the back stairs.

"OK. Remember what I said. Do you remember, Neil?"

"Don't tell Mom."

"Good boy. Okay Deb—do you remember?"

"Um . . ."

"About the vase?"

"Um . . . sshhh. Don't tell Mom."

"Good. That's right. That's right. *Sshhh.* That's it exactly. Everybody remember *shhh.* Great, great."

The back door opens.

In a last-moment fit of encouragement, you desperately whisper, "Don't say anything. There'll be big lollipops for good boys and girls who don't say anything to Mommy—"

Approaching footsteps.

"Right?"

"Right, Dad. Our secret."

"Yep, Dad . . . sshhh."

Mommy enters.

"DAD BROKE THE VASE!"

"HE TOLD US NOT TO TELL!"

In Front of the Kids

Don't be deceived. Kids pick up a lot more of our conversations than we give them credit for.

Of course, it's not always like that. Sometimes I sit the girls down, stare straight into their attentive faces from three feet away and say, "Go and pick up your toys—now."

One minute later, they're running around the house with their toys yet to be picked up.

I say to them, "Didn't I just tell you to pick up your toys?"

"No."

"Nuh."

"I don't think so, Dad."

It's like I'm living in an episode of *The Twilight Zone* or something. I just can't seem to get through to their various brains.

And then there are the other times. The times when they soak up every word I say—and I don't want them to.

Here's a typical example:

We are going to a family lunch in the minivan. In the back, Matilda is asleep, Georgia is singing along loudly with her favorite tape and Rachael is absorbed in a book.

Meredith and I are in the front, talking about the lunch and the members of my family. We are talking quietly even though we know the kids can't hear us.

We arrive at the lunch and everybody stands around the backyard, chatting. It is pleasant and warm. Wine is flowing, the kids are playing with their cousins, the adults are engaging in conversation.

Then the unbelievable happens.

Georgia pipes up with some great line like, "Aunty Sonja, why do you eat like a pig?"

She heard us.

An awful silence grips the gathering and all turn to me with curious expressions.

The only voice that can be heard is Rachael's, scolding Georgia for her rudeness: "Aunty Sonja is only like that because Uncle Roger is a layabout who loses money on cards and horses."

She heard us too.

I smile weakly.

Matilda does not want to disprove the theory that trouble always comes in threes. She grabs Uncle Adam and looks up at him and says, "My Dad says you have a big car 'cause you have a tiny pen—"

"GOSH, IS THAT THE TIME?" I yell.

She, quite clearly, also heard us.

"Time to go, girls. Well, it's been a great afternoon . . . ha, ha. Thanks for having us, Dan. Get your coats, girls. Look, um, we'll be, um . . . bye."

The lesson is, be monumentally careful when talking about anything or anyone in front of your kids.

Because they have big ears.

And long memories.

This also applies to how you speak about them in their presence. This can be to their detriment or their advantage, depending on what you say.

Don't ever put your child down in front of your friends, as if she can't hear you. Avoid

- "Mark is a great kid, but I think he's a little slow."
- "I just don't know what Brittany's problem is."
- "Geez, I wish Sheri were more like Louise."
- "Poor Virginia. She just can't seem to do what she's told."

Also avoid direct putdowns. I was in line at an ATM and heard a mother say to her three-year-old, "You are a horrible little boy. A naughty, naughty boy and I'm sick of you." Admittedly, he had just poured half a milkshake onto her sandled feet, but that's still no excuse. The amount of damage you can do to a child's sense of self-esteem is incalculable. Instead, look for and praise the positive:

- "John has such wonderful manners."
- "I'm so pleased with Stuart—he's very responsible."
- "Did you see the way Carrie took her own plate into the kitchen?"
- "Steve and Kate have been so polite all afternoon."
- "Thanks for giving me some of your milkshake. Maybe next time I could have some in my mouth rather than on my feet."

The amount of good you can do for a child's self-esteem is incalculable.

Sometimes you may want to say something in your child's presence that for one reason or another you don't want her to hear, so you spell out the key words:

- "I bought S-a-r-a that s-l-i-d-e for her upcoming b-i-r-t-h-d-a-y."
- "Is there any c-h-o-c-o-l-a-t-e in the fridge?"
- "When the k-i-d-s are a-s-l-e-e-p, let's have s-e-x."

With such reinforcement, it's no wonder our kids are such good spellers at an early age.

But what can you do once your child learns to spell and you still don't want her to hear certain things? Don't panic. There's still a great trick to keep up your sleeve.

Talk in a convoluted manner with totally archaic vocabulary.

So, instead of "I'm taking Beth to the dentist today," try "You know that man down the road in the white coat whose specialty is molars and crowns? Well, I'm taking our youngest offspring for a visit there today."

> What can you do once your child learns to spell and you still don't want her to hear certain things? Talk in a convoluted manner with totally archaic vocabulary.

Instead of "Ian's surprise birthday party is this Saturday," try "It's been four lots of three-hundred-and-sixty-five days since we came back from the maternity ward that first time with a Lilliputian male tyke and five moons from today we are going to host a commemoration ceremony."

After a while, you'll get quite good at thesaurus-speak. However, you must not do it too often or else your kids will learn those ropes, too. Then at show-and-tell time in kindergarten, they'll come up with beauties, such as "During the recent respite from this educational facility for children, the two older sapiens with whom I currently reside took me to a coastal destination where we constructed citadels out of silicon granules," instead of "Over summer vacation, my parents took me to the beach and we made sandcastles."

CHAPTER 16
Cars

WHEN I was a kid, I had grand schemes and desires about the flashy red sports car I was going to drive when I grew up.

Then I grew up.

Along with "overseas vacation" and "career as an internationally successful rock musician," I have now filed "flashy red sports car" under "U" for Unfulfilled Dreams and instead find myself the owner of an eight-seater family transport vehicle.

And I have no delusions about who the car *really* belongs to.

It belongs to my kids.

It is filled with old, damp towels, buckets, shovels, a broken kite, three bikes of varying sizes, hats, broken sunglasses, odd shoes and socks, empty tubes of sunscreen, several thousand children's cassettes and representative scraps from each of the major food groups.

The back is a three-abreast, car-seat wasteland of sheepskin, Velcro™, buckles and colorful dangly things that someone gave us to amuse the baby.

Once, in an absent-minded fit of neatness, I decided to clean the car. This meant moving all the aforementioned seats, which was fine. What was not fine, however, was the debris of many years lurking in the crevices of the upholstery.

I discovered a colony of mold so advanced it was on the brink of discovering fire, my long-lost car keys, several crusts, pages 4 to 17 of *Green Eggs and Ham*, a chopstick, three bibs, several black apple cores, miscellaneous pieces of plastic jewelry, a doll's head, a hairy lollipop, five diapers (two unused), four broken crayons, three plastic hair combs, two turtle doves and the partner of every single sock in my extensive "where the hell's the other sock" collection.

The point is this.

Your car is going to get trashed. Don't bother trying to vacuum it every weekend. That's just a waste of time.

Car Seats

If you're like me, you remember the deep feeling of inadequacy that crawled up your throat when you assembled your baby's first car seat. You emptied it onto the floor, and there it sat in mocking disarray: a tangle of hooks, webbing, bolts, straps, Velcro, sheepskin and the little orange plastic thing that's always left over at the end.

I have had a great fear of such fit-Part-A-into-Slot-B12-and-pivot-clockwise-type assembly situations ever since, as a boy, I glued my fingers together while attempting to piece the wheel carriage onto the fuselage of a 1:500 scale Lancaster Bomber.

But you obviously conquered your technical ineptitude and are now pretty accomplished with the logistics of transporting a baby around in the car. Now it's part of your regular automotive routine. In fact, like one of those army training guys, you could probably strip and clean your infant car seat in sixty seconds with a blindfold on.

The good news is that it doesn't get any more complicated than that. The problem, however, is that as your baby turns into a toddler, he will be less happy about "lockdown" in his toddler seat.

State laws vary, but most require babies and toddlers to be restrained in an approved, weight-appropriate car seat until age four or five or until they weigh forty pounds. The right kind of seat and a proper fitting are essential. A child's chances of survival in a serious crash are improved by 60 percent if he is in a correct restraint for his size and weight. Unrestrained children are more than five times as likely to die in a car crash than those who are properly fitted into a car seat or harness.

You cannot and should not, must not and will not, hold a child in your lap or under your seatbelt. If you do this, you are an idiot.

So what do you do?

Your toddler is too big to fit into the infant car seat, but if you set him on a normal bucket seat, the upper belt runs across his neck and he'll just slip through and end up on the floor, which defeats the purpose.

So toss out the moldy sheepskin, wrap the infant car seat in plastic and store it in your garage in case you're careless enough to have another baby.

Then get your wallet out (no doubt something you are sickeningly familiar with now that you are a father) and head down to the store to buy a toddler seat, which is a one-piece chunky chair complete with cover and racing harness seatbelt— a larger, racier upright version of the infant car seat. Some models bolt into the frame of the car, much like your car seat, and others use the seat-belt system in the same way the infant car seat did.

Such a seat gives your kid a little more range of motion, a better view of the world around him and a greater projectile vomit range when he becomes carsick. Washable seat covers, usually cotton with groovy patterns, are advisable, particularly if your child is prone to drink-spillage, diaper removal, candy dropping, vomiting or any other accidents involving sticky, colorful or disgusting fluids.

A child seat is appropriate for kids up to forty pounds, but it'll only last to those latter years if your child has a growth deficiency. Pretty soon he'll outgrow it and you'll need to upgrade yet again. This is also because the cover will be too dirty from months of urine, ice cream and stickies.

Toss out the moldy sheepskin, wrap the toddler seat in plastic and store it in your garage in case you're careless enough to have another toddler.

Then, get your wallet out again and buy a hideously expensive slab of molded plastic called a car booster seat, which sits on top of the normal seat and does not actually bolt in.

Make sure that your child's head is supported at the back. This is to avoid whiplash in the event of an accident. If you have a seat with headrests, you need only buy a base to sit on. If, like us, you have a bench seat in the back, buy the complete car booster seat. This has the added advantage of side panels, which are handy when your child falls asleep and his head does that awkward flopping-about thing.

Either way, it is worthwhile getting a harness seatbelt. This bolts in as normal and has two side straps and a cross-your-heart thing at the front, much like the racing harness that motor heads have in their cars. A harness seatbelt will ensure that if you stop suddenly, your child won't find himself sucking on his toes.

Car Seat Guidelines

Following are weight guidelines for typical car seats:

Infant car seat	less than twenty pounds
Infant/toddler convertible seat	up to forty pounds
Toddler seat	twenty to forty pounds
Car booster seat (small)	forty to sixty pounds
Car booster seat (large)	thirty to eighty pounds

Seatbelts

All this talk about seats is fine on paper. But you can't have seats without seatbelts, and therein lies the problem.

Unlike babies, who just lie there in their car seats, toddlers can put up a fight. I've spent plenty of time chasing a toddler around the car, trying to cajole or force her to sit down.

Sometimes I resort to bribery and distraction. Sometimes I have to use my full body weight and all my strength to wrestle and jam her in. And if that fails, I start the engine. It grabs their attention every time. You've never seen a child move faster!

But even once they're in, toddlers have a Houdini-like desire to escape from the confines of the straps. Not only that, they have the manual dexterity to do it. While you're busy driving the car, they're in the back madly working away with a hairpin on the buckle so they can be free to roam the confines of your automobile.

While you're busy driving the car, they're in the back madly working away with a hairpin on the buckle so they can be free to roam the confines of your automobile.

Georgia was particularly adept at escaping. One minute I would strap her into her seat so tightly I feared her arms and legs would turn blue; a few minutes later I'd look in my rearview mirror and see her hanging out of her seat by one kneecap, waving her arms like a windmill in a hurricane.

This raises a serious problem.

For car seats to work, the child needs to stay in them. This is all well and good in the instruction booklet that came with your car seat. On the cover it probably has a picture of a grinning toddler strapped into the seat with a look on his face that says, "I am perfectly happy sitting in this seat. In fact, I love it. I don't ever want to get out. I was made for this seat and this seat was made for me."

But as the father of a toddler, you've already figured out that it just isn't like this in real life.

What do you do if your toddler doesn't like being restricted in his seat? What do you do if your normally placid child goes berserk every time you get into the car? It's bad enough driving home from the supermarket with a screaming tyke in the back, but it's even worse if you're brave enough (or stupid enough) to drive someplace eight hours away on your annual vacation.

Unfortunately, you don't really have much choice in the matter. Laws prevent you from using knockout drugs, handcuffs or muzzles. The hard fact is that children have to stay in their seats whether they like it or not.

Don't be one of those idiots who drives around with a child on his lap. It is dangerous, illegal and stupid. Don't ever give in to the temptation of letting your child out of his seat. A few minutes of quiet just isn't worth the risk of watching them fly through the front windshield.

Ask yourself this question: Would you drop your son or daughter from a third-floor window onto concrete?

Of course not—yet that's the same force as a crash at 35 miles per hour. It's even worse if you're on a highway. A crash at 60 miles per hour is equivalent to dropping your kid off the top of a twelve-story building.

That's a long way up.

And a long way down.

We had to teach Georgia not to escape from her seat. If she managed to free her arms from the seatbelt, I'd tell her to put them back. Then she'd ignore me or ask some inane question about lollipops so I'd tell her again. At this point I'd pull over, get in the back and put her arms back for her and let her know the dire consequences of not wearing a seatbelt: "You wear this seatbelt for your safety. Dad wears a seatbelt. Mom wears a seatbelt. Rachael wears a seatbelt. You do too. Besides, if you take your arms out again, when we get home I'm going to set fire to your dolls."

So I'd drive a little farther, look in the rearview mirror and see her waving at me. I'd pull over, get in the back, put her arms in and then drive another mile until she did it again. And again. And again. Eventually we would get home. And I'd set fire to her favorite doll (only joking). She did, however, learn that the whole seatbelt thing was totally non-negotiable. And I do mean totally non-negotiable.

In fact, our kids are now so seatbelt aware that when I back out of the driveway without my seatbelt on, they start screaming, "SEATBELT, DAD! SEATBELT! DANGER! DANGER!!!" And on the few occasions when I have absent-mindedly forgotten to buckle up their harnesses, they have let me know in no uncertain terms that they are not happy.

So when it comes to seatbelts, be patient, be firm, be cool and be reasonable.

Oh, and get a loud car stereo.

Music

Ultimately, it doesn't really matter what kind of seat you have or whether your child is strapped in. What really counts is the selection of children's muzak you have to offer.

Kids' music is a billion-dollar business. Every children's TV show produces a series of tapes and CDs that are played to death in their airtime so that your child is subliminally programmed to demand them upon entry into your vehicle.

Soon, your Beatles, Springsteen and U2 cassettes will be left behind to make room for several hundred colorful cassettes filled with inane repetitive lyrics and mind-numbingly saccharine tunes. Many of these are produced on budget cassettes that you only play once before they are chewed up and swallowed by your ravenous tape player.

Within weeks you will know literally thousands of idiotic songs, jingles and rhymes. And trust me when I say there's nothing quite like the tingly feeling you get when you're sitting at a set of traffic lights belting out a chorus of "Eensey-Weensey Spider," complete with hand motions, and you look out to see a crowd of people at a bus stop and they're all laughing and pointing at you.

Other Accessories

There are a few other automotive accessories that will make your child's presence in the car safer and more convenient.

Sunshade

Children burn easily, particularly in summer and particularly on long drives. Buy a stick-on sunshade for the car window. They cost only a few bucks, and it's money well spent—that is, until the third day, when your child figures out how to peel it off.

Survival Pack

A young child has the most unnerving habit of urgently needing something when you are at the farthest point away from home. He will do a filthy, explosive, leak-through-all-his-clothes poop in his diaper when you're in a city parking lot. He will require a drink on a hot summer's day when you're halfway between country towns. He will be cold because you dressed him only in undies and a sweater in the middle of winter. He will vomit all over himself just as you arrive at the picnic. It's good to have a small bag of goodies stashed in the back for "emergencies."

- diapers
- tissues
- Band-Aids
- plastic bags
- a towel
- spare clothes
- juice
- a fire extinguisher
- a complete set of children's videos
- a phaser set to *stun*

Luggage Web

In accidents involving station wagons or vans, injuries are often caused by flying objects inside the vehicle. Even the weekly shopping contains deadly, ballistic cans of food that would be dangerous if let loose in the car. Imagine how much worse it would be if you were going on vacation with a kid's bike, a microwave, a cooler and two dozen beers in the back of the car.

Invest in a luggage web or netting to keep your family protected. Elastic netting is inexpensive and can be easily and quickly put in and taken out. However, it is not as strong as a steel screen bolted into the frame of your car.

Vacation Driving

Your vacation has arrived. You made the reservation months ago and if all goes according to plan, in a few hours you'll have sand between your toes and a margarita in your hand. The car is packed and the only thing between you and the resort is 300 miles of road . . . oh, and a toddler who doesn't like being in the car for more than ten minutes.

I'd say you have a problem.

Going on a vacation drive with a small child will test the patience of even the most seasoned of dads.

> The car is packed and the only thing between you and the resort is 300 miles of road . . . oh, and a toddler who doesn't like being in the car for more than ten minutes. I'd say you have a problem.

Be sensible in your expectations. Long car trips can be boring even when you're an adult with another adult or a radio to keep you mentally occupied. Imagine being a two-year-old with a thirty-second attention span, stuck in the back of a hot, stuffy car with nothing to do. You can hardly blame him for getting upset and starting to whine.

There are several things you can do to help the situation if you are planning a long road trip:

- Don't take the kids with you.
- Wear ear plugs.
- Don't be stupid enough to go on a long-distance vacation in the first place. Wait till they're sixteen.

- Leave really early in the morning, avoiding the "tantrum zone."
- Travel at night so the kids go to sleep. This, of course, assumes a shorter trip. There's little point in doing this if you're in danger of nodding off behind the wheel.
- Plan for regular breaks so they can have a drink and run around. This could be at a service station, rest area or a park or, if worst comes to worst, simply a safe spot well off the side of the road.
- A toddler can be kept amused for hours with a good supply of kids' cassettes (see page 143). You run the danger, however, of being driven to the point of insanity by the inane lyrics and repetitive tunes. You may even find that you start entertaining ideas about suddenly turning the car into an oncoming truck to end the torture. Don't do this. Aside from mindless tunes, you can also get a number of inexpensive story tapes of nursery rhymes or films, usually read by someone famous.
- If you're lucky, a preschooler might be occupied for a few hours by his favorite picture- or coloring books.
- Make sure you have a good supply of food, drink and treats so that there's always something in their mouths and they can't do that "arewethereyetIwanttogotothebathroomI'm-boredIwannagohomehetouchedmeI'mgoingtovomit" thing. Usually these supplies will be gone by the time you reach the end of your street, but it'll shut 'em up for a while . . . or at least until the sugar hits their bloodstream.
- Play musical chairs. Every so often, change the seating arrangement, especially if you have more than one child. This will vary the dynamics of conversation and interaction and will also enable your children to annoy a whole range of family members. Make sure, though, that there is always at least one adult in the front, preferably behind the wheel.
- Keep the kids amused by talking to them. A toddler is usually limited in conversational terms to topics like candy and poo-poos. Every time you pass a car, you can say "There's a car!" and they'll say "CAR!" and that's about as

good as it gets. At least with older children, we can play games. My kids enjoy "I spy." This is because they think they win. The routine goes something like this:

"I spy wiv my lill eye sumpink wot is blue."
"Um . . . the sky?"
"Nup."
"Mommy's shirt?"
"Nuh-uh."
"The car in front of us?"
"Nope, you dope." (Riotous laughter.)
"Okay, I give up. What is it?"
"Cow."
"Oh, great."

The other game they love is the tease-the-heck-out-of-each-other-while-Mom-and-Dad-aren't-looking game. This involves one of them putting her finger across the territorial border of her seat, usually marked out by a stitch-line in the upholstery. The routine goes something like this:
We are driving along nicely when a cry comes from the back.
"She touched me."
"Did not. She put her foot on me."
"AAAAagghh. She poked me. Don't touch me! AAAAagghh."
"Daaaaad . . . she's staring at me!"
So I adjust the mirror, trying to catch them at it, and reach back and flap one of my hands madly behind me like a blind snake searching for prey. The kids think that this is the best part of the game.
At this point, Meredith informs me that the car is now on the other side of the road and she would prefer it if I faced the front, put both hands on the wheel and got us back in the righthand lane.

Auto Prisons

I hate seeing a dog stuck in a car on a hot day with the windows rolled up. He pants like crazy and obviously does not enjoy the automotive sauna. He would rather be out running around, chasing sticks and sniffing other dogs' behinds.

While social convention prevents me from doing so, I have often entertained the fantasy of putting a brick through the window of such a vehicle with a note attached to it. Something to the effect of, "Your dog needed some fresh air, so I gave it some."

Similarly, I have never been much impressed by parents who leave their kids in the car, either. Logic would dictate that this is a stupid thing to do, yet it still happens. A car heats up very quickly, and leaving the windows open a little does not really help that much.

I have always vowed that I would never, *never* leave my kids in the car while I ducked into a store.

Not even for a little bit.

Not even for a second.

This is all well and good when I'm going on a major expedition to a shopping mall. I'm certainly no moron and I am obviously not going to leave the kids in the car, especially on a hot day.

But then came the day I had to get a loaf of bread. I parked right outside the twenty-four-hour service station, not nine feet away from the automatic doors and the cash register. I could see the bread stand just inside. Matilda and Georgia were both asleep after a hard morning at the pool. Rachael was sitting in the back quite happily.

"I'll only be a moment," one part of my brain said.

"No. What if something happens?" said another part.

"Oh yeah, like what?"

"Like the fuel tank explodes or a small plane makes an emergency landing in the parking lot or the white slave traders are operating in this suburb . . ."

"Yeah, right," replied the other part as I got out of the car and headed into the station.

Use your common sense. Don't leave them if they are prone to playing with the car's controls, doors or seatbelts. Don't leave them if they'll be out of your sight even for a second. Don't leave them if they'll be distressed by your absence. Don't leave them if the car is parked on a busy road. And don't leave the keys in the car or the engine running. It's best just not to leave them.

Road Sense

Our society is obsessed with the automobile. Like little arteries, our roads spread over the farthest reaches of the nation and dominate our cities. Nearly everyone owns a car or two. Our cities are shrouded in smog produced by these vehicles. You cannot exist in our society and not know about cars.

This is especially the case if you are a boy. Boys spend their lunchtimes talking about what sort of car they're going to get or bragging about their uncle's new BMW. They spend their afternoons designing the perfect car. When they run around, they make car noises.

Then, after all the buildup, they get licenses and buy pathetic little station wagons and try to fix them up, which usually means putting a foam mattress in the back.

The problem, however, is that cars are like guns. They kill. Hundreds of children under the age of five are killed in road-related accidents each year. Thousands are injured.

You and I take our traffic survival skills for granted. We've spent a lifetime developing a sense of speed and distance, a knowledge of traffic flow and road rules, and a healthy fear of cars sporting "Grandma Knows Best" bumper stickers.

Kids have none of these skills. They need to learn from scratch. As soon as he can understand you, you need to teach your child how to deal with cars and roads and make sure he knows how to stay alive around them.

The difficulty really begins when they start to walk. Sure, at first it's two steps, stumble, two steps, stumble, but pretty soon he's wearing his first pair of shoes. Then will come that epic milestone—walking all the way to the corner store without being picked up, which really means you held his hand and dragged him the last 200 yards.

This is where you start entering dangerous territory.

Toddlers can't hear as well as you, nor can they judge speed, distance or the direction of sound. Their peripheral vision is poor. They don't even know what a car is or how long it takes one to stop. They're small, which makes them difficult to see, and their behavior is often unpredictable.

Not only that, they're stupid, too. They have brains the size of peanuts and if they're thinking about lollipops, they won't have the mental space to be thinking about large metal objects bearing down upon them. On top of this, they develop incredible speed and a break-and-run tendency. It takes only a second for them to run off while you're locking the car in a busy parking lot.

Given this, you can do several things to help your child become car-smart.

- Be a good example. Wear a seatbelt yourself. Stop at the curb and look both ways. Check driveways before you cross them.

- Tailor your instructions to his level of understanding. For example, you can start a toddler on a game called, "Who can see a car?"

  As he gets older, he can play a game of spotting when the light changes from red to green. Of course, you'll be holding his hand with a Vulcan death grip at the time.

  With an older child, ask him to tell you when he thinks it's safe to cross the road. On a quiet suburban street, you might even give him independence by not holding his hand. Of course, you're scanning for cars and making sure everything's cool.

  Explain to your child the reasoning behind your rules so he can understand why they're so important. Instead of saying, "Don't step off the road because I say so," try "See those cars there? They travel fast and are dangerous, so never go onto the road without Dad being there to make sure everything's okay."

Several organizations recommend that a child under the age of ten have his hand held by an adult when near traffic.

- Change your tactics according to the location. A quiet suburban street might be good for improving his basic road sense and practicing crossing. When walking in the city or navigating a busy parking lot, however, take extra care. You will need quick reflexes and a strong forearm.

- Teach your child to cross at traffic lights and pedestrian crossings, and even then to look out for and watch all approaching vehicles before stepping out.

> Teach your child to look for good visibility areas and not to cross from behind parked cars, which accounts for about 30 percent of all child-pedestrian fatalities.

Odds are that between your house and the corner store, there are no pedestrian crossings. If so, teach him to look for good visibility areas and not to cross from behind parked cars, which accounts for about 30 percent of all child-pedestrian fatalities.

- Carefully supervise the use of bikes and tricycles. My kids wear approved helmets, even in the backyard. They have never ridden where there's any traffic and will not do so for many years.

- Establish a "safety door" in your car. This means that the traffic-side door is off limits. To get in and out of the car, your child must use the safety door (curb-side door). You can put a colorful sticker on this door so a young child can easily identify it. Weld the other door shut.

- Don't assume your child is safe just because he's not on the road. My kids love nothing more than to chase each other along the sidewalk to the stores. But that sidewalk is intersected about thirty times by little roads called *driveways*.

Some people shoot out of their driveways like Batman responding to the bat signal. Driveway awareness is extremely important. Teach your child to be on the lookout all the time. He is small and can't be seen by people in cars, particularly if these people are backing out of their driveway at speeds close to the sound barrier.

Your child should know to stop, look, listen and evaluate every driveway he comes to before he crosses it.

- Establish safe play areas for your child, where there are gates and fences that prevent road access. The curb and median are not good places to play.
- Warn your child not to stick out his tongue, finger or any other part at the dentally challenged man driving the red pickup one lane over, especially if the pickup has a gun rack in back.
- Treat this as an ongoing education.

At the moment, Matilda still gets carried (actually, dragged) across the road. Georgia has to hang on to me or a piece of my clothing.

Rachael is a mature five-year-old who shows the utmost care in traffic. She is cautious, smart and sensible, and she has proven her skill in dealing with cars for a while now. On our suburban street, she tells me when she thinks it's safe and crosses by my side. On a busy road, however, she also has to hang on to my hand.

I know I'll have to "let them go" at some point, but that won't be for a few years yet.

Rules of the Road

Teach your child these simple rules:

- Stop at the curb.
- In the parking lot, don't leave an adult's side.
- Don't touch any of the driving controls in the car.
- Look for crossings and lights.
- For a young child, never let go of an adult's hand when walking next to or crossing a road.
- For an older child, never break from an adult's side when walking next to or crossing a road.
- Don't play hide-and-seek or any other games near cars.
- Never touch a stranger's Harley Davidson.
- Only use the curb-side car door.
- Don't play near the road.
- Never chase a ball or pet onto the road.
- Always say "excuse me" when you break wind in someone's car.

When they follow these rules, praise and encourage them. When they break them, let them know it's bad news.

CHAPTER 17
Life's Little Lessons

ONE OF THE most important parts of being the father of a young child is getting her ready for life.

When a baby is born, she has no skills whatsoever. The only things she knows is that she was warmer back where she came from and that this nice lady's nipple is good to have in her mouth.

She doesn't know how to walk or talk. She doesn't know how to use a spoon or cross the road or float in the bath or operate a touch-tone phone. She doesn't even know who Elvis is. In short, she doesn't know anything about anything.

It's your job to bring your child up to speed so that one day she will be a decent human being; to show her how to survive in our world and how to deal with people; to reveal to her the wonder of the universe; to give her every opportunity to experience life; to help her grow into a balanced individual, socially, intellectually, spiritually, physically and emotionally; to give her a sense of self-esteem and a respect for others and the environment.

> This is your one chance to exert some influence while she still admires and respects you, before she hits those awkward later years when she thinks you're a moron and her main sphere of influence is some weird-looking rock idol.

Every experience and every day brings new lessons. It is a steep learning curve and a huge task. We must take our responsibility seriously and tackle it with deliberate intent and careful thought. These first years are critical. This is your one chance to exert some influence while she still admires and respects you, before she hits those awkward later years when she thinks you're a moron and her main sphere of influence is some weird-looking rock idol. If you don't act, it won't be long before your child is wearing a black T-shirt and wanting to borrow thirty bucks so she can have her nose pierced.

There are two questions to consider:

1. How does my child learn?

2. What should I teach my child?

Let's look at each of these in turn.

How Does My Child Learn?

Good question.

There are two primary ways that you have an influence on your child and convey information to her.

The first is *active*.

This means you deliberately and purposefully teach her.

You hold up a banana and say "banana" to her.

You give her a lecture about always saying "please" when asking for something.

You show her how to press the button at the traffic lights.

You teach her not to stick a fork into the electrical outlet.

You show her how to program the timer function on the VCR.

You show your son how to aim at the fragrance tablets in the urinal.

You teach your daughter that guys with big cars often have deficiencies in other parts of their life.

You punish her when she spits her food all over the table (mind you, this is for a six-year-old, not a toddler).

These are all *active* teacher-learner situations in which your goal is to get across a point or impart information or knowledge or whatever. Many dads are good at this type of education. It is an obvious and expected part of our paternal duty.

The other way is more subtle and, in some ways, more consequential.

The other way is *passive*.

This means you just go about your normal life and, although you don't know it, your child is watching and listening and copying and learning from you. This can work in either positive or negative ways. Don't ever underestimate the subtle ways in which you can influence your child.

Just being around you and observing the way you interact with other people is a significant learning experience for your child. Many a time I have been horrified when my daughters spout forth a figure of speech that I have used when I thought they weren't paying attention.

> Just being around you and observing the way you interact with other people is a significant learning experience for your child.

I learned this lesson the hard way. One night, I stubbed my toe on the kitchen door. Actually, I stubbed every toe and the pain was so intense I thought I had broken my foot in several places. The force and leg-swing velocity was the kind of kick usually reserved for game-winning goals scored from sixty feet out in the closing minutes of a soccer match.

Anyway, I lay on the floor for five minutes, writhing in agony, moaning and swearing the way you do when you think your leg is going to have to be amputated.

Weeks later, Rachael spilled a drink at the dinner table and recited perfectly some of my more colorful expletives. As you can imagine, Meredith and I almost choked on our tacos.

"Where did you learn that, Rachael?" Meredith asked.

Rachael pointed an accusing finger. "From Dad," she said.

I was dumbstruck. And in trouble with my wife!

So, if you like to swear, don't be surprised if your child adopts your vocabulary. If you never do the dishes, don't be surprised if your child grows up thinking that it's "woman's work." If you throw trash out the car window, expect your child to do the same. If you put your feet up on the table, burp, never say "please" or don't wash your hands after you go to the bathroom, don't be surprised when your child becomes a rude slob.

But your influence can also be positive. If you treat your wife with love and respect, your child will learn about good relationships. If you put your own clothes away and do household chores, your child will learn that you're not just some breadwinning visitor to the house. (I'm not suggesting that your daughter will ever put *her* own clothes away, though.) If you spend time with your child, she'll get the message that she's important to you.

That's right.

Regardless of whether you realize it or are happy about it, you are a role model for your child, positive or negative.

This is an awesome responsibility that really makes you start thinking about how you behave in front of your kid and how you relate to her.

What Should I Teach My Child?

Another good question.

Look, it's not my job to dictate to dads what they should teach their children. That's for you to figure out for yourself. But here's a general list of some things you might like to consider. It doesn't even come vaguely close to approximating an exhaustive list, but it should give you an idea of what I'm talking about.

Survival Skills

You need to show your child how to stay alive and, for the most part, unharmed in our society. Many years ago, such skills were fairly simple. Things like "Don't tease a mastodon" and "Don't take another man's woman" would have done quite nicely.

But survival in our modern society is much more complex. Danger lies behind every corner and around every bend, and it's up to you to teach your child how to deal with it. She has to learn

- how to be a pedestrian *and* a tricycle rider
- about everyday obstacles and dangers (stairs, pool, heights)
- never to take a bone out of a dog's mouth
- not to handle spiders or snakes
- not to touch the testicles on a bull
- how to sit in the bath and not to touch the faucet
- not to believe used-car salesmen or TV commercials
- that the emergency brake in the car is off-limits
- not to play with electricity, matches or her seatbelt
- not to wear an ABBA T-shirt to a heavy metal concert
- not to chew aluminum foil if she has a filling
- not to touch heaters, grills or stove tops

- to wear a hat and sunscreen in the sun
- that dog feces is not an acceptable food source
- not to get into cars with strangers
- what is acceptable touching behavior with adults and other children
- how to swim

Social Skills

Of course, being alive is more than just having a heartbeat. It means existing in society and behaving in appropriate ways with people of all ages. It is your job to teach your child

- socially acceptable nostril-cleansing strategies
- that biting is not a valid way to express affection
- to treat all people with respect (especially her parents)
- how and when to say "please," "thank you" and "excuse me"
- not to hit, scratch, pull hair or call people names (unless really necessary)
- how to "interrupt" in the proper way
- that putting a bowl of food on her head is not funny
- that putting a bowl of food on someone else's head is not funny, either
- how and when to apologize
- how and when to share
- that there are better ways to make friends than pulling their pants down and yelling "WEE-WEE!"
- to clean up after herself and put her things away
- that farting is not funny, except when Dad does it
- tantrums are not enjoyable for anyone in the immediate vicinity
- that she is not the center of the known universe

Dependency Skills

If everything goes according to plan, one day your child will leave the sanctity of your nest to make her own way in the world. You have up until that moment to prepare her for this event. She should know such critical things as

- how to maneuver buckles, buttons, zippers and shoelaces
- how to use a knife, spoon, fork, cup, plate and napkin
- to wipe off the stream of mucus before it touches her upper lip
- how to wash her body, brush her hair and clean her teeth
- how to wipe her behind, wash her hands and, most important of all, flush
- how to cook eggs properly in the microwave
- how to make a good cup of coffee
- how to surf the 'net

Knowledge

As I said before, your child knows little about the world. In fact, she knows nothing. And you certainly don't want her growing up to be stupid, ignorant or unsophisticated about the rich culture and history of our planet.

I would be a fool even to start to catalog the kind of knowledge your child needs to get through an ordinary day, to pass a test at school, to get a good job or even to win a trivia game. To do so would require a truck load of CD-ROMs.

So I'll just leave it all up to you.

Just make sure that somewhere in there you mention faith, Newton's laws, the second verse to the national anthem . . . and, of course, Elvis.

Values

Aside from the cold, hard facts of life, it is up to you to pass on to your child that which you consider to be the important beliefs underlying human existence. These will reflect your philosophy of life, principles, ethics, morals, personal code, religion, upbringing and so on.

I hope, however, that you will choose noble pursuits that will contribute to the furthering of humanity. You might like to think about such things as peace, patience, kindness, self-control, gratitude, self-esteem, honesty, humility, charity, love, beauty, responsibility, truth, justice, the American way and the difference between tax evasion and tax avoidance.

Physical Skills

Every so often, a study comes out suggesting that children's physical capabilities are on the decline. There is a greater percentage of body fat and a general decrease in physical activity among young children, which are attributed to bad diet and an increase in television and computer game usage.

> Over the coming years, you and your child should be toying with balance, coordination, running, hopping, skipping, catching, throwing, jumping, big-game hunting and deep-sea fishing.

While you don't want to be waking your toddler up at five for calisthenics, keep in mind that, over the coming years, you and your child should be toying with balance, coordination, running, hopping, skipping, catching, throwing, jumping, big-game hunting and deep-sea fishing.

Enjoy Life

You must be careful that amid all this teaching and learning you don't fall into the trap of going overboard. Some parents, paranoid that their kids will grow up *behind the others*, push them and drive them harder and harder. Their kids swim when they're a week old, they play the violin before they're out of diapers, they chant the alphabet while they're still in the crib and their parents think they're intellectually backward if they can't navigate the internet.

Watch the film *Parenthood*. Nathan (Rick Moranis) has a singular quest to educate his daughter and make her the perfect human being, expert in all fields of knowledge. She is learning languages, complex numbering systems and martial arts, and he is already talking to her about college, even though she hasn't started school yet.

I can certainly relate to this.

When Rachael was born, I thought her brain was like a computer with an empty hard drive. I thought it was my noble responsibility to make sure that all the cognitive software was good stuff. With my help, she'd grow up to be the very person I wanted her to be and would not appear on the nightly news with a serial number under her chin.

For example, I would install the life applications on "good manners at the table," "health and diet," "obedience to Mom and Dad," "general personal hygiene version 2.5," and "correct attitudes toward education" (with the option to upgrade).

Programs that wouldn't even make it past my PVS (Paternal Virus Scanner) would include "smoking and drinking," "tantrums for beginners" and "the history of ABBA (CD version)."

With me at the keyboard of her mind, she would grow up *exactly* as I planned. She would be flawless, mentally balanced, intelligent, personable, skilled, witty, beautiful, creative . . . just like me.

Dr. Frankenstein would have been proud.

Unfortunately, there's a danger in taking this too far. Sure, learning is important, but as dads we must never forget to let our children have fun and enjoy themselves. Life may well be a rich learning experience, but that doesn't mean we have to run it like a school.

So, as you're teaching your child about the world, let her explore, imagine, laugh, have a good time, play in the mud, sing, and run around naked singing "I done a smelly" at the top of her lungs.

CHAPTER 18
Discipline

dis'cipline n. mental and moral training; system of rules of conduct; behavior according to established rules; order maintained among children; v.t. bring under control; train to obedience and order; drill; punish; chastise; what you call it when you blow your top and yell at your child.

LOOK CAREFULLY at the definitions above. You are reading some of the most important words that relate to your purpose as a father.

Go on. Read it again.

It all sounds easy in theory, but in reality, it's a different matter. Disciplining a child takes effort, time, patience, thought, energy and determination.

The shelves of bookstore parenting sections and countless chapters of parenting books are full of words about discipline. Yet the meaning of those words is open to much interpretation, as illustrated by the vast array of disciplining techniques used by parents.

Some think discipline means spanking the devil out of a child. You know the ones I mean. You see them in supermarkets losing their temper, yelling and swinging their hand at their kid's behind like they're practicing for Wimbledon. This is usually accompanied by a red face and phrases like, "I'm sick of you," or "You little monster, don't you EVER, (smack), EVER (smack) . . ."

This is evidence of a bad temper and a parent who needs a break. Whatever you do, don't ever lash out as a way to release your anger in the mistaken belief that it's an effective act of discipline.

Then there are those who say they're not going to discipline because they are going to reason with their two-year-old. This is a stupid, mindless example of soppy New Age parenting that sounds groovy and modern but in actual fact is ridiculous. Not only does it not work, it assumes that a two-year-old is on the same cognitive-ethical level as an adult and it gives him an elevated view of his position in the grand scheme of the universe.

> Whatever you do, don't ever lash out as a way to release your anger in the mistaken belief that it's an effective act of discipline.

There are also parents who don't discipline or reason with their kids at all, either as part of a deliberate plan or just because they're ignorant or gutless. They don't want to crush their child's creative spirit. They say that these are the formative years when children should explore and do their own thing. The problem is that they grow up like Veruca Salt from *Willy Wonka and the Chocolate Factory*. She is a spoiled brat on a grand scale: whining, complaining, demanding, critical, arrogant, impatient, rude, impertinent and disrespectful.

But it's no wonder, with parents like hers. They are obsequious, fawning, pliable, weak, insipid and innocuous. They give in to her at all times and let her run the show. They let her have what she wants, when she wants it. They totally abdicate their responsibility as disciplinarians.

Parents like this really do exist.

And they have kids like Veruca.

I know because I've met them.

And you will, too.

They will come to visit your house and their child will start biting your child and being rude and demanding things and then breaking stuff and being disobedient. You will look at the parents, waiting hopefully for them to step in, but instead they will look at you and roll their eyes and say something pathetic like, "Little Albert . . . he's a real character. You've no idea. He's so full of beans. Oh well, kids will be kids. Best just to go with the flow."

(All I can think is, "Oh, yeah? Give me thirty seconds with a cattle prod and I'll control him for you.")

Don't think that you'll start disciplining your child when he begins school. By then it will be too late. The damage will have

been done and Veruca will be living in your house where your baby used to be.

> Discipline is something you cannot and must not avoid. You should be disciplining your child from the earliest days.

Discipline is something you cannot and must not avoid. You should be disciplining your child from the earliest days. Routine, structure and order are all forms of discipline. When you enforce nap times and bathe him whether he likes it or not and don't succumb to his complaints about dinner, you are training him to realize that there is a higher power and that he can't have his own way all the time.

Once he enters toddlerdom and starts developing a real sense of right and wrong, and a capacity to communicate and understand, your discipline will need to become more sophisticated than simple routines.

Now, this sounds easy, but we still have to get down to the nuts and bolts of discipline.

What is it and how should you do it?

Discipline is a personal thing and everyone is different. Some parents are solid disciplinarians; others are more lax. Some kids are angels; others you want to stuff in the washing machine. Some discipline is for everyday minor misdemeanors; at other times, it is for something more significant.

I suppose, if anything, I lean toward a traditional, conservative view. Discipline is a good thing. I want to discipline my kids. I want them to be self-disciplined, well adjusted and balanced.

Here's the basic way I try to operate (please note the word "try").

Step One: Clear Expectations

As a starting point, you should make it clear to your child what your behavioral expectations are. He shouldn't have to guess what's right and wrong. You should be telling him and showing him all the time.

He doesn't know that your stereo is not to be touched with ice-cream–covered fingers; that biting isn't an acceptable way to get a toy back; that the road is more dangerous than any other place; that the back stairs are off-limits; that you don't climb across the table to get to the juice. You have to teach him these things.

Your teaching method will obviously be dependent on your child's age and level of understanding.

With a toddler, for example, you might touch an outlet and, with a pained expression, say "no" or "ouch." It's no good talking to him about voltage, amps and ohms when he has only a twenty-word vocabulary, most of which are synonyms for the word "butt."

With a four-year-old, you can (and should) explain to him why you don't want him climbing the tree up to his third-story bedroom window. An understanding of the situation and the logic behind your thinking ("The tree is old and branches may break, and if you fall, you'll die, or at the very least damage your spine or your brain—that is if you miss the tomato stakes in the garden . . .") will have a more lasting impact than "Because I say so."

The old "because I say so" response is a tad authoritarian and, while ultimately true, does not do a lot to explain the workings of the universe.

Guidelines for Setting the Ground Rules

When you establish rules, tell your child why you are doing so:

- "Don't speak to me like that because it's bad manners."
- "You can't have chocolate now because it's dinnertime and we're having spinach instead."
- "Don't run across the road because it's dangerous and you might get hit by a car."
- "I don't want you using those paints because you're wearing your best clothes and they might get dirty."
- "You have to go to bed now because you don't want to be tired for kindergarten tomorrow (and Mom and I need a break)."
- "Don't step on my crotch because it hurts."

Don't expect overnight success or an instant response. You can't get away with telling a toddler that a faucet spits out hot water and then think that he'll never go near it again. Most lessons have to be reinforced over a number of years. You literally have to drum your messages into his head over and over and over again. You have to be patient and prepared to face frustration. (I was twenty-four years old when my mother finally stopped saying, "How many times do I have to tell you?" I thought she stopped because I finally started doing the right thing. She told me later that she just gave up.)

> You can't get away with telling a toddler that a faucet spits out hot water and then think that he'll never go near it again. Most lessons have to be reinforced over a number of years.

Anyway, once your child knows the rules and expectations, he will have one of two responses. He will either

1. obey the rules; or
2. break the rules.

For example, once he knows that he is not supposed to play with the emergency brake in the car, he will either

1. leave the emergency brake alone (which is good); or
2. play with the emergency brake (which is bad).

If he chooses to do the right thing, go to step two.

Step Two: Positive Reinforcement

When your child does the right thing, encourage him. Praise him. Thank him. Tell him you are proud that he didn't walk into the fireplace. Give him a hug as thanks for having good manners at the dinner table. Comment on how grown up he is. Let him "overhear" conversations in which you proudly tell a friend all the good things he's been doing lately.

If he cleans up his toys when you ask him, let him know how happy it makes you. Occasionally give him a treat as a reward for his good behavior. If he bathes and dresses nicely before bed, read him an extra book. Make a fuss over him if he actually does something without being asked. If he sleeps through the night, thank him . . . and beg him to do it again.

One of the best things we've done along these lines has been to create a sticker chart, which lives on the refrigerator door. This is a blank spreadsheet with the girls' names down the left column and the days of the week along the top row. They can get a maximum of three stickers in the appropriate space next to their name on any given day. We selected three categories, one sticker each for

- having good manners at the dinner table
- going to bed peacefully
- helping clean up

When they get to twenty stickers, we reward them with a small treat of their own choosing, such as a bag of chips or a milkshake or that cheap plastic jewelry they are so fond of. It's a tangible way of showing our appreciation for their help.

The girls love doing it because they can see the sticker line growing next to their names and they love getting the reward at the end. They like the acknowledgement and the praise that comes with it.

And for our part, mealtimes and bedtimes have been generally more civil and the house has been neater . . . and all it has cost us is a couple of bucks worth of colored dots with glue on the back.

If you want to establish a similar sticker chart, select two or three aspects of your child's behavior that you want improved.

For example, you might give him a sticker for
- brushing his teeth without complaining
- not crying in the bathtub
- sharing his toys
- not speaking to you in a whiny voice
- putting his shoes away
- not waking you before 7 A.M.
- getting the horses in and shearing the sheep
- not coloring in your crossword puzzle with black marker

Regardless of what you do, when he does something right, let him know that you know that he did something right. Then you'll know that he knows you know. And he'll know that, too. You know? Hopefully, this will make him feel good and proud and more inclined to strive to please you and do "the right thing."

Clear expectations, positive reinforcement and encouragement are important and should be the foundation of your discipline system. However, don't make my mistake. I thought that if I praised my children enough and lavished them with encouragement and paternal warmth, there would be no problems. They would rise to the occasion and would make it their single purpose in life to please their dad.

Sound the buzzer.

Thanks for playing.

Booby prize.

Wrong.

If you think that nice words, cheery smiles and clear explanations are going to get you through the next few years, give me a call when you get back from Fantasy Island.

Sometimes your child will *not* do the right thing. He will play with the emergency brake, reach for the boiling pot, slug his baby brother, speak rudely to you or, in a fit of frustration, hurl his juice in your general direction.

Don't get me wrong. Reason and praise are fine and should be used. But they won't work every time and they won't work on their own. The logic circuitry in a child is built on the false premise that he can do what he wants when he wants because he wants . . . oh, and that his body is the geographic center of the universe.

Sometimes you have to take action.

Step Three: Action

Even a "good kid" will have the occasional bad day. He might be tired, frustrated, excited, angry, irrational, hyped up on sugar or simply not thinking. He will do something stupid or dangerous or rude and will drive you to a level of anger and frustration that you didn't even know existed. He will "cross the line" and for his own benefit will need more than warm, fuzzy hugs and pats on the head. He will need some form of intervention to teach him a lesson and let him know that his actions have consequences.

It all depends on the circumstances.

Sometimes it's best to diffuse the situation before it gets out of hand.

A Word

Sometimes all that is necessary is a sharply delivered word. If Rachael is yelling and singing in bed an hour after the others are asleep, I yell out from my study, "That's enough! Be quiet!" (I actually want to yell other things, but a politically correct reading audience prevents me from going into detail).

A "Talking To"

Sometimes your child may require a "talking to." If Georgia is teasing Matilda by grabbing her blanky, I sit her down and explain it to her: "Georgia, when you do that, it upsets your sister. I know you don't mean to be cruel, but you have to use your brain. You don't like it when Rachael teases you, do you? No. Well, don't do it to Matilda. Give her the blanky back and don't do it again. Okay? Thank you."

A Threat

If a situation is escalating toward a place I don't want to be, I'll use a threat. This lets the transgressor know that there are consequences ahead and it gives her the opportunity to stop doing whatever it is she's doing, thereby saving herself from my wrath and retribution. If Matilda is throwing Brussels sprouts at her sisters during dinner, for example, I will say, "Stop that now. Don't throw any more or I'll make *you* eat them!"

If you make threats, be prepared to carry them out. Be consistent so he knows your rules cannot be broken. Warn him once. Warn him twice. Then act. Fulfill your promise and stick to your threat. Steel yourself against devastating sobs, pitiful stares or last-second attempts to make up for lost ground.

Your child must know that you mean what you say and that nonsense will not be tolerated . . . well, most of the time anyway.

So be careful what you say. Avoid stupid threats such as

- "If you don't eat up, we'll never feed you again."
- "Turn off the TV before I count to three or I'll put a hammer through the screen."
- "If you don't settle down, I'll call off the vacation."

And stay away from parental rhetoricals:

- "Do you want to be in trouble?"
- "Do you want to go to bed right now?"
- "Don't you like Brussels sprouts?"

Your kid will look at you as if to say, "Are you serious?"

Punishment

If the culprit crosses the line and does something hideously naughty or dangerous, spiteful or rude, I will bypass sharp words, friendly talks and threats and will punish right away. You know the kind of stuff I'm talking about. Your child deliberately and flagrantly disobeys you; he bites or punches someone; he is rude, nasty or cruel; he runs away from you in the parking lot; he deliberately knocks a plate off the table; he pushes his brother's head under the water in the bath; he plays with your chainsaw;

he licks all the chocolate off the chocolate chip cookies and then puts them back in the box. In these situations, punishment is swift and instantaneous.

Punishing and chastising your child is a valid and essential part of discipline. Don't be scared of it. Sure, sometimes it's hard to do, particularly if he starts sobbing and staring at you with puppy dog eyes. But at other times it's not hard at all because, to be quite frank, you've *had it up to here* with his carrying on and all of a sudden you have no qualms at all about unleashing rough justice on him.

However, when contemplating punishment, you have to be careful and keep a few things in mind.

Punishment Is for the Benefit of Your Child, Not for Your Satisfaction

You don't punish him to make yourself feel good. It's not a revenge thing. It's not about letting off steam. You're an adult and you should figure out other ways of venting your anger. So when your son empties a bag of flour over your computer, punish him so that he learns how to treat a computer correctly, rather than to appease your rage . . . at least that's what you can tell your friends.

Look, let's be honest here. There will be times when this theory is put to the test. Times when you almost literally feel like throttling them. It's okay to have these feelings. We all do. What you have to be careful of, however, is what you *do* with those feelings.

A Fine Line

It is a fine line between punishment and cruelty and you *must not* cross it. It's vital for the well-being of your child that you don't abuse him, either physically or emotionally.

But in those frustrating, late-night weak moments, the lines can blur.

One night, I was particularly tired and my mind was filled with work deadlines. The girls were in a bad mood and had been whiny and temperamental during dinner. Tantrums, screams and leg-kicking were rampant. They were uncooperative, defiant at every turn and, to cap it all off, it was a hot night. They went to bed at seven and when I went into their room at nine, after two hours of conflict and hysterics, my self-control was at its lowest. Matilda was screaming. Georgia was out of her bed. Rachael was crying and telling me openly that my bedtime rules weren't fair and that I was a "bad daddy." Seconds later I found myself stamping my feet and shouting "I HAVE HAD ENOUGH! BE QUIET—NOW!"

I am amazed and embarrassed at how my own children could transform me from a loving dad into an irrational and frenzied zombie. And to be honest, I'm uncomfortable about declaring my weakness in the pages of this book.

Remember also to avoid psychological abuse. Despite his destructive potential and incredible ability to annoy you, your young child is a fragile creature. It is important that you do not demolish his self-esteem or manipulate him by denying him your love, attention, affection or by playing on his fears.

> If you are annoyed because of something he's said or done, admonish him for his behavior rather than criticizing him personally.

If you are annoyed because of something he's said or done, admonish him for his behavior rather than criticizing him personally. And don't humiliate him, either. For example, don't say, "You stupid little kid. You smashed that cup, you clumsy idiot! How dumb can you be?" Instead try, "You're a sensible boy. That cup broke because you were running. Next time, just walk."

Avoid saying things such as

- "I hate you."
- "You fool!"
- "Don't you have a brain?"
- "You're hopeless!"
- "Sometimes I wish we didn't have children."
- "I'm sick of you and your whining!"
- "If you do that again, I'll let the spiders out of the closet."

Instead, try saying

- "I am annoyed because you disobeyed me."
- "I want you to stop that noise now, please."

- "What you did was dangerous—don't do it again."
- "I don't like that behavior"
- "The plane, Boss, the plane!"

You Shouldn't Punish Him for Accidents

Try not to expect too much from your child. There will be times—hundreds of times—when a cup will smash for no other reason than your child doesn't have the manual dexterity to keep it unsmashed. It will be an accident, pure and simple.

Accidents will happen all the time—little spills, rips and breakages. He is not being disobedient or vindictive. He is just being a kid with kid-level skills and coordination and he must be given the leeway to make mistakes.

You Shouldn't Punish Him if It's Your Fault

If you take your toddler to a party at seven at night, it's not his fault if he doesn't act like an adult. He'll be tired and will probably throw a tantrum or two. The fault is with you, not him.

If you leave a chocolate cake on the coffee table, you hardly have a right to go ballistic if he destroys it when your back is turned. Once again, the fault lies with you, not with him.

Get angry with yourself, but leave the kid out of it.

You Can't Punish Beyond His Years

Take the age and maturity of your child into account before you punish him for something. Don't expect too much of him too soon.

I have slightly different expectations for my three children. Matilda is a toddler and I keep in mind the fact that she is still figuring out what's going on. She is naturally inquisitive and has not yet fully mastered the rules of social conduct. She gets tired and cranky more easily than her sisters and she does not understand things as clearly. If she throws food during dinner, if she runs away from me when I call her name, if she empties the syrup bottle onto the kitchen floor, then I let her know I'm unhappy, but I don't start yelling and then shut her in her room. She's too little.

But if Rachael does those things—look out!

Forms of Punishment

This leaves just one question to answer: *What do you do by way of punishment or chastisement?* If your child needs to get with the program, what methods are at your disposal?

The best punishment is an immediate response to his action. If little Robbie pours paint on his sister on Monday, it does no good to refuse to let him eat pizza on Saturday as punishment. The crime will have no correlation with the punishment, so it won't make sense to him.

> When it comes to punishment, be creative and use different methods for different circumstances.

Make sure that you don't break any laws or breach the International Convention of Human Rights or anything like that. So obviously the cat-o'-nine-tails is out, as is the iron maiden, the guillotine, thumbscrews, the rack, hot pokers and forcing him to listen to line-dancing music.

When it comes to punishment, be creative and use different methods for different circumstances. In our family, for example, all the kids help set the table, which involves getting their own placemat, cup and fork out of the cupboard. One night, Rachael refused and said someone else should do it for her.

We didn't set her a place and explained that if she wanted to be a member of the family, she had to pull her weight. She still refused, so as punishment she ate by herself in a different room. The next night, she was the first to set the table.

Denial of privileges is another alternative. Stop him from doing a favorite activity. Don't allow him to go to a friend's place or watch a favorite TV show. However, note that denial of privileges does not encompass food, water, shelter, education and unconditional love.

Some parents use isolation as a form of punishment. I'm not talking about bread and water in solitary confinement, locked in a closet with half an hour of daylight a day type isolation. I'm talking about being sent to a room by himself or sitting in "the naughty chair" in the corner for a while.

Then, of course, there's spanking.

There are certain issues in parenting circles that prove to be extremely divisive. When discussing such matters, some parents get a little single-minded and self-righteous. For example, there's the breastfeeding versus bottle-feeding argument, the circumcise-or-not-to-circumcise question and the controversy over vaccinations.

But these all pale into insignificance at the sound of the word *spank*. The spanking debate is more divided, contentious, opinionated and fiery than all those other issues put together. Spanking, in short, is a hot topic.

The media is highly critical of parents who spank, characterizing them as short-tempered, out of control and riddled with guilt. Some countries have outlawed spanking. Many organizations, such as UNICEF, are highly critical of spanking and are opposed to any form of physical contact as a means of discipline.

Yet, in the real world, we know that a lot of parents wouldn't bat an eyelid at spanking their three-year-old's behind when he bites his baby sister.

So what are we to make of these two opposing viewpoints? Let's look at the various arguments.

You Must Not Spank Your Child under Any Circumstances

The Arguments

- Physical action against another human is outdated. Society has moved on. We don't beat our criminals, we don't cane our students, we shouldn't spank our children.

- There is no difference between a single spank on the behind and a harsh beating. It is too hard to draw a line between discipline and cruelty.

- The word "spank" is simply a euphemism for hit, strike, slap, belt and so forth.

- It is nonsensical to spank a child as punishment because he hit another child. It is confusing and contradictory.

- There are other disciplinary alternatives available.

- Spanking a child crushes his spirit; is dehumanizing and degrading; teaches him that "might is right"; and makes him fear and resent his parents.

Okay, that's one side's view. Here's the other.

Spanking Is an Acceptable Form of Punishment

The Arguments

- There is a difference between a beating and the occasional spank on the behind.
- Sometimes, there are no alternatives and a quick fix is required. Bribes, reason, threats, begging and loving smiles with encouraging hugs don't work all the time.
- Children need structure and discipline in their lives. They need to know their boundaries and limits, and they need to learn that there are consequences for their actions.
- Spanking a child gives him a healthy respect for his parents. It lets a child know that Mom and Dad are in charge and that in the real world he can't do whatever he feels like.
- Kids today are treated too softly. It's time we established a firmer and harder line instead of this namby-pamby, New Age "let's treat a three-year-old like an adult" nonsense.
- A quick spanking can quickly defuse an escalating situation. It can bring an end to what otherwise might be a nightmare of torment for both parent and child.
- The threat of a spanking in the future will bring quick results.

So, what are we to make of all this?

There are two arguments. One for, one against.

Some people go one way. Some the other. And some, like me, kind of sit in the middle.

For what it's worth, here's what I think.

I stand with UNICEF and other child-protection organizations on some matters. I am totally opposed to repeated, regular or harsh beatings, slaps to the face or knocking a child to the ground. I am opposed to aggressive beltings on bare skin with straps, canes, spoons, belts or paddles. I am opposed to striking a baby or a young toddler who has no idea what's going on. And I am opposed to spanking kids who are school age, because

I believe they have enough intellectual and moral development for other methods to be equally effective.

The gray area for me comes in those awkward middle years around ages three and four—maybe five, tops. Kids of this age have a tiny storehouse of reason and, on occasion, I have found it necessary to bring out the big guns.

So, in answer to your question: Yes, I have spanked each of my children at some point, and I'm don't feel ashamed or guilty about it in the least.

My kids know I love them and they also know that there are behavioral boundaries they are not to cross. They know that the spanking is there as a *last resort in dire situations.*

I am not suggesting that you adopt my views in this regard. Spanking is, and will remain, a contentious issue. If you don't ever want to spank your child, that's fine. But if you lay into your child every day as a primary disciplinary measure, you're a bully and a jerk.

Whatever it is you do, be reasonable, be consistent, be fair, be just, be firm and be bop a lula. Do yourself and your child the favor of thinking before you act, rather than acting in anger on the spur of the moment.

This will be especially helpful when he scrapes the handlebar of his tricycle down the entire length of your car.

CHAPTER 19
Awkward Stuff

WHEN YOU have a baby, your life in some respects can go on as usual. You can walk around naked, take baths with your offspring and let them climb into bed with you in the middle of summer when you're not wearing any pajamas.

But as they grow up, particularly if they're female, this type of behavior will have to be modified. Obviously, you aren't going to be hopping into the tub with your eighteen-year-old daughter.

At least, I hope you don't.

Some parents get a little anxious about nudity and sex and all those other potentially awkward things. For example, there will come a point in the growing awareness of your little girl when she will suddenly realize that you are intrinsically different from her in the physical equipment department.

You're both sitting in the bath playing Frankie the Ferry meets Timmy the Tugboat when your toddler leaps up out of the bath and stares down at you like you are harboring some kind of monster under the water. It's a comical scenario.

She looks at you.

She looks at herself.

She checks you again.

Little boys, noticing that they are physiologically similar—albeit smaller—will stare at you and say something about *how big you are, Dad*. Don't be flattered by this admiration. Remember, he doesn't have much to compare it with.

Little girls, noticing that they seem to be basically lacking the piece of equipment you seem so fondly attached to, will immediately want to know what it is and why they don't have one . . . and where they can get one.

There's no point trying to steer away from the issue or euphemize it to death. Don't, for example, do the old "That's my sausage" routine. This will inevitably lead to disaster next time you go to Grandma's for breakfast.

And don't pretend you didn't hear her or say it's none of her business or cover yourself up as if you're embarrassed. This will just teach her that your body is something naughty.

Just be open and honest. Like this.

"Dabbee, wha's daat?"

"That's my penis."

"Why?"

"Well, um, it just is. That's what it's called."

"Why?"

"I don't know."

"Oh Dad, yooouuu knoooow . . ."

"I don't."

"Whap's id for?"

"Well . . . it helps me . . . um . . . go to the bathroom. You don't have one because you're a girl. Boys have one. Girls don't."

"Why don't girls have one?"

"Um . . . because the dinosaurs became extinct!"

Then again, don't go to the other extreme of over-familiarity, which just breeds contempt. In some circumstances, it can breed pain, too. You don't want your toddler thinking it is some great new Gumby toy. I'm convinced that Matilda believes my organ of creation is a convenient handle for her to keep her balance when standing in the shower with me.

Figure out your own comfortable limits in this regard. Everybody's different. Nudity is not a big deal in our house. We take baths together and towel off together and get dressed together. In summer, if I sleep naked and they come and hop into bed, that's no big deal.

It seems that kids let you know when they've had enough of your nakedness. For me, around age five seems to have been something of a turning point. Rachael at five is still quite happy to get into the bath with me and is still quite happy to let me help her get dressed. But recently she decided that she wanted privacy when she goes to the bathroom and from now on that was off-limits to me.

She also wandered in when I was standing above the toilet and told me that what I was doing was the most disgusting thing she had ever seen and that she never wanted to see it again. I was quite happy about this.

And now that she's at school, I'm not as comfortable about being naked in bed with her when she arrives for a hug in the middle of the night. It's no big deal, but these days I fumble around on the floor next to the bed looking for a pair of boxer shorts to throw on.

Like I said, it's no big deal. Just figure out what you're comfortable with.

Another thing you will eventually encounter will be the *where did I come from?* thing.

You are much better off tackling the question directly and in an appropriate way than postponing it to a later date. There's nothing more embarrassing for an adolescent than watching her parents squirm and stumble through the facts of life even though she found out when she was seven from a friend at school.

> There's nothing more embarrassing for an adolescent than watching her parents squirm and stumble through the facts of life even though she found out when she was seven from a friend at school.

It's a genuine question and one that requires a straight answer. Different parents have different approaches. Some parents emphasize the *fantasy* aspect. The old cabbage patch/stork-brought-you kind of nonsense just messes kids up in later life. There's no reason to tell kids stuff like this, no matter how old they are. I don't know who the heck thought up these answers, but it strikes me as being pointless. I fail to see how "a giant bird dropped you down the chimney" or "we picked you from the garden like a vegetable" is in any way superior to "Mom and Dad made you."

The last decade has seen something of a reaction to this and some parents have begun to emphasize the *technical* aspects. But don't go to extremes and talk to your three-year-old as if she's sixteen. The old "Daddy's penis filled with blood and at a particular time of the month when Mommy was ovulating, he inserted it into . . ." won't cut it either.

Your response needs to be tailored to her level of understanding. Answer her on a *need-to-know* basis. So, for a three-year-old, a simple "you came out of your mommy's tummy" will probably be good enough.

I don't see anything wrong with telling her the truth and the whole truth as long as you put it in a way she understands. The type of question she asks will generally determine how much detail you go into. She'll back off when you've adequately satiated her curiosity.

But be careful. Nothing will kill a conversation at playgroup faster than a kid with a disturbing amount of knowledge who goes around asking the moms about their reproductive organs.

CHAPTER 20
Sanity

LIKE Arnold Schwarzenegger in the action flick *True Lies*, I have a split personality. For you guys who steer clear of Arnie's bulging muscles and classic one-liners, in this movie he is a secret agent with a double life.

By day, he is a world-class super-spy who makes James Bond look like Inspector Clouseau. He can fire incredible weapons, fly jets, set explosives, operate complex computer equipment and deal out rough justice to legions of bad guys.

But at the end of the day, he's a normal dad. He sleeps with an office-working wife, puts on a tie every morning, has a mixed-up teenage daughter, takes the dog for walks and spills his coffee.

We dads are like Schwarzenegger.

I don't mean in the physique department because, like me, you probably have a bicep the size of his wrist; nor do I mean in your ability to deliver witty one-liners before killing people.

What I mean is that, like Arnie, we lead a double life: an adult life and a dad life.

Take, for example, the way we speak.

If you're a teacher, at work you might talk like this: "And so we see that behind the mask, the ebullient fecundity is superbly counterpointed by Menech's use of a procrastinator as protagonist."

If you work in computers, the following words may be familiar to you: "If I can just format the macros on this PC, I'll open a new window and dump some files onto your hard drive through the modem."

If you're a washing-machine repairman: "Yeah, buddy . . . I had to replace this, ah, thingamajiggy here. . . that's gonna cost ya around, ah, let's say . . . three hundred bucks should do it."

It doesn't matter what career you are pursuing or what language you speak in your workplace, when you come home, you speak a totally different dialect. Grown men—competent, intelligent, macho, mature, respected professionals—find themselves coming home at the end of the day, picking up their child and saying, "And how's my baby-waby boy? Have you been a goody-woody goblin? Where's that tummy? Where's that tummy? Where's that tummy? *There* it is!" (If only your friends could see you now!)

And the more you get into dadhood, the worse it gets. This split personality will devour every part of your life.

> It doesn't matter what career you are pursuing or what language you speak in your workplace, when you come home, you speak a totally different dialect.

As an adult, you enjoy fine wine, intelligent conversation, playing sports and reading a good book while listening to Van Morrison. As a dad you spend your time knocking down block towers, coloring, and picking banana pieces off the floor while listening to Barney's Alphabet Jamboree.

As an adult, you go to the video store and rent *Titanic*, *The Matrix*, *Gladiator* and *To Kill a Mockingbird*. As a dad, you are intimately familiar with the regularly rented *Thomas the Tank Engine*, *Land Before Time* and anything with the words "Walt Disney" on it.

As an adult, you like to read Grisham's *The Brethren* and *Sports Illustrated*. As a dad, it's *Gordon the Elephant Buys a Swimsuit*.

As an adult, your favorite restaurant is that great Thai place just down the road. As a dad, you find yourself going through drive-thrus with increasing frequency to pick up family meal deals.

This is, in part, a good thing. It's important that we get into dadhood in a big way and don't try to keep our children as some sort of hidden sideshow that we only interact with every now and then. They shouldn't have to fit in and around our adult existence. They should be an integral part of it.

But there's a danger.

Sometimes I find myself at a dinner party, often with a small group of other "new" parents. They are usually intelligent people who have lead fascinating lives. There's fine wine and a good vibe at the table. So I am often left wondering why, after

two hours, we're still discussing diaper brands, toilet-training, kids' videos and Gretchen's rash ("which just won't go away"). You look back and wonder what happened to your ability to discuss politics, music, food, art, the Bermuda Triangle, the Titanic, religion, the best movie ever made and the difference between imported and domestic beer.

Because a young child is so time consuming, energy draining and demanding, there is a danger that parenthood will consume all aspects of your life till there is nothing left for you. You can fall into a toddler vortex and drown. This situation is even worse if there is a primary caregiver, often the mother, for whom parenting is a full-time occupation.

There is a danger that your life will disappear. There is a danger that your mental well-being will go out the window. There is a danger that you will find yourself at a party and have absolutely nothing to talk about. There is a danger that you and your wife will spend so much time focusing on your child that you'll forget to think about each other, even occasionally. Weeks will pass by and you'll suddenly realize you've been so preoccupied with maintenance of house and child that you haven't spent any time together like you used to.

> There is a saying that the most important thing a father can do for his children is to love their mother.

This is disastrous. There is a saying that the most important thing a father can do for his children is to love their mother. Let your child grow up in a visibly stable relationship, knowing that

Mom and Dad love each other. Show your little one what it means to be a couple who value their partnership.

For this reason, it is vital for your sanity that you keep some small part of your life for yourself; that you recharge your batteries and have a break from parenting on occasion; that you invest time in your marriage. You have to do it for the well-being of your wife, yourself and, ultimately, your child.

Tips for a Balanced Life

There are many things you can do to maintain some semblance of sanity:

- If you have the room, make an "adults only" space in your house; a place that will remain a sacred haven for you to escape to without having to clean crumbs off the floor. It could be a study, living room or your bedroom. Even an off-limits desk where you can keep your stuff without threat of contamination by saliva or stickers is worthwhile.

- Put your child to bed and, when the screaming has finished, eat some takeout with your wife and spend some time actually talking to each other. Leave the TV off. Just for a change, avoid talking about fecal consistency and tantrum resolution tactics.

- Host a dinner party where none of your guests bring kids.

- Make a habit of having an occasional "night out" with your wife. Go on a picnic or out to dinner, or go see a movie or show, play a game of tennis or even take a romantic evening stroll.

- Encourage your wife to go out with her friends and make sure you do the same. Go out with a friend, have a beer, cook a steak and see a movie.

- On the weekend, take turns sleeping in.

- Every night, try to talk with your wife in an adult manner. If you can last five whole minutes without mentioning or even alluding to upcoming birthdays or the other mothers at kindergarten, give yourself a reward.

(continued)

- If you're game and have an excellent support network who can manage your child for a few days, go away with your wife for the weekend. Do something wild and adventurous. Book a resort or go to a local motel. Sleep in, eat well and rediscover *sex as it used to be* (that is, without listening for little footsteps and lasting longer than four minutes).

- If your wife is a full-time mom and you're a full-time worker/part-time dad, find out what life is like *on the other side*. Look after your youngster on your vacations and send your wife off for a few days somewhere by herself. It'll be good for you to spend concentrated time with your child. You'll be able to watch all those videos your wife doesn't like. It'll be good for her to get away from you for a while. And most of all, you'll really appreciate work when you return.

- Tell your wife you love her. Send her flowers, cook her dinner and offer sex whenever she wants it.

Staying sane and maintaining mental balance will make you a better husband and a better dad. And it also means that when your child leaves home many years from now, you might have some life left.

CHAPTER 21
Time

WILLIAM BUTLER YEATS said that the innocent and the beautiful have no enemy but time.

I guess that makes us parents innocent and beautiful.

As young men, we had eighty-six thousand and four hundred seconds in every day to do whatever we wanted, whenever we wanted. Marriage reduces that figure dramatically. But that's fine. The whole reason I got married in the first place was because I wanted to give up my own time to spend with my wife.

As a dad, you will have even less.

With three children under the age of five, I am a time pauper. I am perpetually rushing and often late. Things take three times as long to accomplish. It's like someone put an extra-fast spring in my wristwatch.

I know that, according to the laws of dimensional quantum physics, the universe did not actually change when I became a father, and I know that there are still twenty-four hours in a day. But I don't know where those hours go. They certainly aren't anywhere near me. At the end of every night I get into bed having achieved precious little of what I set out to do.

No doubt you have also discovered this phenomenon. When you introduced a baby into your house, there was less leisure time, less time to go out, less time to sleep, less time to do everything. And if, like me, you have continued to fill up your house with the quaint sounds of pattering feet, you will know that things just get worse.

> I know that, according to the laws of dimensional quantum physics, the universe did not actually change when I became a father, and I know that there are still twenty-four hours in a day. But I don't know where those hours go.

Part of the problem comes from the increase in activity as your child gets older. They start going to swimming lessons or ballet or karate or whatever and you seem to spend ages just driving around and waiting for them to finish. Everything just seems to take so long.

Take, for example, going to the beach.

Just a few years ago, going to the beach was easy. I'd grab my wetsuit and my surfboard and throw them in the back of my Datsun wagon. I could be out the door and in the water in less than ten minutes.

Now it's a different matter.

We spend half an hour searching the house for everybody's swimsuits, beach sandals, hats and favorite towels. Then there's the sunscreen ritual, which takes approximately forever, but I'm not going to go into that because just thinking about it gives me a headache.

After that, we have to pack the beach bag. Goggles. Sunglasses. Sunscreen. Snacks. Drink bottles. By now, each of the girls in turn decides that she has to go to the bathroom, so it's off with the swimsuits and back to square one.

Eventually we make it to the beach, but we still won't be in the water for another thirty minutes because that's how long it takes us to shuffle the half-mile from the car to the beach with all the stuff: umbrella, inner tube, floaties, bubbles, kickboards . . . and inevitably one of the kids will want to go to the bathroom again.

Not only is it hard actually getting out the door, but everything takes so long to do once you get there.

Like going shopping.

In the old days, I could park the car, run to the store, buy stuff and be home in twenty minutes. Now it's an epic journey that takes all day. Friends say to me, "What did you do on the weekend?" and I say, "We went to the store."

> In the old days, I could park the car, run to the store, buy stuff and be home in twenty minutes. Now it's an epic journey that takes all day.

After getting the kids into the car, there's fighting to get them in their seats and struggling to buckle straps and then, at the other end, putting on or taking off jackets.

Next, there's the torture walk. You hold the hand of your eighteen-month-old who loves to walk but only moves three feet a minute. So you shuffle through the parking lot, then shuffle through the mall looking in all the shop windows. Just when you're at the store you want, one of the kids needs to go to the bathroom. You shuffle to the rest rooms. Because of your aversion to public toilets, you spend ten minutes cleaning it before letting her sit on it. What you didn't count on was that today is the day that your child is going to go for the world endurance record for toilet-sitting.

Back in the store, your toddler no longer wants to walk—she wants to be held. With one hand, you get stuff off the shelves while pushing the cart with your groin, which doesn't look so good to the casual observer. Meanwhile your other kids are wreaking havoc; one is about to knock over a twenty-foot-high display of fragile glassware as a protest because you won't buy her all the eye-level kids' goodies; the other decides that it's her turn to go to the bathroom. You abandon your cart and shuffle to the rest room.

After shuffling back to the store and rescuing your cart (half of which has already been emptied by a salesclerk with a chip on her shoulder), you finish your expedition.

But what trip to the store would be complete without those quarter rides that breed outside? Everyone takes a turn on the little train, the little car, the little beetle, the little helicopter and the little spaceship. After half an hour of rocking these irritating machines by hand (because you're too stingy to spend the money), you begin the shuffle back to the car. By this time the kids are exhausted, so you drag them limply along the ground.

You just spent four hours buying batteries and a loaf of bread.

Is there a solution to this dilemma?

No.

The only thing you can do is become a more effective manager of time. Here are four strategies that might help you.

Accept Your Lot in Life

Accept that you will always be rushing. Accept that you will often be late. There's no point comparing yourself to those guys who don't have kids and who have all the time in the world. Because of your family, it's now official—you do not have as much time as everybody else.

Accepting the fact that you cannot operate as you did five years ago is half the battle.

When you are making arrangements to arrive at a friend's place for a barbecue, don't be too specific.

Don't say, "We'll be there at 12:30."

Instead say, "We'll see you sometime between 12:30 and 5:00."

Be Reasonable in Your Expectations

Be aware of how long it takes you to get to the supermarket. Know how long a walk around the block will take. Realize that car trips are fraught with pit stops and detours. Make plans accordingly. Learn from past experience and don't be surprised every time you get to Grandma's late because it took longer than you thought to dress and feed the kids. An hour was a little unreasonable, now that you think about it.

Control Your Time—Don't Let it Control You

As a dad with a toddler or a whole troop of little kids of various ages, time is one of your most precious commodities, one that you cannot afford to waste. Plan exactly how you are going to spend it, in the same way you might pore over a bank statement to map out your budget.

> Plan exactly how you are going to spend your time, in the same way you might pore over a bank statement to map out your budget.

Think about your week and, as much as possible, don't overbook. How much time is needed for work? What time will you be getting home? What social activities have you planned? How long does it take to complete household duties? When exactly are you going to watch those fifteen new release DVDs you got the other day? At what point are you going to spend time with your child? With your wife?

As with so many other aspects of parenting, communication is the key. You should be talking about your time with your wife. If you have something that needs to be done on the weekend, discuss it with her and come to some agreement. You might want to work on the car or complete some office work or mow the lawn or clean the bathroom. She might want to paint a chair, weed the garden or finish that load of papers from work. Map out who's going to do what and when. If you're really clever, you'll only need to spend a few minutes of *quality time* (urgghh) with your child each week.

Create Time

You know those hours you spend in bed each night?

Wasted time!

Start going to bed late or get up early.

Even better, don't go to bed at all!

In the initial stages of writing this book, for example, I got up at four or stayed up till one to get in a few extra hours without the kids wanting to sit on my lap and press the keys while I was typing.

The only drawback was that I became a zombie.

Funny thing is, in a few years your child will leave home, and you'll have more time on your hands than you know what to do with.

CHAPTER 22
Sex

kid'dus interrup'tus n. the experience of having sexual intercourse disrupted by a toddler walking into the room.

I AWOKE on Saturday morning to autumn sun beaming warmly through our bedroom window. Meredith put her arm around me and snuggled up close.

There was no sound from the kids' bedroom.

I stretched and thought, "Life is good."

Moments later we were . . . well, you know how it is. The kids were asleep. The rest of the week is always so busy. Can't throw away opportunities . . .

Suddenly, and with the sort of timing that would impress even Mr. Seiko, a little voice cried out from a bedroom down the corridor, "Daaaddeeee."

Ignore it. Ignore it. Don't think about it. Concentrate.

Then again, louder, "Daaaddeee . . . Daaaddeee . . ."

No. No. I'm imagining it.

Then, another voice, "Dad! DAD! Georgie's calling you . . ."

No she's not.

And a third, "up . . . up."

And then all three at once.

"Dadeeeeee. Momeeeeee."

"DAD! Matilda's awake. She's awake."

No, no, just a minute more. Please.

"Wwwwaaaaaa. Wwwwaaaaaa."

"Daddy, Daddy. Mommy, Mommy."

"DAAAADDD!!!"

"MOOOOMMM!!!"

Our pleasant interlude came to an abrupt end with the thundering of small feet. Rachael and Georgia dragged Matilda down the corridor and exploded onto our bed with their digging elbows, scratching fingers and sloppy kisses. Knees in the groin.

One loaded diaper. Head butts. Books everywhere. Pleas for cookies, cereal and candy. Dribble on my face.

In a flaccid instant, our *married couple time* became *family time*.

But that's pretty much par for the course when you're a dad. No doubt you know what I'm talking about.

There are two reasons for this:

1. You can't just "do it" when you want to. Once upon a time, you could do the wild thing after breakfast, on top of the refrigerator, during lunch, in front of the TV—in fact, anywhere and anytime you wanted, within the bounds of the law, common decency and good taste. There were flashes of spontaneity and hours of sexual adventure.

> In a flaccid instant, our married couple time became family time.

It was a little romantic.

A little erotic.

A little creative.

But the interludes of your young-married-couple stage of life flew out the door the minute you came home from the maternity ward. The baby always cried just at the wrong moment. And you were both tired from the changes to your domestic routine, especially the feeding at all hours of the night. Sex may have lost some of its zing and zap and become more of a clumsy, half-hearted effort.

A little mechanical.

A little dry.

A little routine.

But at least if you were really determined, you could plow on, so to speak, and attend to the babe when you wanted to.

Toddlers just make it worse. Not only are they awake more, but they are mobile as well. (Yep, there's nothing like a toddler stumbling in and climbing on your back while you desperately pretend to be asleep.)

Preschoolers can stroll in and ask you questions about what you're doing. The old "Mommy and Daddy are playing horsy" routine is a good one, unless they start boasting about your equestrian prowess during share time at kindergarten.

2. I'm not quite sure how to phrase this, considering our current cultural climate and its fixation with political correctness, but for what it's worth, here it is: **Males and females think about sex differently.**

There. I said it.

Leonardo da Vinci wasn't too far off when he hypothesized that the penis was directly connected to the lungs, hence the ease of "inflation." But he was wrong. Thanks to the marvels of modern science, we now know that the penis is in fact directly connected to the brain. Supposedly, it dominates our thinking and our outlook. Supposedly, guys want to have sex about two hundred times a day. Supposedly, we are thinking about it when we wake up, when we eat breakfast, when we drive the car, when we read the paper, when we talk to a work colleague who has enormous breasts and a floral-patterned bra and an ever-so-slightly see-through cotton top and moist red lips with that all-too-familiar seductive smile and long black eyelashes that . . . oh, sorry!

Supposedly, we are thinking about it all the time.

And so we end up saying stuff like, "Okay, we've got half an hour before we have to leave—let's have sex," "I haven't seen you all day—let's have sex," "The kids are at our Mom and Dad's? Let's have sex," "*The Simpsons* doesn't start for another ten minutes—let's have sex," "You can't sleep either? Let's have sex."

It's not the same for women, but we are lulled into a false sense of security by those incredible articles in women's magazines that abound in grocery stores: "Ten steps to a better orgasm," "How to please your man," "You can be a better lover," "Your G-spot: Where it is and what to do with it."

Reading these titles makes us guys happy because we think our wives are studying these magazines and that when we get home we will enjoy the fruits of their research.

Not so.

Our wives have a different way of looking at it.

If you're lucky, you might get, "But we had sex last week . . ."

If unlucky, "But we had sex last month . . ."

This seems to be something of an accepted universal experience. At a barbecue or the gym, it only takes one guy to mention sex and all the young fathers start raising their eyebrows.

For most, this shared experience is a source of humor. For others, however, it is a source of frustration.

Maybe it's because we guys are still operating under the heritage of the beach bum whose idea of foreplay was a beer and the words, "Do ya wanna?"

Maybe it's a hormonal thing. Testosterone is more interested in sex than estrogen.

> Maybe it's because we guys are still operating under the heritage of the beach bum whose idea of foreplay was a beer and the words, "Do ya wanna?"

Maybe it's anthropological; some kind of survival of the species thing that causes one member of the reproductive team to want sex all the time. It ensures that our genus will continue.

Or maybe it's because our women are just dead tired because we aren't doing our share of the work.

So what are you supposed to do? Is the zing and zap of good marital sex just to be a dim mammary? I hope not. Sex is an important part of your relationship as husband and wife and should not just be forgotten until you pick up the pieces again when your kids leave home. Because by then your bodies will be old and crusty and sexually repulsive.

There are two things that us dads can do to improve our sexual lot:

1. Choose an appropriate moment. My guess is most of us have a poor awareness when it comes to picking appropriate moments to pursue sex. It's almost as if our libidos are out of chronological synch with our wives. We pick the worst time of day and, therefore, we often face rejection.

As a result, the following phrases are all too familiar:

- "Can't you see I'm busy?"
- "Not now, I'm exhausted."
- "You must be kidding. I've had the kids all day!"
- "I'm asleep. Get your hands off me!"
- "I have to go to work in ten minutes."
- "Can I at least finish buttering this toast first."

We need to think with our brains, not our love machines. We need to realize that some times are better than others.

Midnight after an exhausting dinner party is a bad time. Halfway through the dishwashing is a bad time. When your wife has it in her head that she's got only an hour to get something done is a bad time.

So, when is a good time?

When you take your child out all day, feed, bathe and put him to bed, and then cook dinner for your wife before giving her a foot massage. *That's* a good time.

2. Schedule it in advance. Sex is something that needs to be worked on, talked about and slotted in (sorry!) around the toddler schedule.

You can leave it up to chance and wait till you are both in the mood; not busy, not tired and not doing parenting stuff.

But eighteen years is a long time to wait. Alternatively, you can plan ahead. Some parents actually decide in advance that the next Saturday night will be *the great event*. Others palm off their child on the grandparents and have a romantic evening "like in the old days."

All the same, there are those who find it artificial to plan a sexual encounter ahead of time. It's as if they feel that they're admitting defeat; that their lifestyle is too hectic.

But if that's what it takes, that's what needs to be done. Don't be afraid to discuss sex with your wife. It is beneficial for the parents of small children to talk openly about their needs, desires and frustrations. It's better than letting it become a problem, leaving you sulky and resentful.

If you've never talked about sex before (to your wife, I mean, not your friends) and just relied on your natural drive to get you by, this may be difficult. If you don't know where to start, sit down with your wife and say, "I would like to talk about sex. I would like to have some and am interested to hear your ideas on the matter."

She may say, "Yeah, that sounds good," or "I would like sex, too, but I'm just too tired," or maybe even, "You repulse me."

If you've tried at all the right moments and have openly discussed the issue and are still not satisfied, you have a choice: Either take up a hobby or get castrated.

Of course, not all the blame lies with us guys. We are the victims of misunderstanding. Why can't our wives see that we just want to have sex for their benefit, not our own? Why can't they see it's vital for a healthy marriage? Why can't they see that we want to give of ourselves unselfishly so that they can know the deep communion of sharing?

At least, that's what I read in a book somewhere.

CHAPTER 23
Sibs

WHEN we had Rachael, I didn't give any thought whatsoever to having more children. Not that I was opposed to the idea. I just didn't really think about it. Maybe it was because I was an only child and it just wasn't in my life experience to have multiple children.

Or maybe my mind was dulled by the lack of sleep.

Then we had Georgia. I didn't give any thought whatsoever to having any more children. Not that I was opposed to the idea. I just didn't really think about it. Maybe my mind was full of other things, like how good we had it when we had only one baby.

Then we had Matilda. Around this time we started thinking that maybe some planning and decision-making was in order. Boy, did we have it good when we only had two.

So we stopped with three children, which is a major achievement when you never really even thought about having even one in the first place. One minute we were on our honeymoon, the next we were pushing a triple stroller around the zoo.

Three is plenty to fill our house, our budget, our week and our car, so we called it quits on the baby production line.

Meredith's Fallopian tubes breathed a sigh of relief and my testicles shrank back for several weeks, knowing what inevitably would be coming their way. (For the full story in vivid detail, see page 222.)

You have to ask yourself two questions, punk.

"How many children are you going to have?"

"When are you going to have them?"

If you're smarter than me, this will be a matter of careful consideration rather than fumbling luck.

Consider the variables of your circumstance. Your decision may be influenced by your economic and work situation, your own family, your age, your plans for the future, your experience with your first child, your wife's attitude or ability to go through pregnancy and labor again, the size of your car, the size of your house and your state of mental health.

Don't let anyone else tell you how many children you should have. It should be a decision that you and your wife make after careful thought and lengthy discussion.

> Don't let anyone else tell you how many children you should have. It should be a decision that you and your wife make after careful thought and lengthy discussion.

All kinds of absurd homilies float around parenting circles about how many children you should have:

- "Be happy with one. The next could be a terror."
- "An only child will be lonely, so you should have two."
- "Two's nice, but what if one has an accident?"
- "If you have three, one will always be left out. Four is better."
- "The fifth is always the most enjoyable."
- "If you have twelve, your family can do its own version of Hamlet."

And then there's my pet peeve:

- "Oh, you have three girls? So you'll keep trying till you have a boy?"

Ignore them all.

Our personal guiding motto has been *quit while still ahead.*

To illustrate the significance of this phrase, let me take you back to one night in a summer long ago.

As was family custom, I had some watered-down wine with our evening meal. On this occasion, I felt slightly giddy. I felt good. My fourteen-year-old brain figured out that if one glass made me feel that good, another glass would make me feel twice as good. So I sneaked another . . . and another . . . and another. I felt terrific! Half an hour later, while my parents watched TV, I was out in the kitchen guzzling madly at the tap of a two-gallon cask of moselle.

Fifteen minutes later, I was sitting in the living room with my parents.

That's when things got nasty.

Our whole house was kidnapped by an alien spacecraft because suddenly the floor was where the walls should have been and our brown carpet was spinning madly around my head.

The only warning my parents got was, "I feel . . ." before quarts of cheap wine erupted from my gullet and redecorated the room.

Later, as I crouched quivering in the bathroom, I had time in between each dry retch to consider the error of my ways.

I realized I should have *quit while still ahead.*

I pushed it too far and paid the price.

Having more of something doesn't necessarily mean it's better. This was a valuable lesson to learn.

I am very happy with three children. I might even be happy with four. I don't know. But that fourth might also be the straw that breaks the camel's back. I would rather stop now, while I'm still really enjoying parenting, than keep going till I reach my level of incompetence and suddenly realize I'm in over my head. Better to have a happy camel than a prostrate one . . . if you get what I mean.

Everybody's different. Some parents stop after one child; others after seven. Some parents have their children one after the other; others wait many years. Some dads feel the need to keep going till they get a son so they can play football in the backyard. Some moms want a girl.

Figure it out for yourself and discuss it carefully with your wife. It's rarely a cut-and-dried, set-in-stone, 100 percent obvious answer. Often it's more like a "that's enough, don't you think?" kind of thing, peppered with thoughts of "what if?" You might even change your mind from week to week. Or you might end up having an unplanned child.

If in doubt, spend the afternoon with someone who has a newborn. That'll jog your memory and get you buying condoms within the hour.

The Obvious

Having had three children myself now, I have discovered some interesting points about siblings, which I will now bring to your attention, even though some are pretty obvious:

- If your wife gets pregnant a second or subsequent time, put some thought into introducing a new baby into the home. Hopefully your child will know from the start that "a baby is growing in Mommy's tummy." Depending on her age, she will probably be quite excited about this. Explain to her why Mommy has to go to the hospital. Let her hold the baby—with assistance, obviously.

  When your wife and baby first come home, make sure you address the potential jealousy issue. Let your child help where she can and help her get to know her new brother or sister.

  Many parents buy the older child a doll so she can have a baby as well. This seems to work quite well and it's pretty funny watching a three-year-old try to breastfeed a plastic baby.

  And most important, don't forget to spend time with the older child. If you don't, she might get jealous and grow up with massive insecurities and personality defects and a deep-seated psychosis because no one loves her.

- There is a saying that suggests that once you have one child, the second and third are no big deal.

  This is total and utter nonsense.

  Having an extra child means less free time, more work and less money in your wallet.

  But some benefits kick in after a year or two. It's easier to handle a small group than just one. For example, at bedtime, they all have to clean their teeth and go to bed and because others are with them, they feel that it is less unfair. They also provide company for each other, not only in their beds at night, but also in the mornings and during play. We often get a nice break when all three amuse each other in the toy room rather than wanting us to entertain them. Sometimes, Georgia and Rachael will climb into Matilda's bed and play for thirty minutes in the morning, giving us a pleasant chance to sleep in.

In addition, they look after each other. On a few occasions, Rachael has yelled out that Matilda is vomiting in her crib, or Georgia has pulled a piece of our aforementioned zoo set from Matilda's mouth.

- Carefully consider the gap between your children. All of ours are two years apart and I'm glad they're together. They're good company for each other. They'll do similar kinds of age-related things as they grow up. It's a neat package.

  I know someone who was in twelfth grade when her sister came along. I'm not sure I could handle an eighteen-year gap. Just when you think there's light at the end of the tunnel, you realize it's a train coming to get you.

Having a child is a momentous and life-changing decision that has a huge impact on you. Having subsequent children is no less significant. Sure, you may think, "Hey, my life is chaos anyway, why not really mess it up?" But think about the far-reaching implications.

Here are a few things you might like to keep in mind.

Economic Considerations

You already know that children cost money. You still quake in fear at the memory of that quarterly bank statement after you checked out of the maternity ward and paid off the hospital and doctors.

The Agricultural Research Service of the U.S. Department of Agriculture calculated the weekly cost of raising children, averaged over 18 years. According to their research and depending on your income (if you make more, you spend more), your first child will cost you between $131 and $260 a week.

That's a lot of money.

Some people figure that second and third children cost relatively less than the first because you've already made considerable capital expenditure.

Well, this is true . . . to a point.

You still have to pay all the hospital and doctor bills. You still have to do the whole diaper thing. And, if you're both working, your costs in day care go up accordingly.

Two children will cost you between $235 to $466 per week.
Three children, $316 to $626 per week.

At first, a second or third baby can
slide into the family budget without
too much trouble. A baby doesn't eat
much, and if you've timed it right,
you can do a hand-me-down shuffle
with clothing and the car seats and the
crib/bed situation.

> You need to think ahead.
> Don't fall into the trap of
> assuming that another child
> will cost you only another few
> pieces of toast at breakfast.

But you need to think ahead. Don't fall into the trap of
assuming that another child will cost you only another few
pieces of toast at breakfast.

Hand-me-downs won't work forever, particularly if you have
one girl and one boy. You will need more bedroom furniture.
A few years down the road, perhaps, you'll need to add on to
your home or move to a bigger one. You might have to buy a
bigger car.

Millions of little things that, over the years, will add up to
billions of dollars. Ice creams and drinks when you go out for the
day. Multiple holidays and birthdays and other children's
birthdays. Pocket money. Family passes. Movies. Health
insurance. Entry fees for the pool, the zoo, the museum. Later
on, tuition for ballet or piano or swimming or karate. Fees and
outfits for soccer, volleyball, baseball, basketball and football.

The Department of Agriculture makes these miscellaneous
expenses quite clear. They estimate that the cost of raising one
child to age eighteen is between $123,114 and $242,902. That's
one child. Imagine how many Porsches you could buy. Imagine
the real estate. Imagine the overseas trips.

That's not even counting costs of possible extras like private
school, which could cost you more than one year's salary to get
from preschool through high school graduation . . . to say
nothing of uniforms, field trips and library fines. And, if you
want to go for one of the bigger, traditional private schools, then
you'd better start working nights.

If you thought that was expensive, just wait till you start
buying school shoes. Better cancel your vacations.

Did someone mention family vacations? Accommodation.
Food. Transportation costs. Parents and three children can fit

into one car and one motel room, but you push beyond that and you'll need a car and a trailer and two rooms.

Camping never looked so good.

And what about the weekly grocery bill? That's just going to keep escalating, particularly if your kids are ravenous bottomless pits of hunger.

Next thing you know, they'll all want their own bedrooms, so you'll have to move or add on and you'll be ruined financially.

> There is only one solution: Charge your kids for room and board, starting when they are six years old.

And why?

All because of one moment of passion! There is only one solution: Charge your kids for room and board, starting when they are six years old.

Sibling Rivalry

If you have more than one child, you need to be prepared for the rivalry that will start festering in your home.

The basic problem is that every kid suffers from *Ptolemic Complex*, which leads her to believe that she is not only the center of the family but of the entire universe as well. Everything and everyone revolves around her and her desires and needs.

This is fine if there is only one child in the family. You can give her loads of attention and she can happily live in a state of self-delusion. But once you introduce other little interplanetary bodies (in the form of new children), the finely balanced gravity within the home is thrown into intergalactic turmoil as each little Ptolemian fights for dominance of the domestic galaxy. Every day in your home will be like an episode of *Star Trek*.

Sibling rivalry can and will happen anywhere at anytime. For example, in the car . . .

"She's sitting in my seat."

"You sat here yesterday. IT'S MY TURN!"

"I never get to sit there. This is unfair!"

"GET—"

"AAAGGHH . . ."

"Mom! She scratched me!"

"Did not. Liar. Dad, she told a big lie. LIAR!"

At the table . . .

"I said I wanted the red cup."

"She got one more fry than me. It's not fair."

"Did not."

"How come I have the blue plate? I hate the blue plate!"

"I want to sit there. She always gets to sit there. It's my turn."

"Is not."

"You sat there yesterday. Anyway, if you have the red cup, I get to pick where to sit."

"Do not. That's not a rule."

During play . . .

"That's my doll."

"It's mine. I got it for my birthday."

"Did not. I got it for Christmas."

"AAAGGHH . . . she pulled my hair!"

"No I didn't. Anyway, you scratched me on purpose."

"No I didn't."

"Did."

"Not."

"You're a boy."

"No I'm not. Mo-omm! She said I was a boy!"

"Boy!!"

During domestic disputes . . .

"Okay everyone, come here. Who smashed this jar of peanut butter?"

"Not me."

"Not me."

"Not me."

"Look, someone did it. You're not in trouble. I just want you to tell me when accidents happen, okay?"

"Dad, I think I saw *her* do it."

"Think?"

"Did not. You did it. You said you did it. LIAR!"

"Am not."

During bathtime . . .

"I SAID I WANTED THE PINK TOWEL. I SAID IT FIRST. AND NOW SHE'S GOT THE PINK TOWEL AND THAT'S NOT FAIR. SHE GETS THE PINK TOWEL ALL THE TIME AND . . . AAAAGGGHHHH! SHE HIT ME!"

Teaching Your Kids to Get Along

Are there any solutions to the dilemma of the Ptolemic Complex? It's an uphill battle and you'll never completely tackle the problem, but you can try. Here are a few ideas:

- Make it clear that your household supports the *Copernican Theory of the Universe*—that is, Mom and Dad are the center of the galaxy and everyone else is a little moon with equal rights and privileges.

- Whenever possible, promote and encourage good relationships among your children. Teach values such as sharing and kindness and patience and humility. Teach communication and conflict-resolution skills.

- Explain to your kids your expectations regarding behavior and living together. Remind your older children that they are older and therefore your expectations for them are greater. Tell them they are not to "stoop" to the conduct of the youngest child.

- Reduce conflicts by assigning everyone their own spot in the car, their own toys, their own place setting and placemat, their own seat at the table. Make sure everything is portioned out equally.

- Be a good role model. Don't whine when you don't get your favorite beer glass.

Parenting Style Considerations

When we had our second baby, I would listen to the whining of one-baby parents with a certain amount of arrogance. When we had our third, I realized we'd had it pretty easy with only two. And I'm sure that people with four or five children look at us the same way.

Having more children does change the way you parent. When you had one, it was a new and exciting thing and you probably lavished an inordinate amount of time on that one child. But when you have two (or three or four or five), you have to divide your time to a certain extent. You have the same quantity of time to spend but you have to spread it around more.

Rachael, for example, got buckets of concentrated time from both of us. There was no competition. She was thoroughly pampered and she enjoyed our (mostly) undivided attention. By the time Matilda came along, she was battling for position on my knee during pre-bed story time.

Having more children does change the way you parent.

It's a good idea for you and your wife to figure out what kind of parents you want to be, and then fit the size of your family around that ideal. (Of course, you'll never succeed, but it's good to try anyway!) Having three children is comfortable for me and my style of fathering. If I had six, I'm not sure I'd have the time to be the kind of dad I want to be. And besides, I'd go nuts.

I want to be able to spend a little time alone every so often with each of my children. They are individuals and I don't want them to function as Siamese triplets. On occasion, I'll take just one to the store or for a walk, so I can spend a little time alone with her without a battle with the other two.

Also, as you become more confident as a parent, your style changes. It's like driving a car. When you first get your license, you're extremely careful about everything. You are slightly anxious. You thoroughly consider every single movement. Given a few years, however, you have an unwarranted confidence in your own driving ability so you speed, run red lights and think it's fun to fishtail in snow.

New dads are the same. When you have your first baby, you are attentive to detail and everything is a big deal.

If the baby seems particularly quiet—you go in to check on her.

She coughs—you take her to the doctor.

Diaper changing was messy—you scrub the floor.

As you know, this neurotic behavior doesn't last. After a few years, you end up just like me: a little cocky and indifferent with a hint of nonchalance.

Matilda poops on the floor—I pick it up with my fingers.

Georgia cries at night—I yell out that I'm asleep.

Rachael nearly cuts her finger off with the saw—I give her a Band-Aid.

I'm sure you get the point.

Our first child, Rachael, is a pioneer. She was the first to turn one year old, the first to walk, the first to speak, the first to go to school. She will continue being the first in many things. Matilda, on the other hand, will always be the last.

I have to struggle sometimes to give Matilda the same chance at things and show the same interest and enjoyment in her conquests as I did with Rachael. Rachael got more attention, more video footage, more photos, better parties and more fuss made over every cute new little thing she learned to do. I don't want to deny Matilda these things either. I don't want her to grow up always getting my second (or third) best.

Lifestyle Changes

Aside from your economic situation and parenting skills, you should also think of the impact multiple children will have on other areas of your life.

With each new child, your life becomes more hectic. Sometimes it is almost comical the way our household is a picture of frenzied chaos. Matilda stumbles around the house screaming and undoes the tabs on her brimming diaper.

Georgia has a skull-versus-wall head-banging tantrum because her favorite undies (the ones with the strawberries on them) are in the wash.

Rachael stands half-dressed on the table performing a full-volume rendition of *Beauty and the Beast*. I haven't shaved yet and Meredith has just realized that her black stockings were used by the children to sift flour during a recent cooking episode. And we are already twenty minutes late.

This is certainly a different picture than the luxurious frolic our lives were before we had three children. But, hey . . . we made our bed and now we're sleeping in it, along with all the cookie crumbs. Life with children is hectic and messy, that's all there is to it. If you're looking for an ordered, neat life, don't have more.

Your children modify your ability to have a career, take a vacation, socialize. They don't destroy these things; they just alter them. But if you want to work a seventy-two-hour week, take romantic ski trips and go out to dinner every other night, carefully consider your actions in the fathering game.

CHAPTER 24
Gang Aft a-Gley

TWO hundred years ago, Robert Burns wrote the immortal words

> *The best laid schemes o' mice an' men*
> *Gang aft a-gley*

These words are immortal mainly because none of us scholarly "specialists" know what "gang aft a-gley" means. However, thanks to the marvel of modern translation, we now get the gist of Mr. Burns's intent.

What he's saying is that it doesn't matter how hard you try or how well you plan, at some point your good intentions, your "best laid schemes," will go wrong.

You will screw up, make mistakes, blow it. Don't think of this as a negative thing. It's a valuable lesson for you to learn. We're all amateurs doing our best to become paternal professionals.

Sometimes I'm successful. I'm focused on my job as a dad and deliberately think ahead, plan ahead and prepare myself for situations and dealings with my children. I spend time with them and find that elusive perfect balance between discipline and flexibility. I am fun, in control, full of wise clichés, able to calm all situations and solve all problems. Mike Brady would be proud of me. I am, in short, the best dad on the planet. But it isn't always like this.

> We're all amateurs doing our best to become paternal professionals.

Sometimes I'm a failure. I'm tired, late, short-tempered, unreasonable, in a bad mood and have a lot of things to do. Being a good dad is the last thing on my mind. I'll be impatient with the kids, susceptible to bribery, defeated by tantrums, quick to anger. I am, in short, a confused and guilty failure.

It's hard to maintain the mental focus and energy required to get everything right all the time. Our cognitive capacity to deal

The real world isn't like TV.

with life is finite. Sometimes it's just too hard to juggle mental priorities, and often my skill as a dad suffers.

In parenting circles, there are many formal and informal rules and regulations about what's right and what's not, what you can do and what you can't, what's appropriate and what's not. Unspoken parental sayings lurk in the shadows whenever parents of small children get together. Playgroups and kindergartens have their own unspoken codes of behavior. Older folks at the supermarket give you stares that let you know in no uncertain terms that you are really messing things up. Relatives and friends are quick with clichés and advice.

And, of course, plenty of books are ready to ladle out their own brand of homespun pop psychology . . . just like this book, really, now that I think about it.

> Family barbecues can come to a complete standstill while your parents bring you up to speed on what you're doing wrong as a dad.

No doubt your own parents also have their own set of universal truisms that they are ready to dump on you without the slightest provocation whatsoever. Family barbecues can come to a complete standstill while your parents bring you up to speed on what you're doing wrong as a dad. Your in-laws similarly seem to have an endless store of "things were different in my day" stories.

I'm about to break one of the unspoken rules of parental literature. I'm going to put away my façade of theoretical success for a moment and hang out my paternal dirty laundry.

Here, for your encouragement, is a compilation of rules that I set myself at the start my parenting career.

Unfortunately, I've broken them all.

Rule One: Don't Compare Siblings

Easier said than done. In the heat of the moment I have found myself saying things like

- "Thank you, Rachael, for taking your plate in to the kitchen. You are a good girl. What a pity *some others* aren't as well behaved."

- "Georgia, you're a good girl for getting into your car seat so nicely. Matilda, do you think you could be as good as your sister?"

- "Look at the way Matilda is getting her hair washed! No fuss! I'm impressed that one so young can show up her older sisters!"

All of these come complete with pointed and theatrically hammy stares.

You shouldn't compare siblings because

- You don't want to promote inferiority complexes in your children and a feeling that they can never amount to anything in comparison with the other one.

- You don't want to imply favoritism.

- You want to avoid sibling jealousy and a probable fight the moment you leave the room.

Rule Two: Never Point Your Index Finger and Say All Those Annoying Things Your Parents Used to Say When You Were a Kid

Such as
- "Come here, on the double . . ."
- "If you don't eat your vegetables . . ."
- "How many times do I have to tell you . . ."
- "Do you want to be in trouble?"
- "Because they rot your teeth . . ."
- "I'm not your slave . . ."
- "This is your last warning . . ."
- "There's no ice cream until you eat *all* your dinner . . ."
- "I'm going to count to three . . ."
- "I don't remember you asking to leave the table . . ."
- "What's the magic word?"
- "Do you wanna go pee-pee?"

Rule Three: Don't Offer Bribes

You're going to visit Great-Grandma in the nursing home and you tremble with embarrassment at the memory of the last visit when Miss Three-Years escaped into another ward and trampolined on the bed of Mr. Soames, war veteran and generally grumpy old person, who almost had a heart attack because he had been asleep in the bed.

So at the entrance you crouch down and produce a lollipop.

"If you are good today and behave nicely with polite manners, I will give you this lollipop." (No need for subtlety with a three-year-old.)

One of the problems with this approach is that if you overdo it, your child will grow up expecting material gratification every time you ask her to do something. And as she gets older, the reward will need to get bigger.

If Great-Grandma is still alive when she is Miss Fourteen-Years, you will find yourself saying stuff like, "If you give Great-Grandma a kiss and engage her in five minutes of

(continued)

animated conversation and pretend you are interested in her, I will give you this portable CD player that I have here in my pocket!"

Another problem is that pretty soon your child will learn to haggle. Like so:

"If you are good today and behave nicely with polite manners, I will give you this lollipop."

"Make it two lollipops."

"Um . . . okay—done. It's a deal." "And, ah, Dad?" "Yeah?"

"For two lollipops and an hour of television tonight, I'll tell Nana I love her."

"Half an hour of television . . . and you give her a kiss on the cheek when we leave."

"Um . . . okay, Dad. You drive a hard bargain."

Rule Four: Don't Lose Your Temper

You are at the dinner table. It's the end of a bad day. You are tired, your defenses are down and your mood is lousy. Tempers are short. Your wife has had a bad day, too. Conversation is strained.

Your child is behaving like an animal and is generally uncooperative, disobedient, fussy, whining and so forth. You know he is only three years old, but you don't seem to have a large storehouse of reason or patience or maturity at that particular moment.

Suddenly, he sends the ketchup bottle flying and it hits the floor, where it disintegrates in a glassy explosion of red mush.

Your fuse runs out and you blow your stack. Everybody gets upset and you feel lousy and guilty, which makes your mood even worse.

If you are human, like the rest of us, you may "lose it" sometimes.

Rule Five: Follow Through When You Make a Threat

Kids like to know where they stand. They like consistency and constancy and they need to know that you mean what you say. It is also important for you to maintain a certain sense of discipline. Following through with a threat lets them know that you mean what you say and they are less likely to experiment in the danger area of disobedience.

So whatever you do, don't make an impossible threat in desperation.

Example one: You are about to go to a family bash. Your son is being uncooperative. You reach the end of your rope and say to him, "If you don't come here right now, we're going to leave you here by yourself" (which is a little rough for a two-year-old).

He calls your bluff. He remains uncooperative and yet miraculously is not left behind! He learns that you don't really mean what you say.

Example two: Your daughter is locked into TV mode, and as such, her hearing is not switched to "parental interruption." In desperation you come out with a beauty like, "Heather Ann Smith (using her full name really lets her know that you mean business) . . . Heather Ann Smith, if you don't wash up for dinner right now, you will NEVER, EVER watch television again as long as you live for the rest of your life till the day you die—and that's a promise!"

Of course, little Heather has had you figured out since she was born and gives you one of those "get real, Dad" looks.

Rule Six: Always Have Time for Your Child

I have a psychological paranoia caused by a TV piece that ran a few years back. It shows a beer-swilling slob watching TV while outside his forlorn son is throwing a ball around by himself. The commentary: "You remember last week you said next week you'd play with your kid? It's next week."

Don't get me wrong. It's a good piece. If it made some guys get off their butts and go and play with their kids, that's a worthwhile thing. But I think I've taken it to the extreme.

(continued)

I now feel like I can never reject my children and I can never have any time to myself. I feel like I always have to play when they want to.

Of course, I don't. I'd never have gotten this book written if I had.

But I often feel guilty about it. I sit in my study tapping away at the computer when, suddenly, all three pile in and want to sit on my lap or play with some of the whiz-bang kids' programs we've got or want me to take them down to the bike trail.

Sometimes I do . . . and then feel bad that I'm not getting my work done.

And sometimes I throw them out and shut the door on their despondent faces and go back to the computer. That's when I hear the wind whisper, "You remember last week you said next week you'd play with your kids?"

Sometimes work suffers for the sake of my children.

And sometimes my children suffer for the sake of my work.

But, hey, I'm an adult. I just have to get used to it.

Rule Seven: Never Say "Ask Your Mother"

When guys on TV say "Go ask your mother," I have always considered them to be meek, pathetic, sad, indecisive individuals. Now I am one of them.

Part of the problem is that Meredith takes care of the kids all week and they have a whole system of routines and rules that I never encounter because I'm at work.

I mean, I'm okay on the little things like, "Can I have a drink of water?" But I go to pieces when it comes to things such as what dresses are appropriate for party wear and what they can have to eat only half an hour before dinner.

So I just say, "Ask your mother."

With everyone pushing you in this direction and pulling you in that direction, trying to figure out "the rules" of parenting can be a minefield. But in the end, you need to set your own basic operating parameters and self-imposed laws of fatherhood.

As you continue to walk down the paternal path, you will no doubt discover your own foibles, weaknesses and mistakes. You will no doubt screw up occasionally and realize too late that you were wrong.

That's human. Don't give up on it. Don't throw in the towel. Keep struggling, fighting, striving to be a better dad. Don't be put off when you break your rules or when you encounter harsh criticism from other parenting "experts." Instead, tighten your resolve to overcome your failings.

And if that doesn't work, hand your child back to your wife and say, "Here, honey, you deal with him."

CHAPTER 25

Lemons

THIS IS A guy chapter and women should not read it. It contains personal and secret information that is only for members of the Brotherhood of Dads. So if you are a woman and you just happened to pick up this book off your husband's nightstand and are simply browsing, put the book down—*now*.

Some things should just be kept among the boys.

Okay, now that we've gotten rid of the chicks, let's talk about *contraception*, as in methods or gadgets that prevent conception from taking place and prevent you from being a father again before you're ready for it.

Some people have their kids almost back to back. One's barely out in the world before the next one is in the oven. Others leave a gap. My mother-in-law's closest sibling, for example, is fifteen years older than she. We had our kids less than two years apart from each other, though to be honest, that had less to do with a conscious and carefully planned decision and more to do with a lack of awareness regarding our own fertility.

How many kids you have and when you have them is covered elsewhere in this book (see "Sibs," page 198). But while you're making up your mind, you will have to start being more selective about the destination of your sperm. Somehow, you have to stop any more of them from vacationing on your wife's ovum. Because if you don't, you'll be on the wife's-pregnant-get-your-wallet-out merry-go-round again.

Temporary Solutions

For many years, science has been hard at work and there are now many different options for contraception—some obviously better than others. So, after extensive research, I've compiled a list of things that might help keep you from having another child.

Have Lots of Kids in the First Place

More kids means less sex. Less sex means fewer kids.

Abstinence

Zero percent chance of getting pregnant (unless your name is Mary and you lived two thousand years ago).

No doubt your wife (probably) thinks this is a pretty neat idea. But my guess is that you don't.

Condoms

Four percent chance of getting pregnant in one year.

In the old days, condoms came in plain packaging. Now they have soft-focus shots of people having sex on them, just in case you're not sure what they're for. I mean, you wouldn't want to mistake them for chewing gum. And there are all sorts of types: ribbed, dotted, dimpled, flavored (*you must be kidding*), colored, battery-operated, glow-in-the-dark and ones that play "Happy Birthday" when you unroll them.

Lemons

Marco Polo discovered that it was common practice for the residents of Khanbalik to use half a lemon as a cervical cap. It doesn't work very well, but it sure does smell nice. Also, it's not very pleasant if you have a paper cut on . . . well, you know.

This method is not officially endorsed by the Florida Association of Citrus Growers.

Norplant®

This is a slow-release hormone that is implanted in capsule form under the skin of your wife's arm. It lasts for five years and offers only a 0.09 percent chance of getting pregnant in the first year. It should be removed by the end of the fifth year but a new one can be implanted during the same operation.

Female Pill

Zero-point-two percent chance of getting pregnant in one year.

An effective, common form of contraception, not because it "regulates the tide" as many people believe, but because if your wife takes it, she won't let you near her. And she's probably so crabby that you won't want to touch her anyway.

Billings Method

Twenty percent chance of getting pregnant in one year. This involves monitoring changes in vaginal mucus . . .

Say no more.

Fizzy Drink

High-school mythology had it that if a woman cleansed herself with a certain carbonated drink derived from the cocoa bean that conception could not occur. Don't even think about it.

Cellophane

High-school mythology, part 2: It's just not strong enough.

Depo Provera®

This is a hormone injection that stops ovulation. Same effectiveness as Norplant, but it can have some side effects that won't go away for a few months. Also, it can take up to a year after stopping the injections for your wife to be able to get pregnant again.

Diaphragm

Three and a half percent chance of getting pregnant in one year.

My chorus teacher in high school told me I had a well-developed diaphragm. I can't tell you the confusion this caused me when trying to cope with the knowledge that a diaphragm was somehow involved in the process of stopping sperm.

Anyway, it's not 100 percent reliable, nor is it conducive to romance: "Just wait here, darling, while I slip into something more comfortable . . . and my diaphragm."

The Male Pill

This works in the same way that the female pill does. In other words, it changes hormonal levels to fool the body into shutting down sperm production. In fact, the male pill is said to be more effective than the female pill. One reported side effect has been reduced potassium levels, which can make you incredibly weak and, in some cases, bedridden. Other side effects have been weight gain (great—that's all I need!) and acne (oh, to be a teenager again).

Withdrawal Method (Coitus Interruptus)

Twenty-six percent chance of getting pregnant in one year, which is pretty high in comparison to the other methods. Here's how it goes:

"Oh yeah, baby . . . oh yeah, baby—"

"Be careful . . . don't—"

"I won't. . ."

"Steady . . ."

"Uh-huh . . . mmmmm . . . I . . . I . . . OOOhhhhh—"

"You didn't?"

"I did."

"You idiot."

Can this really work? I don't think so.

Don't.

Cayapo Tribal Method

The ancient Cayapo used a most effective form of contraception. Your wife has to eat nothing but garlic for a week. Before sex, cover her body in chicken claws and moldy cheese and dance around her singing:

> *"Let not my wife's bear spirit be conquered*
> *May she battle and be victorious*
> *And her ancestors not seek vengeance*
> *On my lineage."*

If she does this, she'll never get pregnant.

Femidom

This is the clincher in any argument that all women have penis envy. Not content to let us guys have condoms to ourselves, they invented a polyurethane condom for women. It hasn't really taken off. Which is no surprise to me. It sounds like having sex in a plastic bag.

Vaginal Donut or Sponge

There's a joke in here somewhere. I just can't seem to get it.

This is a donut-shaped foam sponge that fits over the cervix as a barrier to sperm. It also contains spermicides, but in spite of this double protection, it is only 87 percent effective. I haven't seen these around for ages and don't know if they're still made, which is a pity, because they were great for washing the car.

Breastfeeding

Rumors abound that when your wife is breastfeeding, she can't get pregnant. If you rely on this method, you'll be back in the maternity ward before you can say, "What do you mean, old wives' tale?"

Drink More Beer

Nothing like "the droop" to prevent fertilization.

Spermicide

Thirty percent chance of getting pregnant in one year. Pretty high.

This is a foam or gel that is "inserted" to kill sperm. Not particularly romantic. Nor is it all that effective, unless used with another form of contraception (for example, a condom).

Cervix Electric-Shock Machine

Currently being investigated and therefore not available. This little device electrocutes sperm on the way in. The main implication of this is that you shouldn't have sex while standing in the shower or in a puddle.

Permanent Solutions

Temporary options are all well and good if you're planning on adding to the fold later on, or even if you're uncertain. You might want more kids but want to wait for a few years before you go back to square one again.

But there will come a time in your career as dad when you wake up one morning and you and your wife look at each other and say "enough is enough." This is usually the same morning that you wake up at 5 A.M. when your children decide to play trampoline on your blanket, which you happen to be inconveniently and painfully under at the time.

Once you know you've reached your level of incompetence with however many children you happen to have sired, it's time to take some more long-lasting preventive measures. You don't want to spend the next twenty years messing around with plastic gadgets, tablets, foams, creams, injections or citrus fruit.

So after your stud farm/sex slave days are over and you're ready to be put out to reproductive pasture, you may wish to explore some more permanent options.

There are two ways to go.

1. Your Wife Has an Operation

This is a popular choice among husbands.

She can have a *tubal ligation*, often referred to as "having your tubes tied." This blocks the passage so that the eggs can't travel from the ovaries to the womb. It is quite effective, with a failure rate of only one in five hundred.

2. You Have an Operation

This is the hardest section of the book for me to write because my legs keep tying themselves into pretzels.

A *vasectomy* is an increasingly popular choice among couples, perhaps for no other reason than women think it's a good idea to spread around the pain. *They* went through the tribulation and inconvenience of pregnancy and childbirth, so now it's *your* turn.

This is where you regret all your sermons about being a modern father and sharing everything equally—because your wife is going to hold you to it.

A vasectomy is a surgical operation in which the sperm-carrying tubes from your testicles are severed. Hence, I should give you a word of warning. In the following pages you may encounter words such as "snipping," "cutting," "neutered," "hacking" and "slashing."

Call it what you will: losing the balls, severing the nads, breaking ties with Jack and Jill, crunching the squids, sending the boys out to pasture, cracking the chestnuts, being cut from the team. Although technically a small operation, to any man we are talking BIG LEAGUE.

It is a difficult concept to grasp and is something that women just can't understand. Our nads are at the center of our being. They are extremely important to us. We protect them when we play sports. We get told off for holding them while watching TV. And when we see those home-video shows where men get clobbered in the privates with a two-by-four by some smart-alecky kid, we sit bolt upright in a cold sweat. The idea of messing around down there . . . well, it takes some getting used to.

Anyway, if you're still interested, here's what happens.

Making the Decision

You visit the family planning clinic or a surgeon referred by your doctor and say you want a vasectomy. The doctor reaches into a drawer and instead of bringing out a pair of pliers, he pulls out a pad of paper and some brochures.

Welcome to the wonderful world of vasectomy counseling.

It's not just a matter of up on the table, shorts off, snip snip, there you go, thanks for coming, credit card, please. It is a big decision and a major operation and one that should not be entered into too quickly or too lightly . . . kind of like marriage, really.

> The doctor will want to find out how much you know about the procedure and its consequences. He certainly doesn't want to be chopping you up, only to have you sit up and yell, "YOU DID WHAT?"

The doctor will want to find out how much you know about the procedure and its consequences. He certainly doesn't want to be chopping you up, only to have you sit up and yell, "YOU DID WHAT?"

He will pull out a diagram that is the brother sketch to the one-legged woman of the birthing classes you went to years ago. Obviously, however, the squiggles and lumpy parts are in different spots. It usually consists of a massively erect member with huge testicles and gigantic tadpoles racing through the plumbing like spawning salmon.

He will explain the process of the operation and tell you that it is safe, effective, quick and common. I find it interesting that the words "painful," "inconvenient" and "uncomfortable" are conspicuously absent from this list.

A vasectomy should not be considered reversible. This comes as a shock to some guys who believe that they can change their minds a few years down the road and have their space pods reconnected to the mother ship. For a small percentage, this may be the case, but they should be considered the exception rather than the rule.

In addition, the operation can be technically difficult. And expensive.

For this reason, it is not advisable to have a vasectomy if your life is in a temporary state of change, stress or crisis. It may be a decision you regret later on. It should not be viewed as something that will fix any marital or sexual problems.

You and your wife have to be absolutely sure that you don't want any more children.

The doctor will ask you a lot of other questions about your knowledge of contraception, your children, your sex life, health, family history, your reasons for wanting a vasectomy, your credit card number and so forth.

Make sure you've had all your questions answered. Don't forget to inquire about costs. And ask if they use a general or a local anesthetic—or no anesthetic at all.

Next, the doctor will ask you to drop your shorts so he can inspect the area. Some men are surprised by this, not realizing that the initial consultation would involve pants-dropping. They suddenly regret their recent one-hour jog and the fact that their underwear looks like an old dishcloth.

Be prepared for this. A shower beforehand and a fresh pair of underwear with good elastic and no holes are advisable.

Also, be prepared for the fact that your doctor may be female. Some men may not bat an eyelid over this. For others, it may be a concern.

My doctor was female and, while I wasn't particularly bothered by that, it certainly was an odd sensation when after half an hour of discussion, I had to break out the tackle and let her squeeze it. There is a certain sense of strange ridiculousness about being in an office, sun beaming through the window, birds singing outside, and you standing there in your business suit with your pants around your ankles, being felt up by a total stranger. I had seen Meredith delved and explored by male obstetricians as part of her pregnancy check-ups and never gave it a second thought. But when the shoe is on the other foot, it's a different matter.

If after the inspection you are physically okay and it appears that you are a sane and informed individual who is making a carefully considered choice to have your testicles disconnected from the rest of your body, you'll be asked to sign a consent form. This says that you know all about the procedure and accept the risks and possible complications and that you won't sue if your privates swell up to the size of a basketball.

On the way out, make the appointment to get up on the table and face the microsurgeon's scalpel.

Yes—a microsurgeon.

And yes—micro, as in teeny weeny.

Don't take it personally. It is no slur on the magnitude of your organ of creation.

Be Careful

It is a truth universally acknowledged that a man in possession of a vasectomy appointment is ten times more likely than normal to get his wife pregnant.

Yes, it's true. I know plenty of couples who have fallen in the family way in that brief but ironically tragic window of opportunity between the moment they decided not to have any more children and the moment the surgical shears went "click."

For this reason, stay away from your wife. Don't have sex, don't share silverware, use separate bars of soap in the shower . . . in fact, don't even look at her. Sleep in separate beds in different rooms and wear five condoms at all times . . . just in case.

Oh, to Be Clean-Shaven

When you have a vasectomy, you have to be clean-shaven . . . and I don't mean your chin.

Now it's all well and good *talking* about shaving your wrinkled nether region, but doing it is another matter.

Some guys find the thought of squatting in the bath with a razor in one hand and their freshly lathered privates in the other a bit too much to bear.

They would prefer someone else do it.

Someone medical.

Someone trained.

Someone experienced.

A scrotum-shaving professional.

This is where you need to be careful and honest with yourself. Imagine lying down on a bed and having your equipment handled by an eighteen-year-old nurse named Ophelia. She has moist lips, her hair is in a schoolmarm bun and one of the buttons on her blouse is missing . . . and worst of all, she is wearing a nurse's uniform. To divert your attention, you desperately try to think of rotting compost or your grandmother with no clothes on, but in the back of your head you can clearly hear the klaxon wail signifying "up, periscope."

If you can cope with that, fine.

Heck, you might even enjoy it.

Then again you could get a nurse whose only claim to fame in her brief but failed acting career was as a witch in Polanski's *Macbeth*.

If you don't like the idea of someone else getting their hands on your treasure, you'll have to do the job yourself. This is not as easy as it sounds. I don't even like using the words "testicles" and "razor" in the same sentence.

Whatever you do, don't do it when it's cold or you'll end up with a condition commonly referred to in medical circles as "cheese grater syndrome." Remember to work in a downward direction. Never sideways . . . or you'll end up doing the operation yourself.

And there you have it. A baby eagle sitting in your lap with a ridiculous toupee. And I shouldn't have to say this, but I will, just in case.

Don't use aftershave.

Just trust me on this one.

The Night Before

The operation will knock you silly for a couple of days, so you should take care of any pressing business beforehand.

- Don't make any plans for ballroom dancing or house renovations for the next few days.
- Set up a spot on the couch.
- Rent a stack of good videos (with no sex scenes).
- Buy a case of beer and keep them in a cooler by your recliner.
- Make a barrier out of barbed wire so your kids can't jump on your lap.
- Start talking to your wife about what a big sacrifice it is you'll be making tomorrow. Get as much sympathy as you can.
- Don't watch any movies containing scenes of testicular abuse. Avoid *Ice Pirates*, *The Three Musketeers*, *Mississippi Burning* and any of those man and dog films where every five minutes the canine sinks his teeth into some poor guy's crotch.

The Big Day

You are all revved up and ready to go. At the clinic or hospital, you spend a few anxious moments leafing through magazines, but you put them down because they are full of recipes for meatballs.

The assistant comes in and says, "Okay, let's do it."

This is . . . your finest hour.

You go into a room, strip, put on a medical gown and are told that the nurse will be along in a moment to inspect your pruning job. She comes in, you lift your gown, show her your artistry, ask her what she thinks, she says, "Yeah, it's pretty good," and then leaves.

Then another woman comes in and says, "Right, let's inspect the area." You say you just showed it to . . . that's when you see the other woman walking away with a bucket and a mop and a smile on her face. (You may well laugh, but this actually happened to a friend of mine. Hi, Al, how are things?)

After you get over the embarrassment, it's onto the chair or operating table for the anesthetic.

If you're having a general, see you in a few hours.

If you're having a local, keep your eyes and ears firmly shut.

Keep your eyes shut because you don't want to see any hypodermic needles coming toward you while your legs are akimbo. Also, you don't want to see the ridiculous sight of your lonely bald penis cowering in the middle of an expanse of surgical sheets.

Keep your ears shut because then you won't have to listen to the doctor make the standard joke: "It's just a little prick."

Ha, ha.

The operation itself takes about thirty minutes. One or two small vertical incisions are made in the front wall of the scrotum. The two tubes (*vas deferens*) that run to the testicles are fished out, snipped, tied and perhaps cauterized. Then the tubes are stuffed back in.

To finish up, the incision is sealed. This may be done with a few small stitches or just by pressing the skin together and sealing it with a bandage. Interestingly, the scrotum is the only part of the body that can be healed by just squeezing the two sides together.

While it doesn't hurt per se, there is a certain sensation of movement and pulling during the procedure. Some men say that they find the experience to be the testicular version of running your fingernails down a chalkboard.

Recovery

When women have babies, they spend a few days in the hospital getting over their ordeal and nursing their babies. Unfortunately, if you're planning on spending a few days in the hospital getting over your ordeal and nursing your wounded soldier, you will be sorely disappointed.

But that's fair enough when you think about it. I know us guys make a big deal about a vasectomy (*You just can't understand, honey.*), but I think there is a serious order of magnitude problem between having two teensy snips compared with having an eight-pound human pass through your sex organ.

And so you're up and away pretty much as soon as it's finished, even though you now walk like John Wayne. It's a good idea to have a jockstrap or two pairs of cotton briefs to wear home from the surgery. This will keep your wounded soldier nice and snug and will give much-needed support.

You will not be in a position to drive, so make sure you have a ride home. Ask your driver to bring a bag of frozen peas so you can throw them on as soon as you get in the car. This will reduce the swelling and make you feel more comfortable.

When you get home, sit in your recovery chair with your feet up and don't move for two days. Keep applying the peas for ten minutes every hour and use pain killers to ease any discomfort, particularly at night. Sleep with a pillow stuffed between your legs.

I'm sure there are guys out there walking the streets who have had a vasectomy and found it to be as quick and inconvenient as getting a haircut.

But I've never met them.

Whatever you do, don't . . .

- let the kids near you
- lift anything or exercise for at least five days
- read any pornographic magazines, even if it is just for the articles
- have sex for four days
- forget to hold your testicles when you sneeze
- strain too much when sitting on the toilet
- think about your wife wearing a negligee

All you have to do is mention the word "vasectomy" in a room of guys for them to come running, desperate to tell their sad and sorry tales of infection and swollen privates.

"Infection! Hah! Let me tell you about infection."

"Would you like to see the scar?"

"I couldn't do it for ages."

"Swollen! . . . Does the word 'watermelon' mean anything to you?"

"I had a vasectomy . . . then my wife got pregnant again."

"I can't even use a urinal anymore."

"It's the best thing I ever did."

"It's the worst thing I ever did."

"Now my penis picks up FM radio."

Yep, there's nothing like sitting around with the boys, chewing the fat about our collectively severed parts. It's this kind of camaraderie that makes me proud to have testosterone in my veins.

Anyway, there's usually discomfort and some bruising or swelling for a while after the operation. You'll feel like you've been clobbered at close range with a wet football. There may also be two small lumps above your testes for a month or two, but this is normal.

If you're unlucky, you'll get a post-operative infection, which I'm told is like having your privates stuffed in a garbage disposal. Other problems exist but are rare: internal bleeding, sperm granuloma, inflammation of the epididymis and toxification of the scrumdiddlyumptious.

But these are small fry compared to the unbearable itchiness you will encounter when your hair starts to grow back.

Sex

Let's be honest. This is what you want to know about.

After the operation, will you be able to cut it in the bedroom? And even so, will you want do it anyway? Will you still be able to raise the flag, so to speak? Will you start wanting to read Jane Austen novels? Will you be like your dog who was neutered and now just spends his days moping around in front of the fireplace?

If all goes according to plan, there should be no difference in your feeling of masculinity (whatever that means). You won't start speaking in a high voice and you will retain your taste for sports, beer and monster-truck rallies. You will continue to experience pain when your children tread on your groin and shrinkage if you go swimming in icy water.

And there should be no detectable difference in anything vaguely related to sexual activity.

You should have the same sex drive that you always had before (that is, after the bruising and swelling have gone away). You should have the same capacity to develop an erection. You should still have the same sensitivity and so enjoy sex and orgasm just as much as before.

And yes, you should still wake up with one every morning, if you know what I mean.

You should still be firing what is referred to in the books as "ejaculate" (pronounced "ee-jack-ya-lut," not, "ee-jeck-ya-late") and it should look the same as it did before. Sperm accounts for only a few percent of your orgasmic vichyssoise anyway, so there should be no detectable difference . . . unless you look under a microscope.

And what about all the sperm that can't get out anymore?

Sperm is still produced in your testicles, but because the supply line has been severed, it has no way of getting out. Don't worry. When your testicles have ballooned to the size of tennis balls somewhere in the third week, they'll burst of their own volition.

No, no. Only kidding. The sperm simply gets absorbed back into your body.

Urgghh.

The Wait

There is one important point left to cover.

You had a vasectomy in the first place as a contraceptive measure. However, care must be taken. A vasectomy is not instantaneously effective. The supply lines that transport the sperm from the testicles to the outside world have been cut and sealed, but there is still sperm hiding in your plumbing . . . and it will sneak out the next time you have sex . . . and the next, and the next.

In fact, you are possibly fertile for another two months or fifteen to twenty orgasms, whichever comes first.

If you are lucky, you might be able to swing the following scenario with your wife.

She'll come home from a busy day at work, throwing her stuff into the corner and yelling out: "Damn head office! They want that contract in a couple of days. As if I don't have enough work as it is."

To which you, coming down the stairs, will say: "Well, sweetheart, don't make too many plans . . ."

(At this point wafting violins will start to swell in the background. You will eye her hopefully.)

"You mean . . ."

"Yes, darling. I saw Dr Lloyd this afternoon."

(Crescendo of violins. Counter-melody subtly and harmoniously introduced by cellos and violas.)

"You mean . . ."

"Yes, my love. I have to have tests."

(Massive crescendo. Whole symphony joins in.)

"You mean . . ."

"Yes, my honey blossom pancake . . . I have to have . . . (and then the magical words as the whole room starts to spin uncontrollably, accompanied by beautiful orchestral themes) twenty orgasms in the next couple of weeks!"

You will experience the sensation of being lifted off the ground and spun in the clouds as your wife says: "Gosh, that's a lot! But I guess it has to be done . . . let's get started tonight . . . and we can come home early from Mom's tomorrow."

"Yeah, it'll be tough on both of us, but the sooner we get started, the sooner I'll be 'safe.' " *(Yeehaw!)*

If you are unlucky, however, you might experience the following scenario.

Coming home from a busy day at work, your wife will throw her stuff into the corner and yell out: "Damn head office! They want that contract in a couple of days. As if I don't have enough work as it is."

To which you, coming down the stairs, will say: "Well, sweetheart, don't make too many plans . . ."

(At this point you will hear the theme from *Jaws* waft menacingly through the air. She will eye you suspiciously.)

"You mean . . ."

"Darling, I saw Dr. Lloyd this afternoon."

(Crescendo of *Jaws* theme. Aggressive counter-melody suddenly introduced à la staccato stabs from *Psycho*.)

"Yeah, so?"

"Well, I have to have tests."

(Massive crescendo of timpani and other nastily percussive instruments.)

"You mean . . ."

"Yes, my honey blossom pancake . . . I have to have . . . (and then the room will spin sickeningly to the deafening chorus of cannons, breaking glass and sirens) *twenty orgasms in the next couple of weeks!*"

You will experience the sensation of being clubbed across the forehead with a bat as your wife says: "That's a lot! But I guess it has to be done. Well, I'll leave you alone for a while. I've got some shopping to do—"

"No wait—"

"Enjoy yourself. There's a box of tissues in the bathroom."

"Honey . . . but—"

"Have a nice time. Bye."

So as a final check, you have to have a sperm test. They need to see if you're still firing live stuff. Even if the operation has worked, they need to make sure there's none hiding in there, waiting to sneak out and go carousing with an ovum when you least expect it. This also covers the eventuality of *recanalization*, which means the severed vas deferens reconnect of their own accord. The chance of this happening is about one in a thousand.

The sperm test is the final joy of the vasectomy.

You have to prearrange a time with the pathology lab and get a sample to them within the hour.

It's another one of those guy things where you nod your head and are supposed to be mature and clinical, but for some it's a novel thought. Given that not many of us are used to masturbating into a beaker and then handing it over the counter to the young receptionist, I think it's a legitimate concern.

The guys who are in real trouble, however, are the ones who claim not to be able to fly solo, if you know what I mean. This presents certain logistical problems if you need to give a sample. I'm sorry to be the bearer of sad tidings, but the whole thing about obliging nurses and X-rated video libraries is a myth borne of sitcoms.

But once the operation is over and the swelling has gone down and the scar has healed and you can walk like a man and stand erect without that dull ache and you've stopped itching and the lab sends you a letter declaring you're firing blanks, *it's party time!*

No more hassles about the consequences of your desire. No more fumbling with rubber things or gels or pills or thermometers.

It is time to fulfil you destiny as a sex machine.

Yeehaw!

CHAPTER 26
Education

Preschool

WHEN we started the book, your child was just about to take one of the biggest steps of her life . . . namely, her first step. That giant step (or prolonged stumble, as the case may be) heralded a new and exciting stage of your fathering life.

And so it's only fitting that as we reach the end of the book, I leave you with another important step that will mark the beginning of your child's next stage of existence . . . namely, her entry into that formalized prison of education known as *school*.

It begins with preschool, which is like school but isn't *really* considered school. It comes *before* school, hence the letters "p-r-e" on the front. If they weren't there, it would just be school, and that would . . . oh, never mind.

Kids go to preschool for many reasons.

An obvious one is to prepare them for school, which will come when the "pre" part is over. They have to be gradually introduced to a formal setting away from home where other adults are in charge and other children are in attendance. This reinforces a vital social and intellectual function in their development.

A more cynical reason is that both parents can go back to work or the primary caregiver can get some much needed rest from their increasingly demanding child.

And besides, all the other kids are going to preschool and you don't want your child to be educationally disadvantaged.

So, your child is turning three and you want to know about preschool.

What do you need to know?

How Do Preschools Work?

Good question.

There is a tremendous amount of variety in the operation of preschools from state to state and even area to area. Some preschools are gung-ho on educational pursuit, others are more social. Some have computers, others have sandboxes. Some have "normal" school hours while others offer longer hours to serve the needs of working parents.

In fact, the only thing that preschools have in common is that at the end of the day, your child will bring home what is loosely described as "arts and crafts." In some cultures, this is referred to as "junk and garbage."

Your home will become the storehouse for piles of abstract finger paintings, egg cartons with cotton balls stuck to them, nightmare sculptures of pipe-cleaners and corks and, if you're really lucky, bark pictures and maybe even some pasta jewelry (if it doesn't look good, you can always eat it).

The problem is that your child considers it a crime against humanity if you throw them out, so all must stay. Your refrigerator will soon be buried and, like me, you will find yourself making midnight runs to the recycling bin to dump the preschool creations so as not to upset the fine familial balance.

How Do You Choose a Preschool?

In some places, you may not have the luxury of choice. There may be only one preschool in the area. Cost may be prohibitive as may the length of the waiting lists. You may be committed to a particular educational philosophy or religious doctrine, which will further narrow your choice.

However, let's assume that you can shop around. What should you look for?

1. The Physical Environment

- Is it a nice place to be?
- Is it decorated with pictures and posters and other colorful stuff?
- Is there some grass, some space to run around, a few trees, some shade, a sandbox?

- Are there closets and shelves brimming with toys, puzzles, blocks and games?
- Is it bright and airy, and does it generally look clean and in good repair?

2. The Staff

- What are their qualifications and experience?
- How many are there?
- Do they have warm personalities or do they seem cranky and overworked?
- Do they have criminal records for embezzling funds?
- Are they good with kids?
- Do they have that special sing-song voice unique to preschool teachers?

3. Daily Operation

- What do the kids do in a typical day?
- Are parents invited, allowed or expected to be involved?
- What is their education philosophy and disciplinary practice?
- Do they have programs, routines and a semblance of organization?
- Do they communicate with parents?

The best thing, of course, is to visit. Call them and ask if they have an open house or orientation day or ask if you can just show up and take a look around. This will enable you to pick up the "vibe." If it's situated next to a munitions dump and looks like a derelict public toilet and there are fifty kids running riot because the seventeen-year-old running the place is smoking out back with her boyfriend, may I suggest you might want to try somewhere else? It doesn't take long to get a gut reaction to a place and the people there. Look particularly at the children. Are they happy and content or are they tunneling out of the sandbox in a desperate attempt to escape?

Look particularly at the children. Are they happy and content or are they tunneling out of the sandbox in a desperate attempt to escape?

Be quick, though. If you're going to visit, do it early. Those women who reserve their birthing spots in hospitals on the night they conceive are the same ones who register their kids in a preschool an hour after they're born. One preschool near us has a waiting list of three hundred names, with only fifteen new spots opening per year.

What Do Kids Do at Preschool?

Preschool is supposedly about getting ready for school. Given this, you would assume the curriculum would include

- self-defense in the bathroom
- how to talk your way out of detention
- believable excuses for not doing homework
- how to prepare for exams
- the art of the spitball of mysterious origin
- chair-tipping safety
- forging parents' signatures

However, this is not the case.

All are different, but most ordinary preschools have certain common elements:

- storytime
- show and tell
- eating slices of fruit and drinking juice
- playing on the monkey bars or in the sandbox
- nap time
- finger-painting, gluing and coloring
- falling over and skinning knees
- playing games
- the chicken dance

Then, of course, there are hotshot preschools for parents who want their children to get ahead in life, to lead the pack and be on the cutting edge. These preschools have computers, violin lessons, foreign language tuition and seminars on small-group management.

How Can I Prepare My Child for Preschool?

You can do lots of little things to help your child slide into preschool without too much trouble.

The best preparation for preschool takes years of buildup and can't be achieved in just a few days. It's good if your child is used to other adults and other children. It's good if she's been stimulated and is used to games and books and puzzles. It's good if she has manners and a basic understanding of how to interact socially. It's good if she is at least a little independent, especially when it comes to going to the bathroom and getting dressed.

In the weeks leading up to the big day, take her for a walk around the preschool and spend a little time in the playground so she can get used to the place. Meet the staff beforehand. Talk about preschool with your child and describe the sorts of things she will be doing there. Explain that she will be dropped off in the morning and reassure her that she'll be picked up at the end of the day. Talk in positive terms so she knows it's a good thing. If you appear anxious or apprehensive, she will pick up the bad vibes. If she has a friend starting on the same day, go together.

In the weeks leading up to the big day, take her for a walk around the preschool and spend a little time in the playground so she can get used to the place.

Before your child starts, most preschools will provide you with information regarding procedures and expectations on the first day. Some let parents stay for a few hours until their child is settled. Others have a "drop and run" policy.

Either way, no matter how prepared they are, some kids take it in stride and others scream and cry and cling to your leg with a vice-like grip that not even spraying them with mace will shake off. It's best to follow the operating procedure of the staff and, if in doubt, ask for advice. Remember that although this is your first time dropping a child off at preschool, for the staff it's nothing new.

At the end of your child's first day, make a big fuss over her. Pretend that you can actually see the close resemblance in her scribbled portrait of you. Ask her questions about what she did and who she played with. The answers will always be "nothing" and "no one" but don't despair—this is good practice for when she becomes an uncommunicative teenager.

The Modern Dad's Role

There's a lot of fuss made about the "modern father" in parenting circles.

But what does a modern dad do?

How is a modern dad identified?

Well, by changing diapers and getting the bottle in the middle of the night. But what does he do when the diapers and bottles are gone? Does he just revert to being a detached parental relic?

No!

It's easy to let it all go as your child becomes more independent. You have to recommit yourself to being an involved dad. This means that you actively participate in the life and development of your child. You take an interest in her world and her daily routine.

Don't put it off or say that you'll get involved when she hits high school. Get into practice right from the start.

One of the primary ways you can do this is by spending time in activities related to preschool. By doing this you will send a message to your child that says, "You're important to me. I have time for you and your stuff." This also says to your child that you think school is important.

If you work, a regular appearance at preschool will obviously be difficult. But if you have flexible hours or vacation days, try to show your face at least every once in a while. Do the drop-off or the pick-up. On your vacation days, put your name down on the occasional help roster and go and cut up the fruit and help with the crafts.

If they have one, go to the annual concert. Preschool concerts are wild, with tiny kids getting dressed up and running around while all the moms clap enthusiastically and the dads operate video cameras. (If you're really lucky, they'll make you get up for the chicken dance.)

Go to any social bashes that may arise and get to know the other parents. It's likely that you'll be seeing many of them for years to come as you navigate the educational system together. Go to the barbecues, coffee and dessert nights, and fundraising functions.

I have had some fantastic nights at preschool events. Sun setting in the background. Mosquitoes buzzing thickly. The air heavy with the sounds of screaming children smacking heads and toddlers wailing because they've dropped their hot dog in the dirt. And all of us dads congregating around the grill, talking about the capacity of our lawnmower bags.

Some preschools have management committees and support groups. Despite the supposed "sensitive New Age–guy" mentality of our generation of dads, such groups still remain the domain of women.

I went to a kindergarten orientation meeting a few years ago and was surprised to be one of only four guys there. Against twenty-three moms, we were sorely outnumbered.

(That wasn't the only surprise of the night, however. Going to the bathroom in a bowl only slightly bigger than a coffee cup was not easy. It was only made worse by the waist-high stall doors and the large window panel with a clear view to the main room, where all the assembled parents sat. *Talk about stage fright.*)

Anyway, the point is that you should find some way at some time to have some sort of presence at something vaguely associated with the preschool.

School

Preschool is fine for a while, but there will come a time when your child's ever-expanding brain will no longer be satisfied with warm and fuzzy stories, naptime and playing with dollhouses.

It is time for them to move into the big league: *real school.*

Unlike preschool, however, children can't just join up anytime throughout the year. Usually the cutoff for kindergarten tends to be if she turns five before the end of September of that year, give or take a month, depending on the state or province.

For some parents, it's an easy and clear decision. Their child turned five in October of the previous year and is champing at the bit to start. She is bored at preschool and is socially and intellectually ready.

For others, it's a little more complex. Their child turns five in August and she doesn't really seem too mature or confident.

Wearing a school uniform

The choice is to send her or hold her back another year so that she will either be younger or older in comparison to her classmates.

If you're in this situation, consider carefully her social, emotional and intellectual abilities. It would also be advisable to have a chat with her preschool teacher and maybe even the school teacher about her readiness.

Most schools have orientation days toward the end of the year so you can check out the school, the classrooms and the staff. Once again, try to go along, even if it's just to say "hi" to a few familiar faces.

The school probably also produces a list of requirements for students. It's the standard stuff: lunch box and drink thermos, spare undies, bookbag and the mandatory school fashion requirements—one of your shirts with the sleeves ripped off for a painting smock.

Spend some time over the summer preparing her for school. If she goes to a school that requires a uniform, dress her up in it and make a big deal about it. Talk about the differences between preschool and school and the importance of manners and obedience. Take her to visit the school and, if possible, play in the playground.

And then before you know it, the time will come and your child, that same scrunched-up peeled tomato that you saw appear from between your wife's legs, that same wrinkled baby who spent every day squawking from the warmth of her crib, that same toddler who got you a lifetime ban from the local supermarket, that same small child who appeared in your bed every night at 2 A.M. for months on end and gave you the worst nights of your life . . . that same child will be standing on the doorstep, waiting for her first day, carrying a bag almost as big as she is.

Your camera won't have been so busy since that day in the delivery room all those years ago.

This first day is a time of melancholy, realizing that your "baby" is no longer. It is the end of an era. You look back over the past years and wonder where the time went. You look at her birth photos and she almost seems like a different person.

And it is a time of pride as you realize that you have successfully been a parent for several years now and your child has not developed any serious personality disorders. You have made it this far, which means there may be hope for you in the future.

After that, you're on your own.

You're in stage three of fatherhood: the *President of the Fundraising Committee* stage.

Every day will be a blur as you try to keep up with what's going on. Newsletters coming home, parent afternoon gatherings, cute little concerts, parent-teacher meetings, spelling bees and report cards ("for being the best at standing up straight in line").

Soon you'll be spending your days trying to sell your fifty boxes of fundraising candy bars, your afternoons listening to new swear words your child picked up (if you call "Mr. poo-poo dicky ears" swearing) and your nights trying to help think up something creative and original for show and tell next week.

And if you're really lucky, you might even get to take care of the kindergarten pet, who will invariably be Minnie the mouse, Harry the hamster or Rex the rabbit.

If the educational merry-go-round ever seems too much, don't worry. Just remember, you have only thirteen years to go.

CHAPTER 27
The Last Word

*Because the greatness comes not when things go
always good for you, but the greatness comes when
you are really tested, when you take some knocks,
some disappointments, when sadness comes,
because only if you have been in the deepest valley
can you ever know how magnificent it is to be on
the highest mountain.*

— Richard Nixon, 9 August 1974

ONE DAY, you'll be dead.

You'll be just a faded photograph on the mantel and a memory to the friends and family you leave behind. Maybe you'll be old and decrepit and death will be expected. Maybe you'll be tragically snatched in your prime and you won't see it coming. (Maybe it'll be before you finish reading this book! *Read slowly*.) Either way, one day a room full of people will gather together to weep bitterly and blab platitudes about you. I don't know about you, but when I hear the trumpet and leave this dusty rock behind, I don't want to have any regrets. I don't want to look back and think, "If only I'd . . ." Because then it will be too late. You've got one crack at being a dad. One chance to participate in the life of your child. One chance to help him grow up.

> You've got one crack at being a dad. One chance to participate in the life of your child. One chance to help him grow up.

Because once a day goes by, it's gone forever. As the saying goes, "they're only young once." So enjoy it while you can.

Sure, not every moment is going to be fabulous and joyful and full of the wonder experienced by parents on TV commercials. We all have our moments of doubt. For me, it's when I hear my childless friends talking about getting up early on a Saturday . . . at 10 A.M.; when the kids have a triple

tantrum in the grocery store; when I have to take out a bank
loan to buy ballet shoes; when I'm cleaning vomit out of the car;
when I have to leave a dinner party early; when the kids outvote
me at the video store; when small hysterical bodies appear in
our bed in the middle of the night; when there is chaos at the
dinner table when all I want is some peace and quiet; when one
of my girls goes to the bathroom in the movie theater . . . and I
do mean *in* the movie theater.

But while this is true, these moments are overshadowed by
the deep-felt and almost indescribable satisfaction of being a dad
that comes from the most seemingly insignificant events and
encounters.

There are so many daily pleasures: when the kids fall
sleep on my knee or when they snuggle up to me during a
thunderstorm; when they run to me when
I come home from work; when we collect
shells on the beach; when they dress
up as angels for preschool concerts;
when we sit in the bath together until
our skin is all wrinkly; when we talk about
"important stuff"; when we get under a blanket to watch a new
video; when they make me breakfast in bed on Father's Day
(at least I *think* it's breakfast); and, most of all, when all three
sleep through the night . . . in their own beds.

Yep, fatherhood, despite all the frustration and stress, is
pretty fantastic.

I hope you feel the same.

Because you and I, we've still got a long way to go. We're just starting out on our journey up the paternal mountain.

Looking back, my footing as a dad was shaky to start with, but I eventually found my stride, and my wife and I started our ascent. I fell over and grazed my knee a few times while I coped with the changes in lifestyle—lack of time, lack of sex, mess, crying and diapers—but eventually we made it through the foothills of babyhood and arrived at toddler base camp.

By the start of toddlerdom, I considered myself a seasoned mountain climber. The summit was in sight. We encountered the joys of the first steps and the first words as well as the chasms and valleys of tantrums, discipline, bedwetting and birthday parties . . . but my trusty wife usually hauled me out with a rope and we kept travelling in a generally upward direction.

Soon I found myself with three children. And so with a sigh of relief, I took my final arrogant steps to the top of the mountain. I had made it.

To my surprise, rather than a chairlift back to the land of adulthood, I was faced with a whole range of even bigger mountains, as far as the eye could see, that made the mountain I'd just climbed look like a hill . . . and I suddenly realized the secret.

Parenthood gets harder all the time—and better.

And that's where I'm standing now, looking off into the distance with miles and miles to go.

Through the mist ahead I see lots of other travelers walking the road of fatherhood, some moving faster than others, some coping better than others, but all of us putting one foot in front of the other and pushing on. And I can also just make out the signposts along the path: parent-teacher nights, school fundraising committees, menstruation, wet dreams, alcohol, driving lessons, disobedience, music I don't understand, inexplicably large phone bills, hideously expensive fashion, truancy, finding pornography under the bed, slumber parties, broken hearts, teenage angst, "Drop me off here, Dad . . . I'll walk the rest of the way" and finally, "Dad, I'm getting married."

So to you, my paternal brother and fellow traveler, wherever you are on the road, struggle on. Enjoy the peaks. Survive the valleys.

Don't take your family for granted. Don't let your work overcome you. Love your kids. Love your wife. When you die, have no regrets. No "if only's."

Anyway, I have to go now. I've spent far too much time writing this book and it's time for a break.

My journey awaits.

As I head off into the next phase of dadhood, I am both excited and apprehensive. The idea of fathering three girls, especially in their later years, scares the hell out of me. Before I know it, there'll be boys knocking on the door to take my girls out. And I'll spend the rest of the night lying in bed waiting for them to come home.

So I just want to make it clear right now, that if I ever find any pimply-faced adolescent sneaking around my house in the middle of the night, he's dead.

But I'll leave that for the sequel.

See you on the road.

Let the next adventure begin!

CHAPTER 28

What My Friends Had to Say—Part 2

THERE is a lot of television that I don't enjoy: dating games, soap operas, late-night infomercials and anything that features home videos. But one televisual weakness that I profess to (and am currently seeking counseling for) are those "Where Are They Now?" shows about the stars of the sixties and seventies.

I don't know why, but I just love to see what Batman is doing as an old guy (thankfully, his undies are now on the *inside*). I always get a thrill to see that Gilligan is still wearing his stupid hat. I enjoy knowing which of the Partridges is in therapy, and occasionally, I'll even get the ultimate treat of hearing about the sordid behind-the-scenes relationships of the pseudo-incestuous Brady kids.

And so, what a perfect opportunity to do my own "Where Are They Now?"

At the back of my first book, *So You're Going to be a Dad*, I included a section in which all my paternal friends free-associated about their experiences of pregnancy, birth, life, babies, the Clinton administration and so on.

And now here we are . . . a few years down the road. All their babies have turned into toddlers and children and their folds have been added to. Gentlemen, for your reading enjoyment, may I present the sequel, commonly referred to as, "My Friends: Where Are They Now?"

Adrian
Father of Lyndall
Once upon a time, the sharing of things such as going to the bathroom or taking a bath seemed impossible, but now I know how important they are. These are times that a two-year-old holds precious—being in the bathroom with you. Being a dad

has also taught me the meaning of the words "unconditional love." Giving yourself totally to your child, in the bad times as well as the good, helps establish a strong relationship and a person who feels loved and cared for. I love my daughter dearly.

Al

Father of Amy, Beth, Gareth, Josephine and Arnold the dog
Make the most of the time you have with your kids because it will go fast. There will always be more work or commitments or meetings, but your children are only little once. I have to remind myself of this every day. You get them as kids once and once only. If you don't enjoy them, you'll miss out. If you don't get input into their little impressionable minds, someone else will.

So take the time to enjoy your kids.

Andrew

Father of Zoe
In *So You're Going to be a Dad*, Andrew rambled on about how fatherhood wasn't so big and scary and that it would not change his life all that much. I have been counting down the days till this sequel when he would confess that he was overconfident, smug, arrogant and that Pete Downey was right all along.

Unfortunately, Andrew could not submit his own report because he has taken his wife and child to India to set up a development project or something like that.

I think he did it just to taunt me.

–P.D.

Bill

Father of Talitha and Anna
Yep, we've had another one. It certainly ups the stakes when you have a baby and a toddler under the same roof at the same time. A second child doubles the fun (and the torment). Vacations are no longer vacations, a good night's sleep means four hours without interruption, and tantrums are beyond belief. There's no turning back, but why would you?

It's a strangely indescribable feeling when I come home and my daughter gives me hug and with an ear-to-ear grin tells our guests, "That's my Dad, he's my Daddy."

Daniel
Father of Zachary and Rainbow
They say that kids don't cost much, but that's hogwash. They cost a lot. I have to buy stuff all the time, especially shoes, and then a few weeks later they don't fit anymore so we have to get more. I should open a second-hand shoe store.

David
Father of Simon, Timothy and Fetus
Pessimists will tell you that toddlerhood is a nightmare. "After all," they say with a fiendish glint in their eye, "once you make it through the terrible twos, you still have the terrifying threes and the feral fours to go!"

Don't believe them. The toddler years are great, years to savor and treasure. It's a time when your child achieves maximum cuteness, a time when your child is still blissfully unaware of your many flaws, a time when your child has not yet learned the catch phrase "I'm bored," and the world is still a place of wonder and excitement. Enjoy it.

Eric
Father of Harrison and Jordan and man of few words
More work. More fun.

Gabe
Father of Daniel and Joel
The thing about kids is that you can't let them out of your sight for a second, especially when you're out. A few years ago, we all went to a department store to buy clothes. Toddler Joel found a prehistoric jelly bean on the floor. It was covered in dirt and hair and stuff. Although I grabbed it from him, he still managed to get a good lick at it. I thought he would soon die of some weird disease.

Four-year-old Daniel volunteered to get rid of the disgusting, slobbery object. A minute later I found him hiding the jelly bean in the underpants of a lingerie mannequin.

Grant
Father of Alex and William
Our family is supposedly classified as "cash rich—time poor." I'm not too sure about the "cash rich" part, but I can accept the "time poor" description. Now that we have two boys, my time outside work is completely focused on being a father and husband. It's so important to give time to the boys during the week. I don't really believe in planning for quality time, because quality seems spontaneous and I don't think you can actually budget for it. People who focus on quality time look at it from the parent's perspective rather than from the child's.

Life is much richer with a young family, but so much harder than it was before. Linda and I make a point of having long-weekend breaks away from our boys during the year. We find this essential if we are to focus on each other. I don't want our children to be our only common interest in ten years' time.

James
Father of Anna and Edward
I remember when Anna started to eat solid food. I was so determined to do the right thing diet-wise: I was such a great dad, I didn't need any of that canned stuff. Surely I could make stuff that would taste better and be better for her. I slaved over a stove for an hour trying to make stewed apple and she wouldn't even sniff it, let alone taste it.

Out came the can. So much for my ideals.

And now we've just had a son. I'd almost forgotten what a crying baby was like in the middle of the night. The coming weeks are going to be a relearning experience.

Jamie
Father of twins Caleb and Daniel and twins Hannah and Sam and hopefully no more twins
There is only one thing noisier and more chaotic than having four children under two-and-a-half—and that is having four children between two-and-a-half and five.

Life has now settled into a constant routine. It is a boisterous, energetic journey of growth, discovery, change, hard lessons and golden moments.

Our chances of having a third set of twins is high, so we have
to be careful. We find oral sex to be the safest because there's no
chance of Annie getting pregnant when we just talk about it.

There have been many hard times: when all six of us had the
flu, or when all the kids had chickenpox or when the two oldest
had a savage case of ticks.

There have been plenty of funny times: trying to control four
restless little bodies with bribes and threats at the movie theater
or the time I found the boys having a foreskin-stretching
competition.

But the special times, the magic moments, make being a dad
so special. Mornings at the beach, flying a kite, teaching the
kids to ride a bike, playing peek-a-boo in bed on Saturday
morning. I have an unlimited supply of kisses and hugs, games
and story times. And I love it when a stranger says, "Don't they
look like their dad!"

Jeffrey

Father of Nathaniel, Tyler, Lindsay and Tyrone Dawg
First of all, let's get one thing straight. Pete Downey knows
nothing about having toddlers because he only has girls. The
real challenge comes when you have boys. Girls are bright,
shiny and pleasant, even on bad days. Boys get you climbing the
walls a lot faster. However, I have heard rumors that this
changes for both sexes at around the age of twelve, at which
point you want to trade in your girls for boys.

The second thing to remember is that having a toddler is a
learning experience for all involved. You will never be faced
with so many "why" and "why not" questions in your life, often
when you have no idea of the answer.

Third, the biggest shock is realizing that your kid may be
average. Throughout infancy, you are constantly amazed at their
incredible learning capability and you just assume they're
brilliant. But even with good genes and coaching, you may still
be surprised when they run out onto the soccer field and are just
average. Your reaction? "But he was so great in the backyard all
those years!" You feel you've failed, but while all kids are special,
most are average.

My last piece of advice? Let your child be a kid. Let him use his imagination, don't have too many rules and, most of all, don't expect him to act like an adult.

Jim
Father of Michelle, Madeleine and Alana
Justine and I now have three girls and have to decide whether to call it quits or not. The decision is not an easy one for me. I love my girls, and although it was never my motivation in having children in the first place, part of me would like to have had a boy. But to have another child for the sake of trying for a boy does not make sense. I might get a grandson one day, but if not, well, that's life.

The other issue is *who gets the chop?* Both of us are prepared to take action but want to be sure of the procedures and the pros and cons before any scalpels come into sight.

Michelle has started school and is very enthusiastic after all of three weeks. This just reminds me that it's a long haul through the educational system, and we will continually have to focus on trying to help and support them through the years.

John
Father of Angus and Philippa
Well, here we are three years later: more experienced, older and wiser (ha!). What more can I say, what have I learned, what new and wonderful words do I have to share?

None. That's Downey's department. Me, I'm out here struggling away with all the others who never seem too sure of what they're doing either.

My wife told me she wants to write a new book on the subject, because she read all the others and they don't cover children like ours. Are ours really all that strange or are these books written by people who never actually had any kids of their own?

We've learned some interesting things: The idea that "two are as easy as one" is a myth, and at the age of three there is a metamorphosis, but everyone else still thinks they're beautiful and well behaved.

Now that we have come to earth with a resounding crunch from those early days when we were ready to be parental experts, confident that we would show the rest of the world how it is really done; now that we look at it in the cold harsh light of reality, what are my reflections?

It is hard work. It is tiring—no, exhausting—it is frustrating, it is never what you expect, but I wouldn't miss it for the world. It is challenging, exciting, rewarding and the best thing I've ever done.

John

Father of David and Thomas
Being a parent has become increasingly enjoyable as David has grown older. We can talk to each other in the same language; we can kick a soccer ball together; we can watch our favorite TV shows ("Pokemon" *again?*), he can use the potty; he can sleep through the night (and so can we!).

But just as I was beginning to believe that there is life after baby . . . welcome to the real world. We're back at square one! (*Gasp.*)

Malcolm

Father of Rebecca, Joshua and another one due in two months
My children bring me great joy. It's great to see them grow up and develop their own personalities and characteristics.

I see in Rebecca the desire to do things just right as she looks at life with healthy caution. Joshua, on the other hand, looks at life with zeal and little regard for consequences. I'm not sure if this is due to gender difference, though my friends' anecdotes confirm my suspicion that boys are generally more active and more exhausting. Rebecca was never likely to climb onto a mantelpiece and throw a clock off or twice rip the doors off the stereo cabinet.

Having a second child was more work, but now they are able to play nicely together. My colleagues tell me that having a third is like doubling the load again.

I am looking forward, with some trepidation, to the challenge. Lots of work, sure, but in my experience far outweighed by the rewards.

Mark

Father of Laura, Katie and Emma

Parenting—clear evidence of built-in obsolescence. Already Laura has a better memory than me. I rely on her for all the little details I have forgotten, and she keeps track of all the big events I have overlooked. Katie tells the best jokes. Straight-faced and serious in delivery, then exploding with laughter on denouement. Emma—she scuttles across the floor with an eagerness I have long lost, if I ever had it.

Face it. The newer models are smarter, funnier and faster. At our place, they are already mastering that look of bemusement as Daddy struggles to keep up.

Mark

Father of Adam and Matthew

It really was this hard for my Dad.

Matthew

Father of Jordan and The-Almost-Born

After nearly two years of Jordan and seven-ninths of Number 2 incubation, how is life? Well, I don't know if it's a sign of earlier lifestyles, but I can barely remember life without Jordan. He is so integral to our family and all our activities, to consider doing something that doesn't revolve around him (let alone not include him) is hard to imagine.

I remember starting off with gusto trying to ensure his arrival didn't impact on us too much and, in the early stages, was quite successful. When Jordan was small, we survived quite a number of nights with him in a car seat under the restaurant table or in a spare room of a friend's when there for dinner, but that soon tapered off.

With regard to sleeping intrusion, this turned out to be quite minimal, with the exception of a few all-nighters in the hospital casualty department, courtesy of Jordan's asthma.

For someone who prior to parenthood literally refused to hold a newborn, it's amazing how quickly confidence has come. It comes not through standing back and watching, but by doing . . . over and over and over. The rewards are immense,

with every day bringing a new word, thought or deed and
so much of it oozing with such demonstrable love for us,
his parents.

Owen

Father of Sophie, Rosanna and Number 3 (ETA three months)
Starship Household
Captain's Log
Stardate 92-94-96

As the Starship moves not so silently through the
neighborhood, we are preparing for the arrival of our third
alien from the planet Wombus Fertilius. There were early
indications that there may have been two visitors from this
dark and unknown region of the universe. This news sent the
USS Household temporarily into an uncontrolled warp drive
spin, but stability was regained when the ship's doctor
confirmed only a single arrival.

There have been rumors of an uprising from the crew
(aged 2 and 4) ever since First Officer Caroline announced she
was unable to carry the crew from the shuttle to their cabins if
they happened to fall asleep. Her girth continues to cause
suspicion among the crew, who now feel that an extraterrestrial
has been implanted there and plans to take control of the ship.
Little do they know . . .

Further mutiny has been breaking out when the crew is
required to retire for R&R after their morning shift on the
bridge, but Romulan discipline has kept the situation in check.

Unfortunately, *USS Household* was designed for a total of four
crew members, not five, so we will have to live in close quarters
for a while. The alternative, as Dr. Spock would say, is logical—
teleport to a larger starship, but with three crew under four-and-
a-half in our tractor beam, this would put too much strain on
our power reserves.

My only comfort is the knowledge that I am going where
other men have gone before.

Captain, signing off.

Phil

Father of Sam, Laura and Cameron (the Incredible Hulk)

You want to know what life is like with a five-, four- and one-year-old? Here's a typical example of the level of conversation at our breakfast table:

Sam: "Hey, Laura, there's a seagull in your head."

Laura (getting upset): "No there not. No seagull. No seagull."

Sam: "Seagull! Seagull!"

Mom: "It's all right, Laura, you have *brains* in your head. Not a seagull."

Laura (pauses): "I DO NOT HAVE BRAINS IN MY HEAD!"

Mom: "Oh really? Then what do you have?"

Laura (proudly): "Hair."

Ray

Father of Lachlan

In an emotional sense, nothing has changed since Lachlan was a baby. The lows are the pits and the highs are greater than anything I have ever known. One day he throws such a prolonged tantrum that I want to sell him to the gypsies; the next, my wife and I are discussing how we'd divide our assets if we were to divorce (our favorite method of resolving an argument), and my love for Lachlan is so overwhelming that I'm prepared to fight to the death in a custody battle.

Sandy

Father of Jonah and The Unborn, minus six months and counting

I recall my shock at the pregnancy test's reluctance to indicate negative, even after several days. Now I'm glad it didn't. So glad, in fact, that it has happened a second time . . . it's still not turning negative.

It's hard to believe that the lump inside Pascale's stomach has now turned into a stumbling, eating, pooping, portable disaster zone in such a short period of time. One minute he was a little baby, the next he's a toddler. That year goes by so quickly and it is difficult to reconcile the baby who we thought would never roll over with the little boy whose favorite words are "no," "no" and "no," and whose concept of fear around stairs, roads, swimming pools and electrical appliances is nonexistent.

Being a dad is both better and worse than I imagined. But watch out. It all happens so fast.

Simon

Father of The Lump, due any day now
I told you I could do it.

Simon

Father of Christina and Bronte
I'm sitting here with a pink ruffly sunhat having just wrestled the pen from my two-year-old—for the fifth time. I have promised to join the tea party in a minute. Recently one of my friends arrived to find my daughter and I dancing with dolls. Fatherhood sure makes a man out of you.

Wayne

Father of Brittany
When we first discovered that Brittany had serious allergies, we were stunned. After returning from the hospital with a list of only half a dozen foods she probably wouldn't react to, another list of substances that ranged from irritating to life-threatening, and an armful of helpful booklets and brochures, we set about changing our lifestyle and our expectations. As expectant parents, all of this was completely unforeseeable.

A separate, closely monitored diet, special treatment for chronic eczema, dust-mite eradication, asthma maintenance and frequent hospital visits became a regular part of our lives. We read books and articles, found support organizations, talked to other families and eventually regained our balance.

However, the past has passed and the present is much better. Despite every reason to be miserable, Brittany has grown into a happy, intelligent, outgoing, loving and generally wonderful little girl.

Okay, I'm biased.

Glossary

aaahh. The sound made by a man having sex with his wife when a toddler *does not* interrupt by walking into the room.

aarrggh. The sound made by a man having sex with his wife when a toddler *does* interrupt by walking into the room.

afternoon nap. Toddler sleep period, given so that toddler can catch up on some rest and the parents can catch up on some sex.

allergy. A bad reaction to foods or pollens.

and. The third most commonly used word in English.

aquaberg. Toddler feces, released in the bathtub (also known as a *floater*).

Arnold (also: Arn, Arnie, Schwarzie, Mr. Lumpy). Actor Arnold Schwarzenegger, star of the *Terminator* films, *End of Days*, *True Lies*, *Eraser*, *Hercules Goes Bananas* and some stupid flick about a pregnant man.

babababadalgharaghtakammenarronnkonnbronntonnerronnuon nthunurovarrhounawnskawntoohoohoordenentunuk. James Joyce's sound-effect thunder-clap from the novel *Finnegan's Wake*.

baby-sitting. Taking care of a child.

Band-Aids. Strips of plastic used to heal toddler wounds.

bathtub. Large container of water in which one immerses small children in an attempt to keep them clean.

bedtime. A period, often lasting several hours, during which parents attempt to keep their children in their beds.

boompf. Sound made when a toddler falls over and lands on carpet.

"But I'm not tired." The way a preschooler says "good night."

cheezacort. The creamy material found in the creases of a toddler's thighs.

chicken dance. Preschool version of the Hokey-Pokey or Macarena. It involves four finger snaps, four arm flaps, four butt wiggles and four handclaps.

clowder. Collective noun for a group of cats.

condom. A thin rubber sheath worn on an erect penis to prevent sperm entering the vagina.

crapola. When an author passes off his casual anecdotal observations as universal truth.

crash. Collective noun for a group of rhinoceroses.

crudibits. The chunky residue left behind after a young child has attempted unsuccessfully to wipe her own behind.

common sense. Something that small children do not possess.

daylight saving. Time adjustment used in summer for the benefit of vacationers, not parents who want to put their kids to bed in the dark.

déjà vu. The feeling you have when a second or third child is on the way and you're suddenly reminded of your vow not to have any more children because your life has become such a total misery.

Depo Provera. Long-acting synthetic hormone injection for contraceptive purposes.

diaphragm. A flexible rubber cap worn inside the vagina to prevent sperm entering the uterus.

dip? No thanks, it'll spoil my dinner.

diptheria. Infectious bacterial disease characterized by inflammation of the mucous membrane.

doorknob. Your toddler's bedroom should not have one of these on the inside.

drop zone. The geographical point in your house where you want your child's feces deposited.

epididymis. The squishy spot where the vas deferens joins the testicle.

Epididymon. Tragic protagonist in Greek classic of same name.

exaltation. Collective noun for a group of larks.

exorcist. The person you call when your child is having a tantrum.

facial. Pertaining to the human face, not to be confused with fecal.

fecal. Pertaining to human excretion, not to be confused with facial.

granuloma. 1. Tumor of granulation tissue. 2. Collective noun for the grains and oats found in muesli.

hard drive. 1. Non-floppy disc memory-storage system used to house computer information. 2. What you call a car trip when your toddler keeps taking his seatbelt off.

harkoin. The hour immediately before it gets dark, during which it is impossible to put a child to bed.

hepatitis. Inflammation of the liver.

$HOC_6 H_4 C (C_2 H_5) = C (C_2 H_5) C_6 H_4 OH$. A synthetic (*diethylstilbestrol*) that promotes estrogenic activity; formerly used to treat menopausal symptoms.

hysterectomy. 1. The removal of a woman's womb. 2. A historical record of an anal investigation.

hermobat. When the battery of a video recorder dies during the critical moment of a child's birthday party or preschool concert.

impetigo. A skin disease marked by pustular eruptions.

inguinoscrotal condition. I don't really know what this is, but I know I don't want one.

irony. The fact that we all turn out like our parents.

is. The seventh most commonly used word in English.

"I want." The way a preschooler says "please."

knockout. What happens when you change a toddler's diaper eight hours after they've eaten Mexican-style refried beans.

labia. Protagonist in Shakespeare's Roman tragedy *Labia and Vulva*.

me. The geographical center of the universe, according to children under the age of five.

measles. Infectious viral skin disease marked by red spots.

meningitis. Hernia of the membranes surrounding the brain and spinal cord.

miniscule. The size of 1) your toddler's brain or 2) a parent's bank balance.

more. The way a preschooler says "thank you."

mucus. Anything that comes out of a child's nose.

mumps. Infectious viral disease producing swelling of the parotid glands.

nads. Colloquial expression pertaining to the testicles (also known as *jewels* or *nuts*).

no. The way a preschooler says, "I'd rather not, thanks."

palpate the vas. Vasectomy talk meaning "tap the squid."

people mover. 1. A family car with many seats. 2. When a toddler poops his pants in a crowded room.

Peter Downey. Internationally famous funnyman who made his fortune writing parenting books.

pherdyles. Thick, gluggy substances found around a toddler's mouth.

polio (poliomyelitus). Infectious viral inflammation of nerve cells.

poo-poo. Excrement; word used mostly by parents and small children.

potty. 1. Small plastic receptacle for fecal containment, used by toddlers. 2. What happens to parents when they spend too much time alone with their preschooler.

pratesilling (pronounced *prAY-tuh-s'll-ing*). The act of pretending to be asleep in the middle of the night so that your wife will go into the kids' bedroom to see what all the screaming is about.

quietus (pronounced *kwee-EHT-uhs*). The period between when a young child goes to bed and when she starts screaming.

refrigerator. A large white cold object found in the kitchen. Used for food storage and preschool art collection.

road sense. Something that little kids don't have.

rubella (German measles). Infectious viral disease marked by an itchy red rash.

S-bend. Special place for toddlers to stash their parents' jewelry, computer discs and car keys.

scarlet. The color of most dads' faces when they are called up front to do the chicken dance at a preschool concert.

scrotal hematoma. You don't want one.

seminal. Pertaining to reproductive fluids.

semolina. The hard grains left after the process of grinding flour, often used in pasta.

shkegum. The residual smear left in a potty after you've emptied the contents.

shrewdness. Collective noun for a group of apes.

sniddles. Tangled mats of hair on a toddler's scalp, usually the result of some sticky substance such as ice cream or toffee.

So You're Going to be a Dad. Internationally successful parenting text and bible for new parents of the twenty-first century.

sperm. The way a dyslexic spells *sprem*.

SPF 15 (skin protection factor). Recommended grade of sunscreen protection; will allow 15 times normal sun tolerance.

spreem. The trajectory of urine flowing between the body and the toilet.

sterilization. Effective and mostly permanent procedure to render a person unable to reproduce.

supercalifragilisticexpialidocious. Good.

tantrum. To be possessed by evil spirits.

taxidermist. Someone who stuffs creatures (see also *vasectomist*).

television. (also known as TV) The ultimate baby-sitter.

tetanus. Bacterial disease marked by spasm of voluntary muscles.

the. The most commonly used word in English.

thingamajiggy. 1. The clip on the end of the strap connecting a child seat to the body of the car. 2. The technical term for all parts your plumber needs to replace.

thwack. Sound made when a toddler falls over and lands on a tiled floor.

toilet-training. The process of teaching a toddler to empty his bowels into the toilet rather than under the dining room table.

tubal ligation. When a woman has her tubes tied.

Tubal litigation. When Shylock's friend goes to court (a little English teacher humor).

unadulterated rage. The feeling an adult male experiences when he discovers that his preschooler has inserted a slice of cheese into his floppy disk drive.

urgghh. Sound made by a dad when, in the middle of the night, his wife leans over to him and says, "Are you awake?" and he says, "Yes," because he thinks it's leading to sex, but then she says, "It's your turn," and he has to trudge down the hall to a screaming toddler who has pooped in his crib and eaten half of it.

vaccination. To inoculate with vaccine to provide immunity against disease.

vas deferens. "Having this cut will make a *vas deferens* in your ability to impregnate a woman (thank you, and don't forget to tip your waitress)."

vasectomist. Someone who stuffs you (see also *taxidermist*).

vasectomy. When an adult male has his nads separated from the rest of his body for the purpose of contraception.

vasovasostomy. The medical procedure to reverse a vasectomy.

viscum. The thick layer of creamy mucus stretching between a toddler's nose and his chin.

vomit. The act of reverse peristalsis, usually done by small children either in their beds or in the car.

vulva. Swedish motor vehicle owned primarily by people who live in suburban developments.

"wasn't me." The way a preschooler says, "it was me."

whooping cough. A severe lung spasm virus.

windling. When a toddler attempts to use a big toilet, but most of it goes on the floor.

"wish me luck as you wave me goodbye." Traditional ditty sung by testicles on the night before a vasectomy.

withdrawal. Contraceptive method not endorsed by anyone with an ounce of intelligence.

wittisnay. The short period every night between children going to sleep and adults going to bed.

wobbly. The state of a toddler taking his first steps.

wooshdie. Small flame produced when a fart is ignited with a match.

wreeeaaarrnnnggggssshhheeecccchhhh. Sound made when a toddler falls over and lands on the cat.

yuk. The way a preschooler says, "Thanks for cooking me this great dinner."

Attention: Calling All Internet Surfers

COMPUTERS and I don't get along all that well, but nevertheless I have ventured into the cyberworld of the internet. Don't ask me why. It just seemed like a good idea at the time. You can contact my virtual self at author@peterdowney.com and I'll try to reply. But that's not all! You can visit the Peter Downey Dads' home page at www.peterdowney.com which contains all kinds of stuff from my first book, *So You're Going to Be a Dad*, and exciting photos and reviews and interesting dad snippets. No doubt you will also find the words "Elvis" and "Gigantic Bosom" in there, just so lots of people come to look at my site.

Resources

4Dad.com
4Dad.4anything.com

American Coalition for Fathers and Children
1718 M St. NW, Ste. 187
Washington, DC 20036
800-978-DADS
www.acfc.org

Canadian Parents Online
www.canadianparents.com

DualCareerDads.com
www.dualcareerdads.com

Fathers First Online
12333 Exbury St.
Herndon, VA 20170-2518
Tel: 703-430-7287
www.fathersfirst.org

The Fathers Network
16120 NE 8th St.
Bellevue, WA 98008-3937
425-747-4004. ext. 218
www.fathersnetwork.org

Father's Resource Center
1020 2nd St., Ste. A
Encinitas, CA 92024
Tel: 760-634-DADS;
619-702-DADS;
800-515-DADS
Fax: 760-634-3282
www.fathersresourcecenter.com

Father's World
P.O. Box 433
Massapequa, NY 11758
516-795-3096
www.fathersworld.com

National Center for Fathering
P.O. Box 413888
Kansas City, MO 64141
Tel: 800-593-DADS
Fax: 913-384-4665
www.fathers.com

National Fatherhood Initiative
101 Lake Forest Blvd., Ste. 360
Gaithersburg, MD 20877
Tel: 301-948-0599
Fax: 301-948-4325
www.fatherhood.org

Bibliography

SOME of these books and articles I have referred to specifically. Others gave me an idea or two to build on. From some I have taken an obscure piece of information, statistics or quotes. Others were just a curious read and stayed in the bathroom next to the toilet for several weeks.

"Accidents can be prevented," *The Sun-Herald*, 23 October 1994.

Brando, Marlon. *Apocalypse Next Tuesday at Five*. Atlantis: Pseudo Books, 1993.

Bronte, Emily. *Wuthering Heights*. New York: Penguin Classics, 1996. First published, 1847.

Burns, Robert. "To a Mouse" from *The Poetical Works and Letters of Robert Burns with Copious Marginal Explanations of the Scottish Words*. London: Gall & Inglis, (undated).

Byrne, Andrew. "Shock tactics to save young lives," *Sydney Morning Herald*, 17 October 1995.

Byrne, David. *Our House in the Middle of Our Street: Cult Tales of Terror*. Donner Pass, Colo.: Talking Head Publishing, 2003.

Byrne, First Degree. *Ooo, Ooo, Ah, Ah, Ow! That's Hot!* Sao Paulo, Brazil: ¡Si! Press, 1999.

Chung, Kay, "The Impact of Television on the Family: Reactions of Young Children to the Media," IARTV, Victoria, Australia: Seminar Series No. 3, June 1991.

Coleridge, Samuel Taylor. *The Rime of the Ancient Mariner*. A big fat book in my study that has had the whole front section ripped out.

"Dad! She Hit Me!," from *Boxing Greats: Humble Beginnings*. Philadelphia: Rocky Press, 1981.

"Did Not!," from *Sisters of Boxing Greats: Humble Beginnings, My Foot*. Philadelphia: Rocky Press, 1982.

Donaghy, Bronwyn, "Is your child ready for 'big school'?," *Sydney Morning Herald*, 5 January 1996.

Downey, Meredith. *A Comparative Analysis of Demand Factors for Conventional and Organic Fruits and Vegetables*. Department of

Agricultural Economics, University of Sydney, 1989.

"Exercising sensible restraint," *The Sun-Herald*, 23 October 1994.

Gripper, Ali. "15 minute fathers," *Sydney Morning Herald*, 22 January 1996.

Hely, Susan. "The new breed of workaholic," *Business Review Weekly*, 26 May 1989.

Jenny, Jenny, *Who Should I Turn To?* New York: 8675309.

Kamakura, Nikko, and Hakone Yokohama. *Tokyo Travel Guide*. Tokyo: Japan Travel Bureau, 1973.

Let's face it—nobody reads bibliographies anyway, do they? I don't know why I'm bothering. They're pointless if you ask me. You're probably the only person obsessive enough to read this.

Llewellyn-Jones, Derek. *Understanding Sexuality*. Melbourne, Aus.: Oxford University Press, 1980.

Lucas, Jerry. *Championship Card Tricks*. New York: Grossett & Dunlap, 1973.

Macdonald, Iain. *The Perversion of Polly the Dog*. Berkeley: Priority Paid Press, 1996.

Remarque, Erich. *All Quiet on the Western Front*. New York: Ballantine Books, 1996.

Rowlinson, William. *Sprich Mal Deutsch*. UK: Oxford University Press, 1980.

Shakespeare, William. *Othello*. New York: Bantam Classics, 1988.

Still reading are you? Why are you bothering? There are no more jokes.

Trousseau, Madame. *Mr. Sausage and His Fantastic Fun Machine Go Hunting for Zebras*. SK70 Publishers, 1980.

von Feilitzen, C., "Findings of Scandinavian research on child and television in the process of socialization in Prix Jeunesse Seminar" (1976), *Television and Socialization Processes in the Family, Fernsehen und Bildung, Internationale Zeitschrift fur Medienpsychologie und Medienpraxis* (English) Verlag dokumentation, Munchen, pp. 54-84.

Whippersnapper, Young. *"Center of the Universe" and Other Ways to Address Me*. Tucson, Ariz.: Full Court Press, 2010.

OK. That's it. There's no more. Now, stop reading and go play with your child.

Index